The Marrow of Tradition

CHARLES W. CHESNUTT

The Marrow of Tradition

Transaction Publishers
New Brunswick (U.S.A.) and London (U.K.)

147931

Library of Congress Catalog Number: 99–14583
ISBN: 1–56000–493–2
Printed in the United States of America

Library of Congress Cataloging-in-Publication Data

Chesnutt, Charles Waddell, 1858–1932.
    The marrow of tradition / Charles W. Chesnutt.
      p. (large print) cm.
    ISBN 1–56000–493–2 (alk. paper)
    1. Afro-Americans—North Carolina—Wilmington Fiction.   2. Riots-
-North Carolina—Wilmington Fiction.   3. Large type books.
4. Wilmington (N.C.) Fiction.   I. Title.
[PS1292.C6M3   1999]
813'.4—dc21   99–14583
                                       CIP

CONTENTS

THE MARROW OF TRADITION

I
AT BREAK OF DAY

"Stay here beside her, major. I shall not be needed for an hour yet. Meanwhile I'll go downstairs and snatch a bit of sleep, or talk to old Jane."

The night was hot and sultry. Though the windows of the chamber were wide open, and the muslin curtains looped back, not a breath of air was stirring. Only the shrill chirp of the cicada and the muffled croaking of the frogs in some distant marsh broke the night silence. The heavy scent of magnolias, overpowering even the strong smell of drugs in the sickroom, suggested death and funeral wreaths, sorrow and tears, the long home, the last sleep. The major shivered with apprehension as the slender hand which he held in his own contracted nervously and in a spasm of pain clutched his fingers with a vise-like grip.

Major Carteret, though dressed in brown linen, had thrown off his coat for greater comfort. The stifling heat, in spite of the palm-leaf fan which he plied mechanically, was scarcely less oppressive than his own thoughts. Long ago, while yet a mere boy in years, he had come back from Appomattox to find his family, one of the oldest and proudest in the state, hopelessly impoverished by the war,—even their ancestral home swallowed up in the common ruin. His elder brother had sacrificed his life on the bloody altar of the lost cause, and his father, broken and chagrined, died not many years later, leaving the major the last of his line. He had tried in various pursuits to gain a foothold in the new life, but with indifferent success until he won the hand of Olivia Merkell, whom he had seen grow from a small girl to glorious womanhood. With her money he had founded the Morning Chronicle, which he had made the leading organ of his party and the most influential paper in the State. The fine old house in which they lived was hers. In this very room she had first drawn the breath of life; it had been their nuptial chamber; and here, too, within a few hours, she might die, for it seemed impossible that one could long endure such frightful agony and live.

One cloud alone had marred the otherwise perfect serenity of their happiness. Olivia was childless. To have children to perpetuate the name of which he was so proud, to write it still higher on the roll of honor, had been his dearest hope. His disappointment had been proportionately keen. A few months ago this dead hope had revived, and altered the whole aspect of their lives. But as time went on, his wife's age had begun to tell upon her, until even Dr. Price, the most cheerful and optimistic of physicians, had warned him, while hoping for the best, to be prepared for the worst. To add to the danger, Mrs. Carteret had only this day suffered from a nervous shock, which, it was feared, had hastened by several weeks the expected event.

Dr. Price went downstairs to the library, where a dim light was burning. An old black woman, dressed in a gingham frock, with a red bandana handkerchief coiled around her head by way of turban, was seated by an open window. She rose and curtsied as the doctor entered and dropped into a willow rocking-chair near her own.

"How did this happen, Jane?" he asked in a subdued voice, adding, with assumed severity, "You ought to have taken better care of your mistress."

"Now look a-hyuh, Doctuh Price," returned the old woman in an unctuous whisper, "you don' wanter come talkin' none er yo' foolishness 'bout my not takin' keer er Mis' 'Livy. *She* never would 'a' said sech a thing! Seven er eight mont's ago, w'en she sent fer me, I says ter her, says I:—

"'Lawd, Lawd, honey! You don' tell me dat after all dese long wary years er waitin' de good Lawd is done heared yo' prayer an' is gwine ter sen' you de chile you be'n wantin' so long an' so bad? Bless his holy name! Will I come an' nuss yo' baby? Why, honey, I nussed you, an' nussed yo' mammy thoo her las' sickness, an' laid her out w'en she died. I would n' *let* nobody e'se nuss yo' baby; an' mo'over, I'm gwine ter come an' nuss you too. You're young side er me, Mis' 'Livy, but you're ove'ly ole ter be havin' yo' fus' baby, an' you'll need somebody roun', honey, w'at knows all 'bout de fam'ly, an' deir ways an' deir weaknesses, an' I don' know who dat'd be ef it wa'n't me.'

"'Deed, Mammy Jane,' says she, 'dere ain' nobody e'se I'd have but you. You kin come ez soon ez you wanter an' stay ez long ez you mineter.'

"An hyuh I is, an' hyuh I'm gwine ter stay. Fer Mis' 'Livy is my ole mist'ess's daughter, an' my ole mist'ess wuz good ter me, an' dey ain' none er her folks gwine ter suffer ef ole Jane kin he'p it."

"Your loyalty does you credit, Jane," observed the doctor; "but you have n't told me yet what happened to Mrs. Carteret to-day. Did the horse run away, or did she see something that frightened her?"

"No, suh, do hoss did n' git skeered at nothin', but Mis' 'Livy did see somethin', er somebody; an' it wa'n't no fault er mine ner her'n neither,—it goes fu'ther back, suh, fu'ther dan dis day er dis year. Does you 'member de time w'en my ole mist'ess, Mis' 'Livy upstairs's mammy, died? No? Well, you wuz prob'ly 'way ter school den, studyin' ter be a doctuh. But I'll tell you all erbout it.

"W'en my ole mist'ess, Mis' 'Liz'beth Merkell,—an' a good mist'ess she wuz,—tuck sick fer de las' time, her sister Polly—ole Mis' Polly Ochiltree w'at is now—come ter de house ter he'p nuss her. Mis' 'Livy upstairs yander wuz erbout six years ole den, de sweetes' little angel you ever laid eyes on; an' on her dyin' bed Mis' 'Liz'beth ax' Mis' Polly fer ter stay hyuh an' take keer er her chile, an' Mis' Polly she promise'. She wuz a widder fer de secon' time, an' did n' have no child'en, an' could jes' as well come as not.

"But dere wuz trouble after de fune'al, an' it happen' right hyuh in dis lib'ary. Mars Sam wuz settin' by de table, w'en Mis' Polly come downstairs, slow an' solemn, an' stood dere in de middle er de flo', all in black, till Mars Sam sot a cheer fer her.

"'Well, Samuel,' says she, 'now dat we 've done all we can fer po' 'Liz'beth, it only 'mains fer us ter consider Olivia's future.'

"Mars Sam nodded his head, but did n' say nothin'.

"'I don' need ter tell you,' says she, 'dat I am willin' ter carry out de wishes er my dead sister, an' sac'ifice my

4

own comfo't, an' make myse'f yo' housekeeper an' yo' child's nuss, fer my dear sister's sake. It wuz her dyin' wish, an' on it I will ac', ef it is also yo'n.'

"Mars Sam did n' want Mis' Polly ter come, suh; fur he did n' like Mis' Polly. He wuz skeered er Miss Polly."

"I don't wonder," yawned the doctor, "if she was anything like she is now."

"Wuss, suh, fer she wuz younger, an' stronger. She always would have her say, no matter 'bout what, an' her own way, no matter who 'posed her. She had already be'n in de house fer a week, an' Mars Sam knowed ef she once come ter stay, she 'd be de mist'ess of eve'ybody in it an' him too. But w'at could he do but say yas?

"'Den it is unde'stood, is it,' says Mis' Polly, w'en he had spoke, 'dat I am ter take cha'ge er de house?'

"'All right, Polly,' says Mars Sam, wid a deep sigh.

"Mis, Polly 'lowed he wuz sighin' fer my po' dead mist'ess, fer she did n' have no idee er his feelin's to'ds her,—she alluz did 'low dat all de gent'emen wuz in love wid 'er.

"'You won' fin' much ter do,' Mars Sam went on, 'fer Julia is a good housekeeper, an' kin ten' ter mos' eve'ything, under yo' d'rections.'

"Mis' Polly stiffen' up like a ramrod. 'It mus' be unde'stood, Samuel,' says she, 'dat w'en I 'sumes cha'ge er yo' house, dere ain' gwine ter be no 'vided 'sponsibility; an' as fer dis Julia, me an' her could n' git 'long tergether nohow. Ef I stays, Julia goes.'

"W'en Mars Sam heared dat, he felt better, an' 'mence' ter pick up his courage. Mis' Polly had showed her han' too plain. My mist'ess had n' got col' yit, an' Mis' Polly, who'd be'n a widder fer two years dis las' time, wuz al-

5

ready fig'rin' on takin' her place fer good, an' she did n' want no other woman roun' do house dat Mars Sam might take a' intrus' in.

"'My dear Polly,' says Mars Sam, quite determine', 'I could n' possibly sen' Julia 'way. Fac' is, I could n' git 'long widout Julia. She 'd be'n runnin' dis house like clockwo'k befo' you come, an' I likes her ways. My dear, dead 'Liz'beth sot a heap er sto' by Julia, an' I'm gwine ter keep her here fer Liz'beth's sake.'

"Mis' Polly's eyes flash' fire.

"'Ah,' says she, 'I see—I see! You perfers her house-keepin' ter mine, indeed! Dat is a fine way ter talk ter a lady! An' a heap er rispec' you is got fer de mem'ry er my po' dead sister!'

"Mars Sam knowed w'at she 'lowed she seed wa'n't so; but he did n' let on, fer it only made him de safer. He wuz willin' fer her ter 'magine w'at she please', jes, so long ez she kep' out er his house an' let him alone.

"'No, Polly,' says he, gittin' bolder ez she got madder, 'dere ain' no use talkin'. Nothin' in de worl' would make me part wid Julia.'

"Mis' Polly she r'ared an' she pitch', but Mars Sam belt on like grim death. Mis' Polly would n' give in neither, an' so she fin'lly went away. Dey made some kind er 'rangement afterwa'ds, an' Miss Polly tuck Mis' 'Livy ter her own house. Mars Sam paid her bo'd an' 'lowed Mis' Polly somethin' fer takin' keer er her."

"And Julia stayed?"

"Julia stayed, suh, an' a couple er years later her chile wuz bawn, right here in dis house."

"But you said," observed the doctor, "that Mrs. Ochiltree was in error about Julia."

"Yas, suh, so she wuz, w'en my ole mist'ess died. But dis wuz two years after,—an' w'at has ter be has ter be. Julia had a easy time; she had a black gal ter wait on her, a buggy to ride in, an' eve'ything she wanted. Eve'ybody s'posed Mars Sam would give her a house an' lot, er leave her somethin' in his will. But he died suddenly, and did n' leave no will, an' Mis' Polly got herse'f 'pinted gyardeen ter young Mis' 'Livy, an' driv Julia an' her young un out er de house, an' lived here in dis house wid Mis' 'Livy till Mis' 'Livy ma'ied Majah Carteret."

"And what became of Julia?" asked Dr. Price.

Such relations, the doctor knew very well, had been all too common in the old slavery days, and not a few of them had been projected into the new era. Sins, like snakes, die hard. The habits and customs of a people were not to be changed in a day, nor by the stroke of a pen. As family physician, and father confessor by brevet, Dr. Price had looked upon more than one hidden skeleton; and no one in town had had better opportunities than old Jane for learning the undercurrents in the lives of the old families.

"Well," resumed Jane, "eve'ybody s'posed, after w'at had happen', dat Julia'd keep on livin' easy, fer she wuz young an' good-lookin'. But she did n'. She tried ter make a livin' sewin', but Mis' Polly would n' let de bes' w'ite folks hire her. Den she tuck up washin', but did n' do no better at dat; an' bimeby she got so discourage' dat she ma'ied a shif'less yaller man, an' died er consumption soon after,—an' wuz 'bout ez well off, fer dis man could n' hardly feed her nohow."

"And the child?"

"One er de No'the'n w'ite lady teachers at de mission

7

school tuck a likin' ter little Janet, an' put her thoo school, an' den sent her off ter de No'th fer ter study ter be a school teacher. W'en she come back, 'stead er teachin' she ma'ied ole Adam Miller's son."

"The rich stevedore's son, Dr. Miller?"

"Yas, suh, dat's de man,—you knows 'im. Dis yer boy wuz jes' gwine 'way fer ter study ter be a doctuh, an' he ma'ied dis Janet, an' tuck her 'way wid 'im. Dey went off ter Europe, er Irope, er Orope, er somewhere er 'nother, 'way off yander, an' come back here las' year an' sta'ted dis yer horspital an' school fer ter train de black gals fer nusses."

"He's a very good doctor, Jane, and is doing a useful work. Your chapter of family history is quite interesting,—I knew part of it before, in a general way; but you have n't yet told me what brought on Mrs. Carteret's trouble."

"I 'm jes' comin' ter dat dis minute, suh,—w'at I be'n tellin' you is all a part of it. Dis yer Janet, w'at is Mis' 'Livy's half-sister, is ez much like her ez ef dey wuz twins. Folks sometimes takes 'em fer one ernudder,—I s'pose it tickles Janet mos' ter death, but it do make Mis' 'Livy rippin'. An' den 'way back yander jes' after de wah, w'en de ole Carteret mansion had ter be sol', Adam Miller bought it, an' dis yer Janet an' her husban' is be'n livin' in it ever sence ole Adam died, 'bout a year ago; an' dat makes de majah mad, 'ca'se he don' wanter see cullud folks livin' in de ole fam'ly mansion w'at he wuz bawn in. An' mo'over, an' dat 's de wust of all, w'iles Mis' 'Livy ain' had no child'en befo', dis yer sister er her'n is got a fine-lookin' little yaller boy, w'at favors de fam'ly so dat ef Mis' 'Livy'd see de chile anywhere, it 'd mos' break her heart fer ter think 'bout her not havin' no child'en herse'f. So ter-day, w'en Mis' 'Livy wuz out ridin' an' met dis yer Janet wid her boy, an' w'en Mis' 'Livy got ter studyin' 'bout her own chances, an' how she mought not come thoo safe, she jes' had a fit er hysterics right dere in de buggy. She wuz mos' home, an' William got her here, an' you knows de res'."

Major Carteret, from the head of the stairs, called the doctor anxiously.

"You had better come along up now, Jane," said the doctor.

For two long hours they fought back the grim spectre that stood by the bedside. The child was born at dawn. Both mother and child, the doctor said, would live.

"Bless its 'ittle hea't!" exclaimed Mammy Jane, as she held up the tiny mite, which bore as much resemblance to mature humanity as might be expected of an infant which had for only a few minutes drawn the breath of life. "Bless its 'ittle hea't! it 's de ve'y spit an' image er its pappy!"

The doctor smiled. The major laughed aloud. Jane's unconscious witticism, or conscious flattery, whichever it might be, was a welcome diversion from the tense strain of the last few hours.

"Be that as it may," said Dr. Price cheerfully, "and I'll not dispute it, the child is a very fine boy,—a very fine boy, indeed! Take care of it, major," he added with a touch of solemnity, "for your wife can never bear another."

With the child's first cry a refreshing breeze from the distant ocean cooled the hot air of the chamber; the heavy odor of the magnolias, with its mortuary suggestiveness, gave place to the scent of rose and lilac and honeysuckle. The birds in the garden were singing lustily.

All these sweet and pleasant things found an echo in the major's heart. He stood by the window, and looking toward the rising sun, breathed a silent prayer of thanksgiving. All nature seemed to rejoice in sympathy with his happiness at the fruition of this long-deferred hope, and to predict for this wonderful child a bright and glorious future.

Old Mammy Jane, however, was not entirely at ease concerning the child. She had discovered, under its left ear, a small mole, which led her to fear that the child was born for bad luck. Had the baby been black or yellow, or poor-white, Jane would unhesitatingly have named, as his ultimate fate, a not uncommon form of taking off, usually resultant upon the infraction of certain laws, or, in these swift modern days, upon too violent a departure from established social customs. It was manifestly impossible that a child of such high quality as the grandson of her old mistress should die by judicial strangulation; but nevertheless the warning was a serious thing, and not to be lightly disregarded.

Not wishing to be considered as a prophet of evil omen, Jane kept her own counsel in regard to this significant discovery. But later, after the child was several days old, she filled a small vial with water in which the infant had been washed, and took it to a certain wise old black woman, who lived on the farther edge of the town and was well known to be versed in witchcraft and conjuration. The conjure woman added to the contents of the bottle a bit of calamus root, and one of the cervical vertebræ from the skeleton of a black cat, with several other mysterious ingredients, the nature of which she did not disclose. Following instructions given her, Aunt Jane buried the bottle in Carteret's back yard, one night during the full moon, as a good-luck charm to ward off evil from the little grandson of her dear mistress, so long since dead and gone to heaven.

II
THE CHRISTENING PARTY

THEY named the Carteret baby Theodore Felix. Theodore was a family name, and had been borne by the eldest son for several generations, the major himself being a second son. Having thus given the child two beautiful names, replete with religious and sentimental significance, they called him—"Dodie."

The baby was christened some six weeks after its birth, by which time Mrs. Carteret was able to be out. Old Mammy Jane, who had been brought up in the church, but who, like some better informed people in all ages, found religion not inconsistent with a strong vein of superstition, felt her fears for the baby's future much relieved when the rector had made the sign of the cross and sprinkled little Dodie with the water from the carved marble font, which had come from England in the reign of King Charles the Martyr, as the ill-fated son of James I. was known to St. Andrew's. Upon this special occasion Mammy Jane had been provided with a seat downstairs among the white people, to her own intense satisfaction, and to the secret envy of a small colored attendance in the gallery, to whom she was ostentatiously pointed out by her grandson Jerry, porter at the Morning Chronicle office, who sat among them in the front row.

On the following Monday evening the major gave a christening party in honor of this important event. Owing to Mrs. Carteret's still delicate health, only a small number of intimate friends and family connections were invited to attend. These were the rector of St. Andrew's; old Mrs. Polly Ochiltree, the god-mother; old Mr. Delamere, a distant relative and also one of the sponsors; and his grandson, Tom Delamere. The major had also invited Lee Ellis, his young city editor, for whom he had a great liking apart from his business value, and who was a frequent visitor at the house. These, with the family itself, which consisted of the major, his wife, and his half-sister, Clara Pemberton, a young woman of about eighteen, made up the eight persons for whom covers were laid.

Ellis was the first to arrive, a tall, loose-limbed young man, with a slightly freckled face, hair verging on auburn, a firm chin, and honest gray eyes. He had come half an hour early, and was left alone for a few minutes in the parlor, a spacious, high-ceilinged room, with large windows, and fitted up in excellent taste, with stately reminiscences of a past generation. The walls were hung with figured paper. The ceiling was whitewashed, and decorated in the middle with a plaster centre-piece, from which hung a massive chandelier sparkling with prismatic rays from a hundred crystal pendants. There was a handsome mantel, set with terra-cotta tiles, on which fauns and satyrs, nymphs and dryads, disported themselves in idyllic abandon. The furniture was old, and in keeping with the room.

At seven o'clock a carriage drove up, from which alighted an elderly gentleman, with white hair and mustache, and bowed somewhat with years. Short of breath and painfully weak in the legs, he was assisted from the carriage by a colored man, apparently about forty years old, to whom short side-whiskers and spectacles imparted an air of sobriety. This attendant gave his arm respectfully to the old gentleman, who leaned upon it heavily, but with as little appearance of dependence as possible. The servant, assuming a similar unconsciousness of the weight resting upon his arm, assisted the old gentleman carefully up the steps.

"I'm all right now, Sandy," whispered the gentleman as soon as his feet were planted firmly on the piazza. "You may come back for me at nine o'clock."

Having taken his hand from his servant's arm, he advanced to meet a lady who stood in the door awaiting him, a tall, elderly woman, gaunt and angular of frame, with a mottled face, and high cheekbones partially covered by bands of hair entirely too black and abundant for a person of her age, if one might judge from the lines of her mouth, which are rarely deceptive in such matters.

"Perhaps you'd better not send your man away, Mr. Delamere," observed the lady, in a high shrill voice, which grated upon the old gentleman's ears. He was slightly hard of hearing, but, like most deaf people, resented being screamed at. "You might need him before nine o'clock. One never knows what may happen after one has had the second stroke. And moreover, our butler has fallen down the back steps—negroes are so careless!—and sprained his ankle so that he can't stand. I'd like to have Sandy stay and wait on the table in Peter's place, if you don't mind."

"I thank you, Mrs. Ochiltree, for your solicitude," replied Mr. Delamere, with a shade of annoyance in his voice, "but my health is very good just at present, and I do not anticipate any catastrophe which will require my servant's presence before I am ready to go home. But I have no doubt, madam," he continued, with a courteous inclination, "that Sandy will be pleased to serve you, if you desire it, to the best of his poor knowledge."

"I shill be honored, ma'am," assented Sandy, with a bow even deeper than his master's, "only I'm 'feared I ain't rightly dressed fer ter wait on table. I wuz only goin' ter pra'r-meetin', an' so I did n' put on my bes' clo's. Ef Mis' Ochiltree ain' gwine ter need me fer de nex' fifteen minutes, I kin ride back home in de ca'ige an' dress myse'f suitable fer de occasion, suh."

"If you think you 'll wait on the table any better," said Mrs. Ochiltree, "you may go along and change your clothes; but hurry back, for it is seven now, and dinner will soon be served."

Sandy retired with a bow. While descending the steps to the carriage, which had waited for him, he came face to face with a young man just entering the house.

"Am I in time for dinner, Sandy?" asked the newcomer.

"Yas, Mistuh Tom, you're in plenty er time. Dinner won't be ready till *I* git back, which won' be fer fifteen minutes er so yit."

Throwing away the cigarette which he held between his fingers, the young man crossed the piazza with a light step, and after a preliminary knock, for an answer to which he did not wait, entered the house with the air of one thoroughly at home. The lights in the parlor had been lit, and Ellis, who sat talking to Major Carteret when the newcomer entered, covered him with a jealous glance.

Slender and of medium height, with a small head of almost perfect contour, a symmetrical face, dark almost to swarthiness, black eyes, which moved somewhat restlessly, curly hair of raven tint, a slight mustache, small hands and feet, and fashionable attire, Tom Delamere, the grandson of the old gentleman who had already arrived, was easily the handsomest young man in Wellington. But no discriminating observer would have characterized his beauty as manly. It conveyed no impression of strength, but did possess a certain element, feline rather than feminine, which subtly negatived the idea of manliness.

He gave his hand to the major, nodded curtly to Ellis, saluted his grandfather respectfully, and inquired for the ladies.

"Olivia is dressing for dinner," replied the major "Mrs. Ochiltree is in the kitchen, struggling with the servants. Clara—Ah, here she comes now!"

Ellis, whose senses were preternaturally acute where Clara was concerned, was already looking toward the hall and was the first to see her. Clad in an evening gown of simple white, to the close-fitting corsage of which she had fastened a bunch of pink roses, she was to Ellis a dazzling apparition. To him her erect and well-moulded form was the embodiment of symmetry, her voice sweet music, her movements the perfection of grace; and it scarcely needed a lover's imagination to read in her fair countenance a pure heart and a high spirit,—the truthfulness that scorns a lie, the pride which is not haughtiness. There were suggestive depths of tenderness, too, in the curl of her lip, the droop of her long lashes, the glance of her blue eyes,—depths that Ellis had long since divined, though he had never yet explored them. She gave Ellis a friendly nod as she came in, but for the smile with which she greeted Delamere, Ellis would have given all that he possessed,—not a great deal, it is true, but what could a man do more?

"You are the last one, Tom," she said reproachfully. "Mr. Ellis has been here half an hour."

Delamere threw a glance at Ellis which was not exactly friendly. Why should this fellow always be on hand to emphasize his own shortcomings?

"The rector is not here," answered Tom triumphantly. "You see I am not the last."

"The rector," replied Clara, "was called out of town at six o'clock this evening, to visit a dying man, and so cannot be here. You are the last, Tom, and Mr. Ellis was the first."

Ellis was ruefully aware that this comparison in his favor was the only visible advantage that he had gained from his early arrival. He had not seen Miss Pemberton a moment sooner by reason of it. There had been a certain satisfaction in being in the same house with her, but Delamere had arrived in time to share or, more correctly, to monopolize, the sunshine of her presence.

Delamere gave a plausible excuse which won Clara's pardon and another enchanting smile, which pierced Ellis like a dagger. He knew very well that Delamere's excuse was a lie. Ellis himself had been ready as early as six o'clock, but judging this to be too early, had stopped in at the Clarendon Club for half an hour, to look over the magazines. While coming out he had glanced into the card-room, where he had seen his rival deep in a game of cards, from which Delamere had evidently not been able to tear himself until the last moment. He had accounted for his lateness by a story quite inconsistent with these facts.

The two young people walked over to a window on the opposite side of the large room, where they stood talking to one another in low tones. The major had left the room for a moment. Old Mr. Delamere, who was watching his grandson and Clara with an indulgent smile, proceeded to rub salt into Ellis's wounds.

"They make a handsome couple," he observed. "I remember well when her mother, in her youth an ideally beautiful woman, of an excellent family, married Daniel Pemberton, who was not of so good a family, but had made money. The major, who was only a very young man then, disapproved of the match; he considered that his mother, although a widow and nearly forty, was marrying beneath her. But he has been a good brother to Clara, and a careful guardian of her estate. Ah, young gentleman, you cannot appreciate, except in imagination, what it means, to one standing on the brink of eternity, to feel sure that he will live on in his children and his children's children!"

Ellis was appreciating at that moment what it meant, in cold blood, with no effort of the imagination, to see the girl whom he loved absorbed completely in another man. She had looked at him only once since Tom Delamere had entered the room, and then merely to use him as a spur with which to prick his favored rival.

"Yes, sir," he returned mechanically, "Miss Clara is a beautiful young lady."

"And Tom is a good boy—a fine boy," returned the

old gentleman. "I am very well pleased with Tom, and shall be entirely happy when I see them married."

Ellis could not echo this sentiment. The very thought of this marriage made him miserable. He had always understood that the engagement was merely tentative, a sort of family understanding, subject to confirmation after Delamere should have attained his majority, which was still a year off, and when the major should think Clara old enough to marry. Ellis saw Delamere with the eye of a jealous rival, and judged him mercilessly,— whether correctly or not the sequel will show. He did not at all believe that Tom Delamere would make a fit husband for Clara Pemberton; but his opinion would have had no weight,—he could hardly have expressed it without showing his own interest. Moreover, there was no element of the sneak in Lee Ellis's make-up. The very fact that he might profit by the other's discomfiture left Delamere secure, so far as he could be affected by anything that Ellis might say. But Ellis did not shrink from a fair fight, and though in this one the odds were heavily against him, yet so long as this engagement remained indefinite, so long, indeed, as the object of his love was still unwed, he would not cease to hope. Such a sacrifice as this marriage clearly belonged in the catalogue of impossibilities. Ellis had not lived long enough to learn that impossibilities are merely things of which we have not learned, or which we do not wish to happen.

Sandy returned at the end of a quarter of an hour, and dinner was announced. Mr. Delamere led the way to the dining-room with Mrs. Ochiltree. Tom followed with Clara. The major went to the head of the stairs and came down with Mrs. Carteret upon his arm, her beauty rendered more delicate by the pallor of her countenance and more complete by the happiness with which it glowed. Ellis went in alone. In the rector's absence it was practically a family party which sat down, with the exception of Ellis, who, as we have seen, would willingly have placed himself in the same category.

The table was tastefully decorated with flowers, which grew about the house in lavish profusion. In warm climates nature adorns herself with true feminine vanity.

"What a beautiful table! " exclaimed Tom, before they were seated.

"The decorations are mine," said Clara proudly. "I cut the flowers and arranged them all myself."

"Which accounts for the admirable effect," rejoined Tom with a bow, before Ellis, to whom the same thought had occurred, was able to express himself. He had always counted himself the least envious of men, but for this occasion he coveted Tom Delamere's readiness.

"The beauty of the flowers," observed old Mr. Delamere, with sententious gallantry, "is reflected upon all around them. It is a handsome company."

Mrs. Ochiltree beamed upon the table with a dry smile.

"I don't perceive any effect that it has upon you or me," she said. "And as for the young people, 'Handsome is as handsome does.' If Tom here, for instance, were as good as he looks"—

"You flatter me, Aunt Polly," Tom broke in hastily, anticipating the crack of the whip; he was familiar with his aunt's conversational idiosyncrasies.

"If you are as good as you look," continued the old lady, with a cunning but indulgent smile, "some one has been slandering you."

"Thanks, Aunt Polly! Now you don't flatter me."

"There is Mr. Ellis," Mrs. Ochiltree went on, "who is not half so good-looking, but is steady as a clock, I dare say."

"Now, Aunt Polly," interposed Mrs. Carteret, "let the gentlemen alone."

"She does n't mean half what she says," continued Mrs. Carteret apologetically, "and only talks that way to people whom she likes."

Tom threw Mrs. Carteret a grateful glance. He had been apprehensive, with the sensitiveness of youth, lest his old great-aunt should make a fool of him before Clara's family. Nor had he relished the comparison with Ellis, who was out of place, anyway, in this family party. He had never liked the fellow, who was too much of a plodder and a prig to make a suitable associate for a whole-souled, generous-hearted young gentleman. He tolerated him as a visitor at Carteret's and as a member of the Clarendon Club, but that was all.

"Mrs. Ochiltree has a characteristic way of disguising her feelings," observed old Mr. Delamere, with a touch of sarcasm.

Ellis had merely flushed and felt uncomfortable at the reference to himself. The compliment to his character hardly offset the reflection upon his looks. He knew he was not exactly handsome, but it was not pleasant to have the fact emphasized in the presence of the girl he loved; he would like at least fair play, and judgment upon the subject left to the young lady.

Mrs. Ochiltree was quietly enjoying herself. In early life she had been accustomed to impale fools on epigrams, like flies on pins, to see them wriggle. But with advancing years she had lost in some measure the faculty of nice discrimination,—it was pleasant to see her victims squirm, whether they were fools or friends. Even one's friends, she argued, were not always wise, and were sometimes the better for being told the truth. At her niece's table she felt at liberty to speak her mind, which she invariably did, with a frankness that sometimes bordered on brutality. She had long ago outgrown the period where ambition or passion, or its partners, envy and hatred, were springs of action in her life, and simply retained a mild enjoyment in the exercise of an old habit, with no active malice whatever. The ruling passion merely grew stronger as the restraining faculties decreased in vigor.

A diversion was created at this point by the appearance of old Mammy Jane, dressed in a calico frock, with clean white neckerchief and apron, carrying the wonderful baby in honor of whose naming this feast had been given. Though only six weeks old, the little Theodore had grown rapidly, and Mammy Jane declared was already quite large for his age, and displayed signs of an unusually precocious intelligence. He was passed around the table and duly admired. Clara thought his hair was fine. Ellis inquired about his teeth. Tom put his finger in the baby's fist to test his grip. Old Mr. Delamere was unable to decide as yet whether he favored most his father or his mother. The object of these attentions endured them patiently for several minutes, and then protested with a vocal vigor which led to his being taken promptly back upstairs. Whatever fate might be in store for him, he manifested no sign of weak lungs.

"Sandy," said Mrs. Carteret when the baby had retired,

"pass that tray standing upon the side table, so that we may all see the presents."

Mr. Delamere had brought a silver spoon, and Tom a napkin ring. Ellis had sent a silver watch; it was a little premature, he admitted, but the boy would grow to it, and could use it to play with in the mean time. It had a glass back, so that he might see the wheels go round. Mrs. Ochiltree's present was an old and yellow ivory rattle, with a handle which the child could bite while teething, and a knob screwed on at the end to prevent the handle from slipping through the baby's hand.

"I saw that in your cedar chest, Aunt Polly," said Clara, "when I was a little girl, and you used to pull the chest out from under your bed to get me a dime."

"You kept the rattle in the right-hand corner of the chest," said Tom, "in the box with the red silk purse, from which you took the gold piece you gave me every Christmas."

A smile shone on Mrs. Ochiltree's severe features at this appreciation, like a ray of sunlight on a snow-bank.

"Aunt Polly's chest is like the widow's cruse," said Mrs. Carteret, "which was never empty."

"Or Fortunatus's purse, which was always full," added old Mr. Delamere, who read the Latin poets, and whose allusions were apt to be classical rather than scriptural.

"It will last me while I live," said Mrs. Ochiltree, adding cautiously, "but there'll not be a great deal left. It won't take much to support an old woman for twenty years."

Mr. Delamere's man Sandy had been waiting upon the table with the decorum of a trained butler, and a gravity all his own. He had changed his suit of plain gray for a long blue coat with brass buttons, which dated back to the fashion of a former generation, with which he wore a pair of plaid trousers of strikingly modern cut and pattern. With his whiskers, his spectacles, and his solemn air of responsibility, he would have presented, to one unfamiliar with the negro type, an amusingly impressive appearance. But there was nothing incongruous about Sandy to this company, except perhaps to Tom Delamere, who possessed a keen eye for contrasts and always regarded Sandy, in that particular rig, as a very comical darkey.

"Is it quite prudent, Mrs. Ochiltree," suggested the major at a moment when Sandy, having set down the tray, had left the room for a little while, "to mention, in the presence of the servants, that you keep money in the house?"

"I beg your pardon, major," observed old Mr. Delamere, with a touch of stiffness. "The only servant in hearing of the conversation has been my own and Sandy is as honest as any man in Wellington."

"You mean, sir," replied Carteret, with a smile, "as honest as any *negro* in Wellington."

"I make no exceptions, major," returned the old gentleman, with emphasis. "I would trust Sandy with my life,—he saved it once at the risk of his own."

"No doubt," mused the major, "the negro is capable of a certain doglike fidelity,—I make the comparison in a kindly sense,—a certain personal devotion which is admirable in itself, and fits him eminently for a servile career. I should imagine, however, that one could more safely trust his life with a negro than his portable property."

"Very clever, major! I read your paper, and know that your feeling is hostile toward the negro, but"—

The major made a gesture of dissent, but remained courteously silent until Mr. Delamere had finished.

"For my part," the old gentleman went on, "I think they have done very well, considering what they started from, and their limited opportunities. There was Adam Miller, for instance, who left a conformable estate. His son George carries on the business, and the younger boy, William, is a good doctor and stands well with his profession. His hospital is a good thing, and if my estate were clear, I should like to do something for it."

"You are mistaken, sir, in imagining me hostile to the negro," explained Carteret. "On the contrary, I am friendly to his best interests. I give him employment; I pay taxes for schools to educate him, and for court-houses and jails to keep him in order. I merely object to being governed by an inferior and servile race."

Mrs. Carteret's face wore a tired expression. This question was her husband's hobby, and therefore her own nightmare. Moreover, she had her personal grievance against the negro race, and the names mentioned by old Mr. Delamere had brought it vividly before her mind. She had no desire to mar the harmony of the occasion by the discussion of a distasteful subject.

Mr. Delamere, glancing at his hostess, read something of this thought, and refused the challenge to further argument.

"I do not believe, major," he said, "that Olivia relishes the topic. I merely wish to say that Sandy is an exception to any rule which you may formulate in derogation of the negro. Sandy is a gentleman in ebony!"

Tom could scarcely preserve his gravity at this characterization of old Sandy, with his ridiculous air of importance, his long blue coat, and his loud plaid trousers. That suit would make a great costume for a masquerade. He would borrow it some time,—there was nothing in the world like it.

"Well, Mr. Delamere," returned the major good-humoredly, "no doubt Sandy is an exceptionally good negro,—he might well be, for he has had the benefit of your example all his life,—and we know that he is a faithful servant. But nevertheless, if I were Mrs. Ochiltree, I should put my money in the bank. Not all negroes are as honest as Sandy, and an elderly lady might not prove a match for a burly black burglar."

"Thank you, major," retorted Mrs. Ochiltree, with spirit, "I'm not yet too old to take care of myself. That cedar chest has been my bank for forty years, and I shall not change my habits at my age."

At this moment Sandy reëntered the room. Carteret made a warning gesture, which Mrs. Ochiltree chose not to notice.

"I've proved a match for two husbands, and am not afraid of any man that walks the earth, black or white, by day or night. I have a revolver, and know how to use it. Whoever attempts to rob me will do so at his peril."

After dinner Clara played the piano and sang duets with Tom Delamere. At nine o'clock Mr. Delamere's carriage came for him, and he went away accompanied by Sandy. Under cover of the darkness the old gentleman leaned on his servant's arm with frank dependence, and Sandy lifted him into the carriage with every mark of devotion.

Ellis had already excused himself to go to the office and look over the late proofs for the morning paper. Tom remained a few minutes longer than his grandfather, and upon taking his leave went round to the Clarendon Club, where he spent an hour or two in the card-room with a couple of congenial friends. Luck seemed to favor him, and he went home at midnight with a comfortable balance of winnings. He was fond of excitement, and found a great deal of it in cards. To lose was only less exciting than to win. Of late he had developed into a very successful player,—so successful, indeed, that several members of the club generally found excuses to avoid participating in a game where he made one.

III
THE EDITOR AT WORK

To go back a little, for several days after his child's birth Major Carteret's chief interest in life had been confined to the four walls of the chamber where his pale wife lay upon her bed of pain, and those of the adjoining room where an old black woman crooned lovingly over a little white infant. A new element had been added to the major's consciousness, broadening the scope and deepening the strength of his affections. He did not love Olivia the less, for maternity had crowned her wifehood with an added glory; but side by side with this old and tried attachment was a new passion, stirring up dormant hopes and kindling new desires. His regret had been more than personal at the thought that with himself an old name should be lost to the State; and now all the old pride of race, class, and family welled up anew, and swelled and quickened the current of his life.

Upon the major's first appearance at the office, which took place the second day after the child's birth, he opened a box of cigars in honor of the event. The word had been passed around by Ellis, and the whole office force, including reporters, compositors, and pressmen, came in to congratulate the major and smoke at his expense. Even Jerry, the colored porter,—Mammy Jane's grandson and therefore a protégé of the family,—presented himself among the rest, or rather, after the rest. The major shook hands with them all except Jerry, though he acknowledged the porter's congratulations with a kind nod and put a good cigar into his outstretched palm, for which Jerry thanked him without manifesting any consciousness of the omission. He was quite aware that under ordinary circumstances the major would not have shaken hands with white workingmen, to say nothing of negroes; and he had merely hoped that in the pleasurable distraction of the moment the major might also overlook the distinction of color. Jerry's hope had been shattered, though not rudely; for the major had spoken pleasantly and the cigar was a good one. Mr. Ellis had once shaken hands with Jerry,—but Mr. Ellis was a young man, whose Quaker father had never owned any slaves, and he could not be expected to have as much pride as one of the best "quality," whose families had possessed land and negroes for time out of mind. On the whole, Jerry preferred the careless nod of the editor-in-chief to the more familiar greeting of the subaltern.

Having finished this pleasant ceremony, which left him with a comfortable sense of his new dignity, the major turned to his desk. It had been much neglected during the week, and more than one matter claimed his attention; but as typical of the new trend of his thoughts, the first subject he took up was one bearing upon the future of his son. Quite obviously the career of a Carteret must not be left to chance,—it must be planned and worked out with a due sense of the value of good blood.

There lay upon his desk a letter from a well-known promoter, offering the major an investment which promised large returns, though several years must elapse before the enterprise could be put upon a paying basis. The element of time, however, was not immediately important. The Morning Chronicle provided him an ample income. The money available for this investment was part of his wife's patrimony. It was invested in a local cotton mill, which was paying ten per cent., but this was a beggarly return compared with the immense profits promised by the offered investment,—profits which would enable his son, upon reaching manhood, to take a place in the world commensurate with the dignity of his ancestors, one of whom, only a few generations removed, had owned an estate of ninety thousand acres of land and six thousand slaves.

This letter having been disposed of by an answer accepting the offer, the major took up his pen to write an editorial. Public affairs in the state were not going to his satisfaction. At the last state election his own party, after an almost unbroken rule of twenty years, had been defeated by the so-called "Fusion" ticket, a combination of Republicans and Populists. A clean sweep had been made of the offices in the state, which were now filled by new men. Many of the smaller places had gone to colored men, their people having voted almost solidly for the Fusion ticket. In spite of the fact that the population of Wellington was two thirds colored, this state of things was gall and wormwood to the defeated party, of which the Morning Chronicle was the acknowledged organ. Major Carteret shared this feeling. Only this very morning, while passing the city hall, on his way to the office, he had seen the steps of that noble building disfigured by a fringe of job-hunting negroes, for all the world—to use a local simile—like a string of buzzards sitting on a rail, awaiting their opportunity to batten upon the helpless corpse of a moribund city.

Taking for his theme the unfitness of the negro to participate in government,—an unfitness due to his limited education, his lack of experience, his criminal tendencies, and more especially to his hopeless mental and physical inferiority to the white race,—the major had demonstrated, it seemed to him clearly enough, that the ballot in the hands of the negro was a menace to the commonwealth. He had argued, with entire conviction, that the white and black races could never attain social and political harmony by commingling their blood; he had proved by several historical parallels that no two unassimilable races could ever live together except in the relation of superior and inferior; and he was just dipping his gold pen into the ink to indite his conclusions from the premises thus established, when Jerry, the porter, announced two visitors.

"Gin'l Belmont an' Cap'n McBane would like ter see you, suh."

"Show them in, Jerry."

The man who entered first upon this invitation was a dapper little gentleman with light-blue eyes and a Vandyke beard. He wore a frock coat, patent leather shoes, and a Panama hat. There were crow's-feet about his eyes, which twinkled with a hard and, at times, humorous shrewdness. He had sloping shoulders, small hands and feet, and walked with the leisurely step characteristic of those who have been reared under hot suns.

Carteret gave his hand cordially to the gentleman thus described.

"How do you do, Captain McBane," he said, turning to the second visitor.

The individual thus addressed was strikingly different in appearance from his companion. His broad shoulders, burly form, square jaw, and heavy chin betokened strength, energy, and unscrupulousness. With the exception of a small, bristling mustache, his face was clean shaven, with here and there a speck of dried blood due to a carelessly or unskillfully handled razor. A single deep-set gray eye was shadowed by a beetling brow, over which a crop of coarse black hair, slightly streaked with gray, fell almost low enough to mingle with his black, bushy eyebrows. His coat had not been brushed for several days, if one might judge from the accumulation of dandruff upon the collar, and his shirt-front, in the middle of which blazed a showy diamond, was plentifully stained with tobacco juice. He wore a large slouch hat, which, upon entering the office, he removed and held in his hand.

Having greeted this person with an unconscious but quite perceptible diminution of the warmth with which he had welcomed the other, the major looked around the room for seats for his visitors, and perceiving only one chair, piled with exchanges, and a broken stool propped against the wall, pushed a button, which rang a bell in the hall, summoning the colored porter to his presence.

"Jerry," said the editor when his servant appeared, "bring a couple of chairs for these gentlemen."

While they stood waiting, the visitors congratulated the major on the birth of his child, which had been announced in the Morning Chronicle, and which the prominence of the family made in some degree a matter of public interest.

"And now that you have a son, major," remarked the gentleman first described, as he lit one of the major's cigars, "you'll be all the more interested in doing something to make this town fit to live in, which is what we came up to talk about. Things are in an awful condition! A negro justice of the peace has opened an office on Market Street, and only yesterday summoned a white man to appear before him. Negro lawyers get most of the business in the criminal court. Last evening a group of young white ladies, going quietly along the street arm-in-arm, were forced off the sidewalk by a crowd of negro girls. Coming down the street just now, I saw a spectacle of social equality and negro domination that made my blood boil with indignation,—a white and a black convict, chained together, crossing the city in charge of a negro officer! We cannot stand that sort of thing, Carteret,—it is the last straw! Something must be done, and that quickly!"

The major thrilled with responsive emotion. There was something prophetic in this opportune visit. The matter was not only in his own thoughts, but in the air; it was the spontaneous revulsion of white men against the rule of an inferior race. These were the very men, above all others in the town, to join him in a movement to change these degrading conditions.

General Belmont, the smaller of the two, was a man of good family, a lawyer by profession, and took an active part in state and local politics. Aristocratic by birth and instinct, and a former owner of slaves, his conception of the obligations and rights of his caste was nevertheless somewhat lower than that of the narrower but more sincere Carteret. In serious affairs Carteret desired the approval of his conscience, even if he had to trick that docile organ into acquiescence. This was not difficult to do in politics, for he believed in the divine right of white men and gentlemen, as his ancestors had believed in and died for the divine right of kings. General Belmont was not without a gentleman's distaste for meanness, but he permitted no fine scruples to stand in the way of success. He had once been minister, under a Democratic administration, to a small Central American state. Political rivals had characterized him as a tricky demagogue, which may of course have been a libel. He had an amiable disposition, possessed the gift of eloquence, and was a prime social favorite.

Captain George McBane had sprung from the poor-white class, to which, even more than to the slaves, the abolition of slavery had opened the door of opportunity. No longer overshadowed by a slaveholding caste, some of this class had rapidly pushed themselves forward. Some had made honorable records. Others, foremost in negro-baiting and election frauds, had done the dirty work of politics, as their fathers had done that of slavery, seeking their reward at first in minor offices,—for which men of gentler breeding did not care,—until their ambition began to reach out for higher honors.

Of this class McBane—whose captaincy, by the way, was merely a polite fiction—had been one of the most successful. He had held, until recently, as the reward of questionable political services, a contract with the State for its convict labor, from which in a few years he had realized a fortune. But the methods which made his contract profitable had not commended themselves to humane people, and charges of cruelty and worse had been preferred against him. He was rich enough to escape serious consequences from the investigation which followed, but when the Fusion ticket carried the state he lost his contract, and the system of convict labor was abolished. Since then McBane, had devoted himself to politics: he was ambitious for greater wealth, for office, and for social recognition. A man of few words and self-engrossed, he seldom spoke of his aspirations except where speech might favor them, preferring to seek his ends by secret "deals" and combinations rather than to challenge criticism and provoke rivalry by more open methods.

At sight, therefore, of these two men, with whose careers and characters he was entirely familiar, Carteret felt sweep over his mind the conviction that now was the time and these the instruments with which to undertake the redemption of the state from the evil fate which had befallen it.

Jerry, the porter, who had gone downstairs to the counting-room to find two whole chairs, now entered with one in each hand. He set a chair for the general, who gave him an amiable nod, to which Jerry responded with a bow and a scrape. Captain McBane made no acknowledgment, but fixed Jerry so fiercely with his single eye that upon placing the chair Jerry made his escape from the room as rapidly as possible.

"I don' like dat Cap'n McBane," he muttered, upon reaching the hall. "Dey says he got dat eye knock' out tryin' ter whip a cullud 'oman, when he wuz a boy, an' dat he ain' never had no use fer niggers sence—'cep'n' fer what he could make outen 'em wid his convic' labor contrac's. His daddy wuz a' overseer befo' 'im, an' it come nachul fer him ter be a nigger-driver. I don' want dat one eye er his'n restin' on me no longer 'n I kin he'p, an' I don' know how I'm gwine ter like dis job ef he's gwine ter be comin' roun' here. He ain' nothin' but po' w'ite trash nohow; but Lawd! Lawd! look at de money he's got,—livin' at de hotel, wearin' di'mon's, an' colloguin' wid de bes' quality er dis town! 'Pears ter me de bottom rail is gittin' mighty close ter de top. Well, I s'pose it all comes f'm bein' w'ite. I wush ter Gawd I wuz w'ite!"

After this fervent aspiration, having nothing else to do for the time being, except to remain within call, and having caught a few words of the conversation as he went in with the chairs, Jerry, who possessed a certain amount of curiosity, placed close to the wall the broken stool upon which he sat while waiting in the hall, and applied his ear to a hole in the plastering of the hallway. There was a similar defect in the inner wall, between the same two pieces of studding, and while this inner opening was not exactly opposite the outer, Jerry was enabled, through the two, to catch in a more or less fragmentary way what was going on within.

He could hear the major, now and then, use the word "negro," and McBane's deep voice was quite audible when he referred, it seemed to Jerry with alarming frequency, to "the damned niggers," while the general's suave tones now and then pronounced the word "niggro,"—a sort of compromise between ethnology and the vernacular. That the gentlemen were talking politics seemed quite likely, for gentlemen generally talked politics when they met at the Chronicle office. Jerry could hear the words "vote," "franchise," "eliminate," "constitution," and other expressions which marked the general tenor of the talk, though he could not follow it all,— partly because he could not hear everything distinctly, and partly because of certain limitations which nature had placed in the way of Jerry's understanding anything very difficult or abstruse.

He had gathered enough, however, to realize, in a vague way, that something serious was on foot, involving his own race, when a bell sounded over his head, at which he sprang up hastily and entered the room where the gentlemen were talking.

"Jerry," said the major, "wait on Captain McBane."

"Yas suh," responded Jerry, turning toward the captain, whose eye he carefully avoided meeting directly.

"Take that half a dollar, boy," ordered McBane, "an' go 'cross the street to Mr. Sykes's, and tell him to send me three whiskies. Bring back the change, and make has'e."

The captain tossed the half dollar at Jerry, who, looking to one side, of course missed it. He picked the money up, however, and backed out of the room. Jerry did not like Captain McBane, to begin with, and it was clear that the captain was no gentleman, or he would not have thrown the money at him. Considering the source, Jerry might have overlooked this discourtesy had it not been coupled with the remark about the change, which seemed to him in very poor taste.

Returning in a few minutes with three glasses on a tray, he passed them round, handed Captain McBane his change, and retired to the hall.

"Gentlemen," exclaimed the captain, lifting his glass, "I propose a toast: 'No nigger domination.'"

"Amen!" said the others, and three glasses were solemnly drained.

"Major," observed the general, smacking his lips, "I should like to use Jerry for a moment, if you will permit me."

Jerry appeared promptly at the sound of the bell. He had remained conveniently near,—calls of this sort were apt to come in sequence.

"Jerry," said the general, handing Jerry half a dollar, "go over to Mr. Brown's,—I get my liquor there,—and tell them to send me three glasses of my special mixture. And, Jerry,—you may keep the change!"

"Thank y', gin'l, thank y', marster," replied Jerry, with unctuous gratitude, bending almost double as he backed out of the room.

"Dat's a gent'eman, a rale ole-time gent'eman," he said to himself when he had closed the door. "But dere 's somethin' gwine on in dere,—dere sho' is! 'No nigger damnation!' Dat soun's all right,—I'm sho' dere ain' no nigger I knows w'at wants damnation, do' dere's lots of 'em w'at deserves it; but ef dat one-eyed Cap'n McBane got anything ter do wid it, w'atever it is, it don' mean no good fer de niggers,—damnation 'd be better fer 'em dan

36

dat Cap'n McBane! He looks at a nigger lack he could jes' eat 'im alive."

"This mixture, gentlemen," observed the general when Jerry had returned with the glasses, "was originally compounded by no less a person than the great John C. Calhoun himself, who confided the recipe to my father over the convivial board. In this nectar of the gods, gentlemen, I drink with you to 'White Supremacy!'"

"White Supremacy everywhere!" added McBane with fervor.

"Now and forever!" concluded Carteret solemnly.

When the visitors, half an hour later, had taken their departure, Carteret, inspired by the theme, and in less degree by the famous mixture of the immortal Calhoun, turned to his desk and finished, at a white heat, his famous editorial in which he sounded the tocsin of a new crusade.

At noon, when the editor, having laid down his pen, was leaving the office, he passed Jerry in the hall without a word or a nod. The major wore a rapt look, which Jerry observed with a vague uneasiness.

"He looks jes' lack he wuz walkin' in his sleep," muttered Jerry uneasily. "Dere's somethin' up, sho's you bawn! 'No nigger damnation!' Anybody'd 'low dey wuz all gwine ter heaven; but I knows better! W'en a passel er w'ite folks gits ter talkin' 'bout de niggers lack dem in yander, it's mo' lackly dey're gwine ter ketch somethin' e'se dan heaven! I got ter keep my eyes open an' keep up wid w'at's happenin'. Ef dere's gwine ter be anudder flood 'roun' here, I wants ter git in de ark wid de w'ite folks,—I may haf ter be anudder Ham, an' sta't de cullud race all over ag'in."

IV
THEODORE FELIX

THE young heir of the Carterets had thriven apace, and at six months old was, according to Mammy Jane, whose experience qualified her to speak with authority, the largest, finest, smartest, and altogether most remarkable baby that had ever lived in Wellington. Mammy Jane had recently suffered from an attack of inflammatory rheumatism, as the result of which she had returned to her own home. She nevertheless came now and then to see Mrs. Carteret. A younger nurse had been procured to take her place, but it was understood that Jane would come whenever she might be needed.

"You really mean that about Dodie, do you, Mammy Jane?" asked the delighted mother, who never tired of hearing her own opinion confirmed concerning this wonderful child, which had come to her like an angel from heaven.

"Does I mean it!" exclaimed Mammy Jane, with a tone and an expression which spoke volumes of reproach. "Now, Mis' 'Livy, what is I ever uttered er said er spoke er done dat would make you s'pose I could tell you a lie 'bout yo' own chile?"

"No, Mammy Jane, I'm sure you would n't."

"'Deed, ma'am, I'm tellin' you de Lawd's truf. I don' haf ter tell no lies ner strain no p'ints 'bout my ole mist'ess's gran'chile. Dis yer boy is de ve'y spit an' image er yo' brother, young Mars Alick, w'at died w'en he wuz 'bout eight mont's ole, w'iles I wuz laid off havin' a baby er my own, an' could n' be roun' ter look after 'im. An' dis chile is a rale quality chile, he is,—I never seed a baby wid sech fine hair fer his age, nor sech blue eyes, ner sech a grip, ner sech a heft. W'y, dat chile mus' weigh 'bout twenty-fo' poun's, an' he not but six mont's ole. Does dat gal w'at does de nussin' w'iles I 'm gone ten' ter dis chile right, Mis' 'Livy?

"She does fairly well, Mammy Jane, but I could hardly expect her to love the baby as you do. There's no one like you, Mammy Jane."

"'Deed dere ain't, honey; you is talkin' de gospel truf now! None er dese yer young folks ain' got de trainin' my ole mist'ess give me. Dese yer newfangle' schools don' l'arn 'em nothin' ter compare wid it. I'm jes' gwine ter give dat gal a piece er my min', befo' I go, so she'll ten' ter dis chile right."

The nurse came in shortly afterwards, a neat-looking brown girl, dressed in a clean calico gown, with a nurse's cap and apron.

"Look a-here, gal," said Mammy Jane sternly, "I wants you ter understan' dat you got ter take good keer er dis chile; for I nussed his mammy dere, an' his gran'mammy befo' 'im, an' you is got a priv'lege dat mos' lackly you don' 'preciate. I wants you to 'member, in yo' incomin's an' out goin's, dat I got my eye on you, an' am gwine ter see dat you does yo' wo'k right."

"Do you need me for anything, ma'am?" asked the young nurse, who had stood before Mrs. Carteret, giving Mammy Jane a mere passing glance, and listening impassively to her harangue. The nurse belonged to the younger generation of colored people. She had graduated from the mission school, and had received some instruction in Dr. Miller's class for nurses. Standing, like most young people of her race, on the border line between two irreconcilable states of life, she had neither the picturesqueness of the slave, nor the unconscious dignity of those of whom freedom has been the immemorial birthright; she was in what might be called the chip-on-the-shoulder stage, through which races as well as individuals must pass in climbing the ladder of life,—not an interesting, at least not an agreeable stage, but an inevitable one, and for that reason entitled to a paragraph in a story of Southern life, which, with its as yet imperfect blending of old with new, of race with race, of slavery with freedom, is like no other life under the sun.

Had this old woman, who had no authority over her, been a little more polite, or a little less offensive, the nurse might have returned her a pleasant answer. These old-time negroes, she said to herself, made her sick with their slavering over the white folks, who, she supposed, favored them and made much of them because they had once belonged to them,—much the same reason why they fondled their cats and dogs. For her own part, they gave her nothing but her wages, and small wages at that, and she owed them nothing more than equivalent service. It was purely a matter of business; she sold her time for their money. There was no question of love between them.

Receiving a negative answer from Mrs. Carteret, she left the room without a word, ignoring Mammy Jane completely, and leaving that venerable relic of antebellum times gasping in helpless astonishment.

"Well, I nevuh!" she ejaculated, as soon as she could get her breath, "ef dat ain' de beatinis' pe'fo'mance I ever seed er heared of! Dese yer young niggers ain' got de manners dey wuz bawned wid! I don' know w'at dey 're comin' to, w'en dey ain' got no mo' rispec' fer ole age—I don' know—I don' know!"

"Now what are you croaking about, Jane?" asked Major Carteret, who came into the room and took the child into his arms.

Mammy Jane hobbled to her feet and bobbed a curtsy. She was never lacking in respect to white people of proper quality; but Major Carteret, the quintessence of aristocracy, called out all her reserves of deference. The major was always kind and considerate to these old family retainers, brought up in the feudal atmosphere now so rapidly passing away. Mammy Jane loved Mrs. Carteret; toward the major she entertained a feeling bordering upon awe.

"Well, Jane," returned the major sadly, when the old nurse had related her grievance, "the old times have vanished, the old ties have been ruptured. The old relations of dependence and loyal obedience on the part of the colored people, the responsibility of protection and kindness upon that of the whites, have passed away forever. The young negroes are too self-assertive. Education is spoiling them, Jane; they have been badly taught. They are not content with their station in life. Some time they will overstep the mark. The white people are patient, but there is a limit to their endurance.

"Dat's w'at I tells dese young niggers," groaned Mammy Jane, with a portentous shake of her turbaned head, "w'en I hears 'em gwine on wid deir foolishniss; but dey don' min' me. Dey 'lows dey knows mo' d'n I does, 'ca'se dey be'n l'arnt ter look in a book. But, pshuh! my ole mist'ess showed me mo' d'n dem niggers 'll l'arn in a thousan' years! I's fetch' my gran'son' Jerry up ter be 'umble, an' keep in 'is place. An' I tells dese other niggers dat of dey'd do de same, an' not crowd do w'ite

41

folks, dey'd git ernuff ter eat, an' live out deir days in peace an' comfo't. But dey don' min' me—dey don' min' me!"

"If all the colored people were like you and Jerry, Jane," rejoined the major kindly, "there would never be any trouble. You have friends upon whom, in time of need, you can rely implicitly for protection and succor. You served your mistress faithfully before the war; you remained by her when the other negroes were running hither and thither like sheep without a shepherd; and you have transferred your allegiance to my wife and her child. We think a great deal of you, Jane."

"Yes, indeed, Mammy Jane," assented Mrs. Carteret, with sincere affection, glancing with moist eyes from the child in her husband's arms to the old nurse, whose dark face was glowing with happiness at these expressions of appreciation, "you shall never want so long as we have anything. We would share our last crust with you."

"Thank y', Mis' 'Livy," said Jane with reciprocal emotion, "I knows who my frien's is, an' I ain' gwine ter let nothin' worry me. But for de Lawd's sake, Mars Philip, gimme dat chile, an' lemme pat 'im on de back, er he 'll choke hisse'f ter death!"

The old nurse had been the first to observe that little Dodie, for some reason, was gasping for breath. Catching the child from the major's arms, she patted it on the back, and shook it gently. After a moment of this treatment, the child ceased to gasp, but still breathed heavily, with a strange, whistling noise.

"Oh, my child!" exclaimed the mother, in great alarm, taking the baby in her own arms, "what can be the matter with him, Mammy Jane?"

"Fer de Lawd's sake, ma'am, I don' know, 'less he's swallered somethin'; an' he ain' had nothin' in his han's but de rattle Mis' Polly give 'im."

Mrs. Carteret caught up the ivory rattle, which hung suspended by a ribbon from the baby's neck.

"He has swallowed the little piece off the end of the handle," she cried, turning pale with fear, "and it has lodged in his throat. Telephone Dr. Price to come immediately, Philip, before my baby chokes to death! Oh, my baby, my precious baby!"

An anxious half hour passed, during which the child lay quiet, except for its labored breathing. The suspense was relieved by the arrival of Dr. Price, who examined the child carefully.

"It's a curious accident," he announced at the close of his inspection. "So far as I can discover, the piece of ivory has been drawn into the trachea, or windpipe, and has lodged in the mouth of the right bronchus. I'll try to get it out without an operation, but I can't guarantee the result."

At the end of another half hour Dr. Price announced his inability to remove the obstruction without resorting to more serious measures.

"I do not see," he declared, "how an operation can be avoided."

"Will it be dangerous?" inquired the major anxiously, while Mrs. Carteret shivered at the thought.

"It will be necessary to cut into his throat from the outside. All such operations are more or less dangerous, especially on small children. If this were some other child, I might undertake the operation unassisted; but I know how you value this one, major, and I should prefer to share the responsibility with a specialist."

"Is there one in town? " asked the major.

"No, but we can get one from out of town."

"Send for the best one in the country," said the major, "who can be got here in time. Spare no expense, Dr. Price. We value this child above any earthly thing."

"The best is the safest," replied Dr. Price. "I will send for Dr. Burns, of Philadelphia, the best surgeon in that line in America. If he can start at once, he can reach here in sixteen or eighteen hours, and the case can wait even longer, if inflammation does not set in."

The message was dispatched forthwith. By rare good fortune the eminent specialist was able to start within an hour or two after the receipt of Dr. Price's telegram. Meanwhile the baby remained restless and uneasy, the doctor spending most of his time by its side. Mrs. Carteret, who had never been quite strong since the child's birth, was a prey to the most agonizing apprehensions.

Mammy Jane, while not presuming to question the opinion of Dr. Price, and not wishing to add to her mistress's distress, was secretly oppressed by forebodings which she was unable to shake off. The child was born for bad luck. The mole under its ear, just at the point where the hangman's knot would strike, had foreshadowed dire misfortune. She had already observed several little things which had rendered her vaguely anxious.

For instance, upon one occasion, on entering the room where the baby had been left alone, asleep in her crib, she had met a strange cat hurrying from the nursery, and, upon examining closely the pillow upon which the child lay, had found a depression which had undoubtedly been due to the weight of the cat's body. The child was restless and uneasy, and Jane had ever since believed that the cat had been sucking little Dodie's breath, with what might have been fatal results had she not appeared just in the nick of time.

This untimely accident of the rattle, a fatality for which no one could be held responsible, had confirmed the unlucky omen. Jane's duties in the nursery did not permit her to visit her friend the conjure woman; but she did find time to go out in the back yard at dusk, and to dig up the charm which she had planted there. It had protected the child so far; but perhaps its potency had become exhausted. She picked up the bottle, shook it vigorously, and then laid it back, with the other side up. Refilling the hole, she made a cross over the top with the thumb of her left hand, and walked three times around it.

What this strange symbolism meant, or whence it derived its origin, Aunt Jane did not know. The cross was there, and the Trinity, though Jane was scarcely conscious of these, at this moment, as religious emblems. But she hoped, on general principles, that this performance would strengthen the charm and restore little Dodie's luck. It certainly had its moral effect upon Jane's own mind, for she was able to sleep better, and contrived to impress Mrs. Carteret with her own hopefulness.

V
A JOURNEY SOUTHWARD

As the south-bound train was leaving the station at Philadelphia, a gentleman took his seat in the single sleeping-car attached to the train, and proceeded to make himself comfortable. He hung up his hat and opened his newspaper, in which he remained absorbed for a quarter of an hour. When the train had left the city behind, he threw the paper aside, and looked around at the other occupants of the car. One of these, who had been on the car since it had left New York, rose from his seat upon perceiving the other's glance, and came down the aisle.

"How do you do, Dr. Burns?" he said, stopping beside the seat of the Philadelphia passenger.

The gentleman looked up at the speaker with an air of surprise, which, after the first keen, incisive glance, gave place to an expression of cordial recognition.

"Why, it's Miller!" he exclaimed, rising and giving the other his hand, "William Miller—Dr. Miller, of course. Sit down, Miller, and tell me all about yourself,—what you're doing, where you've been, and where you're going. I'm delighted to meet you, and to see you looking so well—and so prosperous."

"I deserve no credit for either, sir," returned the other, as he took the proffered seat, "for I inherited both health and prosperity. It is a fortunate chance that permits me to meet you."

The two acquaintances, thus opportunely thrown together so that they might while away in conversation the tedium of their journey, represented very different and yet very similar types of manhood. A celebrated traveler, after many years spent in barbarous or savage lands, has said that among all varieties of mankind the similarities are vastly more important and fundamental than the differences. Looking at these two men with the American eye, the differences would perhaps be the more striking, or at least the more immediately apparent, for the first was white and the second black, or, more correctly speaking, brown; it was even a light brown, but both his swarthy complexion and his curly hair revealed what has been described in the laws of some of our states as a "visible admixture" of African blood.

Having disposed of this difference, and having observed that the white man was perhaps fifty years of age and the other not more than thirty, it may be said that they were both tall and sturdy, both well dressed, the white man with perhaps a little more distinction; both seemed from their faces and their manners to be men of culture and accustomed to the society of cultivated people. They were both handsome men, the elder representing a fine type of Anglo-Saxon, as the term is used in speaking of our composite white population; while the mulatto's erect form, broad shoulders, clear eyes, fine teeth, and pleasingly moulded features showed nowhere any sign of that degeneration which the pessimist so sadly maintains is the inevitable heritage of mixed races.

As to their personal relations, it has already appeared that they were members of the same profession. In past years they had been teacher and pupil. Dr. Alvin Burns was professor in the famous medical college where Miller had attended lectures. The professor had taken an interest in his only colored pupil, to whom he had been attracted by his earnestness of purpose, his evident talent, and his excellent manners and fine physique. It was in part due to Dr. Burns's friendship that Miller had won a scholarship which had enabled him, without drawing too heavily upon his father's resources, to spend in Europe, studying in the hospitals of Paris and Vienna, the two most delightful years of his life. The same influence had strengthened his natural inclination toward operative surgery, in which Dr. Burns was a distinguished specialist of national reputation.

Miller's father, Adam Miller, had been a thrifty colored man, the son of a slave, who, in the olden time, had bought himself with money which he had earned and saved, over and above what he had paid his master for his time. Adam Miller had inherited his father's thrift, as well as his trade, which was that of a stevedore, or contractor for the loading and unloading of vessels at the port of Wellington. In the flush turpentine days following a few years after the civil war, he had made money. His savings, shrewdly invested, had by constant accessions become a competence. He had brought up his eldest son to the trade; the other he had given a professional education, in the proud hope that his children or his grandchildren might be gentlemen in the town where their ancestors had once been slaves.

Upon his father's death, shortly after Dr. Miller's return from Europe, and a year or two before the date at which this story opens, he had promptly spent part of his inheritance in founding a hospital, to which was to be added a training school for nurses, and in time perhaps a medical college and a school of pharmacy. He had been strongly tempted to leave the South, and seek a home for his family and a career for himself in the freer North, where race antagonism was less keen, or at least less oppressive, or in Europe, where he had never found his color work to his disadvantage. But his people had needed him, and he had wished to help them, and had sought by means of this institution to contribute to their uplifting. As he now informed Dr. Burns, he was returning from New York, where he had been in order to purchase equipment for his new hospital, which would soon be ready for the reception of patients.

"How much I can accomplish I do not know," said Miller, "but I'll do what I can. There are eight or nine million of us, and it will take a great deal of learning of all kinds to leaven that lump."

"It is a great problem, Miller, the future of your race," returned the other, "a tremendously interesting problem. It is a serial story which we are all reading, and which grows in vital interest with each successive installment. It is not only your problem, but ours. Your race must come up or drag ours down."

"We shall come up," declared Miller; "slowly and painfully, perhaps, but we shall win our way. If our race had made as much progress everywhere as they have made in Wellington, the problem would be well on the way toward solution."

"Wellington?" exclaimed Dr. Burns. "That's where I'm going. A Dr. Price, of Wellington, has sent for me to perform an operation on a child's throat. Do you know Dr. Price?"

"Quite well," replied Miller, "he is a friend of mine."

"So much the better. I shall want you to assist me. I read in the Medical Gazette, the other day, an account of a very interesting operation of yours. I felt proud to number you among my pupils. It was a remarkable case—a rare case. I must certainly have you with me in this one."

"I shall be delighted, sir," returned Miller, "if it is agreeable to all concerned."

Several hours were passed in pleasant conversation while the train sped rapidly southward. They were already far down in Virginia, and had stopped at a station beyond Richmond, when the conductor entered the car.

"All passengers," he announced, "will please transfer to the day coaches ahead. "The sleeper has a hot box, and must be switched off here."

Dr. Burns and Miller obeyed the order, the former leading the way into the coach immediately in front of the sleeping-car.

"Let's sit here, Miller," he said, having selected a seat near the rear of the car and deposited his suitcase in a rack. "It's on the shady side."

Miller stood a moment hesitatingly, but finally took the seat indicated, and a few minutes later the journey was again resumed.

When the train conductor made his round after leaving the station, he paused at the seat occupied by the two doctors, glanced interrogatively at Miller, and then spoke to Dr. Burns, who sat in the end of the seat nearest the aisle.

"This man is with you?" he asked, indicating Miller with a slight side movement of his head, and a keen glance in his direction.

"Certainly," replied Dr. Burns curtly, and with some surprise. "Don't you see that he is?"

The conductor passed on. Miller paid no apparent attention to this little interlude, though no syllable had escaped him. He resumed the conversation where it had been broken off, but nevertheless followed with his eyes the conductor, who stopped at a seat near the forward end of the car, and engaged in conversation with a man whom Miller had not hitherto noticed.

As this passenger turned his head and looked back toward Miller, the latter saw a broad-shouldered, burly white man, and recognized in his square-cut jaw, his coarse, firm mouth, and the single gray eye with which he swept Miller for an instant with a scornful glance, a well-known character of Wellington, with whom the reader has already made acquaintance in these pages. Captain McBane wore a frock coat and a slouch hat; several buttons of his vest were unbuttoned, and his solitaire diamond blazed in his soiled shirt-front like the headlight of a locomotive.

The conductor in his turn looked back at Miller, and retraced his steps. Miller braced himself for what he feared was coming, though he had hoped, on account of his friend's presence, that it might be avoided.

"Excuse me, sir," said the conductor, addressing Dr. Burns, "but did I understand you to say that this man was your servant?"

"No, indeed!" replied Dr. Burns indignantly. "The gentleman is not my servant, nor anybody's servant, but is my friend. But, by the way, since we are on the subject, may I ask what affair it is of yours?"

"It's very much my affair," returned the conductor, somewhat nettled at this questioning of his authority. "I'm sorry to part *friends*, but the law of Virginia does not permit colored passengers to ride in the white cars.

You'll have to go forward to the next coach," he added, addressing Miller this time.

"I have paid my fare on the sleeping-car, where the separate-car law does not apply," remonstrated Miller.

"I can't help that. You can doubtless get your money back from the sleeping-car company. But this is a day coach, and is distinctly marked 'White,' as you must have seen before you sat down here. The sign is put there for that purpose."

He indicated a large card neatly framed and hung at the end of the car, containing the legend, "White," in letters about a foot long, painted in white upon a dark background, typical, one might suppose, of the distinction thereby indicated.

"You shall not stir a step, Miller," exclaimed Dr. Burns wrathfully. "This is an outrage upon a citizen of a free country. You shall stay right here."

"I'm sorry to discommode you," returned the conductor, "but there's no use kicking. It's the law of Virginia, and I am bound by it as well as you. I have already come near losing my place because of not enforcing it, and I can take no more such chances, since I have a family to support."

"And my friend has his rights to maintain," returned Dr. Burns with determination. "There is a vital principle at stake in the matter."

"Really, sir," argued the conductor, who was a man of peace and not fond of controversy, "there's no use talking—he absolutely cannot ride in this car."

"How can you prevent it?" asked Dr. Bums, lapsing into the argumentative stage.

"The law gives me the right to remove him by force.

I can call on the train crew to assist me, or on the other passengers. If I should choose to put him off the train entirely, in the middle of a swamp, he would have no redress—the law so provides. If I did not wish to use force, I could simply switch this car off at the next siding, transfer the white passengers to another, and leave you and your friend in possession until you were arrested and fined or imprisoned."

"What he says is absolutely true, doctor," interposed Miller at this point. "It is the law, and we are powerless to resist it. If we made any trouble, it would merely delay your journey and imperil a life at the other end. I'll go into the other car."

"You shall not go alone," said Dr. Burns stoutly, rising in his turn. "A place that is too good for you is not good enough for me. I will sit wherever you do."

"I'm sorry again," said the conductor, who had quite recovered his equanimity, and calmly conscious of his power, could scarcely restrain an amused smile; "I dislike to interfere, but white passengers are not permitted to ride in the colored car."

"This is an outrage," declared Dr. Burns, "a d—d outrage! You are curtailing the rights, not only of colored people, but of white men as well. I shall sit where I please!"

"I warn you, sir," rejoined the conductor, hardening again, "that the law will be enforced. The beauty of the system lies in its strict impartiality—it applies to both races alike."

"And is equally infamous in both cases," declared Dr. Burns. "I shall immediately take steps"—

"Never mind, doctor," interrupted Miller, soothingly,

"it's only for a little while. I'll reach my destination just as surely in the other car, and we can't help it, anyway. I'll see you again at Wellington."

Dr. Burns, finding resistance futile, at length acquiesced and made way for Miller to pass him.

The colored doctor took up his valise and crossed the platform to the car ahead. It was an old car, with faded upholstery, from which the stuffing projected here and there through torn places. Apparently the floor had not been swept for several days. The dust lay thick upon the window sills, and the water-cooler, from which he essayed to get a drink, was filled with stale water which had made no recent acquaintance with ice. There was no other passenger in the car, and Miller occupied himself in making a rough calculation of what it would cost the Southern railroads to haul a whole car for every colored passenger. It was expensive, to say the least; it would be cheaper, and quite as considerate of their feelings, to make the negroes walk.

The car was conspicuously labeled at either end with large cards, similar to those in the other car, except that they bore the word "Colored" in black letters upon a white background. The author of this piece of legislation had contrived, with an ingenuity worthy of a better cause, that not merely should the passengers be separated by the color line, but that the reason for this division should be kept constantly in mind. Lest a white man should forget that he was white,—not a very likely contingency,— these cards would keep him constantly admonished of the fact; should a colored person endeavor, for a moment, to lose sight of his disability, these staring signs would remind him continually that between him and the rest of mankind not of his own color, there was by law a great gulf fixed.

Having composed himself, Miller had opened a newspaper, and was deep in an editorial which set forth in glowing language the inestimable advantages which would follow to certain recently acquired islands by the introduction of American liberty, when the rear door of the car opened to give entrance to Captain George McBane, who took a seat near the door and lit a cigar. Miller knew him quite well by sight and by reputation, and detested him as heartily. He represented the aggressive, offensive element among the white people of the New South, who made it hard for a negro to maintain his self-respect or to enjoy even the rights conceded to colored men by Southern laws. McBane had undoubtedly identified him to the conductor in the other car. Miller had no desire to thrust himself upon the society of white people, which, indeed, to one who had traveled so much and so far, was no novelty; but he very naturally resented being at this late day—the law had been in operation only a few months—branded and tagged and set apart from the rest of mankind upon the public highways, like an unclean thing. Nevertheless, he preferred even this to the exclusive society of Captain George McBane.

"Porter," he demanded of the colored train attaché who passed through the car a moment later, "is this a smoking car for white men?"

"No, suh," replied the porter, "but they comes in here sometimes, when they ain' no cullud ladies on the kyar."

"Well, I have paid first-class fare, and I object to that man's smoking in here. You tell him to go out."

"I'll tell the conductor, suh," returned the porter in a low tone. "I'd jus' as soon talk ter the devil as ter that man."

The white man had spread himself over two seats, and was smoking vigorously, from time to time spitting carelessly in the aisle, when the conductor entered the compartment.

"Captain," said Miller, "this car is plainly marked 'Colored.' I have paid first-class fare, and I object to riding in a smoking car."

"All right," returned the conductor, frowning irritably. "I'll speak to him."

He walked over to the white passenger, with whom he was evidently acquainted, since he addressed him by name.

"Captain McBane," he said, "it's against the law for you to ride in the nigger car."

"Who are you talkin' to?" returned the other. "I'll ride where I damn please."

"Yes, sir, but the colored passenger objects. I'm afraid I'll have to ask you to go into the smoking-car."

"The hell you say!" rejoined McBane. "I'll leave this car when I get good and ready, and that won't be till I've finished this cigar. See?"

He was as good as his word. The conductor escaped from the car before Miller had time for further expostulation. Finally McBane, having thrown the stump of his cigar into the aisle and added to the floor a finishing touch in the way of expectoration, rose and went back into the white car.

Left alone in his questionable glory, Miller buried himself again in his newspaper, from which he did not look up until the engine stopped at a tank station to take water.

As the train came to a standstill, a huge negro, covered thickly with dust, crawled off one of the rear trucks unobserved, and ran round the rear end of the car to a watering-trough by a neighboring well. Moved either by extreme thirst or by the fear that his time might be too short to permit him to draw a bucket of water, he threw himself down by the trough, drank long and deep, and plunging his head into the water, shook himself like a wet dog, and crept furtively back to his dangerous perch.

Miller, who had seen this man from the car window, had noticed a very singular thing. As the dusty tramp passed the rear coach, he cast toward it a glance of intense ferocity. Up to that moment the man's face, which Miller had recognized under its grimy coating, had been that of an ordinarily good-natured, somewhat reckless, pleasure-loving negro, at present rather the worse for wear. The change that now came over it suggested a concentrated hatred almost uncanny in its murderousness. With awakened curiosity Miller followed the direction of the negro's glance, and saw that it rested upon a window where Captain McBane sat looking out. When Miller looked back, the negro had disappeared.

At the next station a Chinaman, of the ordinary laundry type, boarded the train, and took his seat in the white car without objection. At another point a colored nurse found a place with her mistress.

"White people," said Miller to himself, who had seen these passengers from the window, "do not object to the negro as a servant. As the traditional negro,—the servant,—he is welcomed; as an equal, he is repudiated."

Miller was something of a philosopher. He had long ago had the conclusion forced upon him that an educated man of his race, in order to live comfortably in the United States, must be either a philosopher or a fool; and since he wished to be happy, and was not exactly a fool, he had cultivated philosophy. By and by he saw a white man, with a dog, enter the rear coach. Miller wondered whether the dog would be allowed to ride with his master, and if not, what disposition would be made of him. He was a handsome dog, and Miller, who was fond of animals, would not have objected to the company of a dog, as a dog. He was nevertheless conscious of a queer sensation when he saw the porter take the dog by the collar and start in his own direction, and felt consciously relieved when the canine passenger was taken on past him into the baggage-car ahead. Miller's hand was banging over the arm of his seat, and the dog, an intelligent shepherd, licked it as he passed. Miller was not entirely sure that he would not have liked the porter to leave the dog there; he was a friendly dog, and seemed inclined to be sociable.

Toward evening the train drew up at a station where quite a party of farm laborers, fresh from their daily toil, swarmed out from the conspicuously labeled colored waiting-room, and into the car with Miller. They were a jolly, good-natured crowd, and, free from the embarrassing presence of white people, proceeded to enjoy themselves after their own fashion. Here an amorous fellow sat with his arm around a buxom girl's waist. A musically inclined individual—his talents did not go far beyond inclination—produced a mouth-organ and struck up a tune, to which a limber-legged boy danced in the aisle. They were noisy, loquacious, happy, dirty, and malodorous. For a while Miller was amused and pleased. They were his people, and he felt a certain expansive warmth toward them in spite of their obvious shortcomings. By and by, however, the air became too close, and he went out upon the platform. For the sake of the democratic ideal, which meant so much to his race, he must have endured the affliction. He could easily imagine that people of refinement, with the power in their hands, might be tempted to strain the democratic ideal in order to avoid such contact; but personally, and apart from the mere matter of racial sympathy, these people were just as offensive to him as to the whites in the other end of the train. Surely, if a classification of passengers on trains was at all desirable, it might be made upon some more logical and considerate basis than a mere arbitrary, tactless, and, by the very nature of things, brutal drawing of a color line. It was a veritable bed of Procrustes, this standard which the whites had set for the negroes. Those who grew above it must have their heads cut off, figuratively speaking,— must be forced back to the level assigned to their race; those who fell beneath the standard set had their necks stretched, literally enough, as the ghastly record in the daily papers gave conclusive evidence.

Miller breathed more freely when the lively crowd got off at the next station, after a short ride. Moreover, he had a light heart, a conscience void of offense, and was only thirty years old. His philosophy had become somewhat jaded on this journey, but he pulled it together for a final effort. Was it not, after all, a wise provision of nature that had given to a race, destined to a long servitude and a slow emergence therefrom, a cheerfulness of spirit which enabled them to catch pleasure on the wing, and endure with equanimity the ills that seemed inevitable? The ability to live and thrive under adverse circumstances is the surest guaranty of the future. The race which at the last shall inherit the earth—the residuary legatee of civilization—will be the race which remains longest upon it. The negro was here before the Anglo-Saxon was evolved, and his thick lips and heavy-lidded eyes looked out from the inscrutable face of the Sphinx across the sands of Egypt while yet the ancestors of those who now oppress him were living in caves, practicing human sacrifice, and painting themselves with woad—and the negro is here yet.

"'Blessed are the meek,'" quoted Miller at the end of these consoling reflections, "'for they shall inherit the earth.' If this be true, the negro may yet come into his estate, for meekness seems to be set apart as his portion."

The journey came to an end just as the sun had sunk into the west.

Simultaneously with Miller's exit from the train, a great black figure crawled off the trucks of the rear car, on the side opposite the station platform. Stretching and shaking himself with a free gesture, the black man, seeing himself unobserved, moved somewhat stiffly round the end of the car to the station platform.

"'Fo de Lawd!" he muttered, "ef I had n' had a cha'm' life, I'd 'a' never got here on dat ticket, an' dat's a fac'—it sho' am! I kind er 'lowed I wuz gone a dozen times, ez it wuz. But I got my job ter do in dis worl', an' I knows I ain' gwine ter die 'tel I've 'complished it. I jes' want one mo' look at dat man, an' den I'll haf ter git somethin' ter eat; fer two raw turnips in twelve hours is slim pickin's fer a man er my size!"

VI
JANET

As the train drew up at the station platform, Dr. Price came forward from the white waiting-room, and stood expectantly by the door of the white coach. Miller, having left his car, came down the platform in time to intercept Burns as he left the train, and to introduce him to Dr. Price.

"My carriage is in waiting," said Dr. Price. "I should have liked to have you at my own house, but my wife is out of town. We have a good hotel, however, and you will doubtless find it more convenient."

"You are very kind, Dr. Price. Miller, won't you come up and dine with me?"

"Thank you, no," said Miller, "I am expected at home. My wife and child are waiting for me in the buggy yonder by the platform."

"Oh, very well; of course you must go; but don't forget our appointment. Let's see, Dr. Price, I can eat and get ready in half an hour—that will make it"—

"I have asked several of the local physicians to be present at eight o'clock," said Dr. Price. "The case can safely wait until then."

"Very well, Miller, be on hand at eight. I shall expect you without fail. Where shall he come, Dr. Price?"

"To the residence of Major Philip Carteret, on Vine Street."

"I have invited Dr. Miller to be present and assist in the operation," Dr. Burns continued, as they drove toward the hotel. "He was a favorite pupil of mine, and is a credit to the profession. I presume you saw his article in the Medical Gazette?"

"Yes, and I assisted him in the case," returned Dr. Price. "It was a colored lad, one of his patients, and he called me in to help him. He is a capable man, and very much liked by the white physicians."

Miller's wife and child were waiting for him in fluttering anticipation. He kissed them both as he climbed into the buggy.

"We came at four o'clock," said Mrs. Miller, a handsome young woman, who might be anywhere between twenty-five and thirty, and whose complexion, in the twilight, was not distinguishable from that of a white person, "but the train was late two hours, they said. We came back at six, and have been waiting ever since."

"Yes, papa," piped the child, a little boy of six or seven, who sat between them, "and I am very hungry."

Miller felt very much elated as he drove homeward through the twilight. By his side sat the two persons whom he loved best in all the world. His affairs were prosperous. Upon opening his office in the city, he had been received by the members of his own profession with a cordiality generally frank, and in no case much reserved. The colored population of the city was large, but in the main poor, and the white physicians were not unwilling to share this unprofitable practice with a colored doctor worthy of confidence. In the intervals of the work upon his hospital, he had built up a considerable practice among his own people; but except in the case of some poor unfortunate whose pride had been lost in poverty or sin, no white patient had ever called upon him for treatment. He knew very well the measure of his powers,—a liberal education had given him opportunity to compare himself with other men,—and was secretly conscious that in point of skill and knowledge he did not suffer by comparison with any other physician in the town. He liked to believe that the race antagonism which hampered his progress and that of his people was a mere temporary thing, the outcome of former conditions, and bound to disappear in time, and that when a colored man should demonstrate to the community in which he lived that he possessed character and power, that community would find a way in which to enlist his services for the public good.

He had already made himself useful, and had received many kind words and other marks of appreciation. He was now offered a further confirmation of his theory: having recognized his skill, the white people were now ready to take advantage of it. Any lurking doubt he may have felt when first invited by Dr. Burns to participate in the operation, had been dispelled by Dr. Price's prompt acquiescence.

On the way homeward Miller told his wife of this appointment. She was greatly interested; she was herself a mother, with an only child. Moreover, there was a stronger impulse than mere humanity to draw her toward the stricken mother. Janet had a tender heart, and could have loved this white sister, her sole living relative of whom she knew. All her life long she had yearned for a kind word, a nod, a smile, the least thing that imagination might have twisted into a recognition of the tie between them. But it had never come.

And yet Janet was not angry. She was of a forgiving temper; she could never bear malice. She was educated, had read many books, and appreciated to the full the social forces arrayed against any such recognition as she had dreamed of. Of the two barriers between them a man might have forgiven the one; a woman would not be likely to overlook either the bar sinister or the difference of race, even to the slight extent of a silent recognition. Blood is thicker than water, but, if it flow too far from conventional channels, may turn to gall and wormwood. Nevertheless, when the heart speaks, reason falls into the background, and Janet would have worshiped this sister, even afar off, had she received even the slightest encouragement. So strong was this weakness that she had been angry with herself for her lack of pride, or even of a decent self-respect. It was, she sometimes thought, the heritage of her mother's race, and she was ashamed of it as part of the taint of slavery. She had never acknowledged, even to her husband, from whom she concealed nothing else, her secret thoughts upon this lifelong sorrow. This silent grief was nature's penalty, or society's revenge, for whatever heritage of beauty or intellect or personal charm had come to her with her father's blood. For she had received no other inheritance. Her sister was rich by right of her birth; if Janet had been fortunate, her good fortune had not been due to any provision made for her by her white father.

She knew quite well how passionately, for many years, her proud sister had longed and prayed in vain for the child which had at length brought joy into her household, and she could feel, by sympathy, all the sickening suspense with which the child's parents must await the result of this dangerous operation.

"O Will," she adjured her husband anxiously, when he had told her of the engagement, "you must be very careful. Think of the child's poor mother! Think of our own dear child, and what it would mean to lose him!"

VII
THE OPERATION

DR. PRICE was not entirely at ease in his mind as the two doctors drove rapidly from the hotel to Major Carteret's. Himself a liberal man, from his point of view, he saw no reason why a colored doctor might not operate upon a white male child,—there are fine distinctions in the application of the color line,—but several other physicians had been invited, some of whom were men of old-fashioned notions, who might not relish such an innovation.

This, however, was but a small difficulty compared with what might be feared from Major Carteret himself. For he knew Carteret's unrelenting hostility to anything that savored of recognition of the negro as the equal of white men. It was traditional in Wellington that no colored person had ever entered the front door of the Carteret residence, and that the luckless individual who once presented himself there upon alleged business and resented being ordered to the back door had been unceremoniously thrown over the piazza railing into a rather thorny clump of rose-bushes below. If Miller were going as a servant, to hold a basin or a sponge, there would be no difficulty; but as a surgeon—well, he would n't borrow trouble. Under the circumstances the major might yield a point.

But as they neared the house the major's unyielding disposition loomed up formidably. Perhaps if the matter were properly presented to Dr. Burns, he might consent to withdraw the invitation. It was not yet too late to send Miller a note.

"By the way, Dr. Burns," he said, "I'm very friendly

to Dr. Miller, and should personally like to have him with us to-night. But—I ought to have told you this before, but I couldn't very well do so, on such short notice, in Miller's presence—we are a conservative people, and our local customs are not very flexible. We jog along in much the same old way our fathers did. I'm not at all sure that Major Carteret or the other gentlemen would consent to the presence of a negro doctor."

"I think you misjudge your own people," returned Dr. Burns, "they are broader than you think. We have our prejudices against the negro at the North, but we do not let them stand in the way of anything that we want. At any rate, it is too late now, and I will accept the responsibility. If the question is raised, I will attend to it. When I am performing an operation I must be *aut Cæsar, aut nullus.*"

Dr. Price was not reassured, but he had done his duty and felt the reward of virtue. If there should be trouble, he would not be responsible. Moreover, there was a large fee at stake, and Dr. Burns was not likely to prove too obdurate.

They were soon at Carteret's, where they found assembled the several physicians invited by Dr. Price. These were successively introduced as Drs. Dudley, Hooper, and Ashe, all of whom were gentlemen of good standing, socially and in their profession, and considered it a high privilege to witness so delicate an operation at the hands of so eminent a member of their profession.

Major Carteret entered the room and was duly presented to the famous specialist. Carteret's anxious look lightened somewhat at sight of the array of talent present. It suggested, of course, the gravity of the impending event, but gave assurance of all the skill and care which science could afford.

Dr. Burns was shown to the nursery, from which he returned in five minutes.

"The case is ready," he announced. "Are the gentlemen all present?"

"I believe so," answered Dr. Price quickly.

Miller had not yet arrived. Perhaps, thought Dr. Price, a happy accident, or some imperative call, had detained him. This would be fortunate indeed. Dr. Burns's square jaw had a very determined look. It would be a pity if any acrimonious discussion should arise on the eve of a delicate operation. If the clock on the mantel would only move faster, the question might never come up.

"I don't see Dr. Miller," observed Dr. Burns, looking around the room. "I asked him to come at eight. There are ten minutes yet."

Major Carteret looked up with a sudden frown.

"May I ask to whom you refer? " he inquired, in an ominous tone.

The other gentlemen showed signs of interest, not to say emotion. Dr. Price smiled quizzically.

"Dr. Miller, of your city. He was one of my favorite pupils. He is also a graduate of the Vienna hospitals, and a surgeon of unusual skill. I have asked him to assist in the operation."

Every eye was turned toward Carteret, whose crimsoned face had set in a look of grim determination.

"The person to whom you refer is a negro, I believe?" he said.

"He is a colored man, certainly," returned Dr. Burns, "though one would never think of his color after knowing him well."

"I do not know, sir," returned Carteret, with an effort at self-control, "what the customs of Philadelphia, or Vienna may be; but in the South we do not call negro doctors to attend white patients. I could not permit a negro to enter my house upon such an errand."

"I am here, sir," replied Dr. Burns with spirit, "to perform a certain operation. Since I assume the responsibility, the case must be under my entire control. Otherwise I cannot operate."

"Gentlemen," interposed Dr. Price, smoothly, "I beg of you both—this is a matter for calm discussion, and any asperity is to be deplored. The life at stake here should not be imperiled by any consideration of minor importance."

"Your humanity does you credit, sir," retorted Dr. Burns. "But other matters, too, are important. I have invited this gentleman here. My professional honor is involved, and I merely invoke my rights to maintain it. It is a matter of principle, which ought not to give way to a mere prejudice."

"That also states the case for Major Carteret," rejoined Dr. Price, suavely. "He has certain principles,—call them prejudices, if you like,—certain inflexible rules of conduct by which he regulates his life. One of these, which he shares with us all in some degree, forbids the recognition of the negro as a social equal."

"I do not know what Miller's social value may be," replied Dr. Burns, stoutly, "or whether you gain or lose by your attitude toward him. I have invited him here in a strictly professional capacity, with which his color is not at all concerned."

"Dr. Burns does not quite appreciate Major Carteret's point of view," said Dr. Price. "This is not with him an unimportant matter, or a mere question of prejudice, or even of personal taste. It is a sacred principle, lying at the very root of our social order, involving the purity and prestige of our race. You Northern gentlemen do not quite appreciate our situation; if you lived here a year or two you would act as we do. Of course," he added, diplomatically, "if there were no alternative—if Dr. Burns were willing to put Dr. Miller's presence on the ground of imperative necessity"—

"I do nothing of the kind, sir," retorted Dr. Burns with some heat. "I have not come all the way from Philadelphia to undertake an operation which I cannot perform without the aid of some particular physician. I merely stand upon my professional rights."

Carteret was deeply agitated. The operation must not be deferred; his child's life might be endangered by delay. If the negro's presence were indispensable he would even submit to it, though in order to avoid so painful a necessity, he would rather humble himself to the Northern doctor. The latter course involved merely a personal sacrifice—the former a vital principle. Perhaps there was another way of escape. Miller's presence could not but be distasteful to Mrs. Carteret for other reasons. Miller's wife was the living evidence of a painful episode in Mrs. Carteret's family, which the doctor's presence would inevitably recall. Once before, Mrs. Carteret's life had been endangered by encountering, at a time of great nervous strain, this ill-born sister and her child. She was even now upon the verge of collapse at the prospect of her child's suffering, and should be protected from the intrusion of any idea which might add to her distress.

"Dr. Burns," he said, with the suave courtesy which was part of his inheritance, "I beg your pardon for my heat, and throw myself upon your magnanimity, as between white men"—

"I am a gentleman, sir, before I am a white man," interposed Dr. Burns, slightly mollified, however, by Carteret's change of manner.

"The terms should be synonymous," Carteret could not refrain from saying. "As between white men, and gentlemen, I say to you, frankly, that there are vital, personal reasons, apart from Dr. Miller's color, why his presence in this house would be distasteful. With this statement, sir, I throw myself upon your mercy. My child's life is worth more to me than any earthly thing, and I must be governed by your decision."

Dr. Burns was plainly wavering. The clock moved with provoking slowness. Miller would be there in five minutes.

"May I speak with you privately a moment, doctor?" asked Dr. Price.

They withdrew from the room and were engaged in conversation for a few moments. Dr. Burns finally yielded.

"I shall nevertheless feel humiliated when I meet Miller again," he said, "but of course if there is a personal question involved, that alters the situation. Had it been merely a matter of color, I should have maintained my position. As things stand, I wash my hands of the whole affair, so far as Miller is concerned, like Pontius Pilate—yes, indeed, sir, I feel very much like that individual."

"I'll explain the matter to Miller," returned Dr. Price, amiably, "and make it all right with him. We Southern people understand the negroes better than you do, sir.

70

Why should we not? They have been constantly under our interested observation for several hundred years. You feel this vastly more than Miller will. He knows the feeling of the white people, and is accustomed to it. He wishes to live and do business here, and is quite too shrewd to antagonize his neighbors or come where he is not wanted. He is in fact too much of a gentleman to do so."

"I shall leave the explanation to you entirely," rejoined Dr. Burns, as they reëntered the other room.

Carteret led the way to the nursery, where the operation was to take place. Dr. Price lingered for a moment. Miller was not likely to be behind the hour, if he came at all, and it would be well to head him off before the operation began.

Scarcely had the rest left the room when the door-bell sounded, and a servant announced Dr. Miller.

Dr. Price stepped into the hall and met Miller face to face.

He had meant to state the situation to Miller frankly, but now that the moment had come he wavered. He was a fine physician, but he shrank from strenuous responsibilities. It had been easy to theorize about the negro; it was more difficult to look this man in the eyes—whom at this moment he felt to be as essentially a gentleman as himself—and tell him the humiliating truth.

As a physician his method was to ease pain—he would rather take the risk of losing a patient from the use of an anæsthetic than from the shock of an operation. He liked Miller, wished him well, and would not wittingly wound his feelings. He really thought him too much of a gentleman for the town, in view of the restrictions with which he must inevitably be hampered. There was something melancholy, to a cultivated mind, about a sensitive, educated man who happened to be off color. Such a person was a sort of social misfit, an odd quantity, educated out of his own class, with no possible hope of entrance into that above it. He felt quite sure that if he had been in Miller's place, he would never have settled in the South—he would have moved to Europe, or to the West Indies, or some Central or South American state where questions of color were not regarded as vitally important.

Dr. Price did not like to lie, even to a negro. To a man of his own caste, his word was his bond. If it were painful to lie, it would be humiliating to be found out. The principle of *noblesse oblige* was also involved in the matter. His claim of superiority to the colored doctor rested fundamentally upon the fact that he was white and Miller was not; and yet this superiority, for which he could claim no credit, since he had not made himself, was the very breath of his nostrils,—he would not have changed places with the other for wealth untold; and as a gentleman, he would not care to have another gentleman, even a colored man, catch him in a lie. Of this, however, there was scarcely any danger. A word to the other surgeons would insure their corroboration of whatever he might tell Miller. No one of them would willingly wound Dr. Miller or embarrass Dr. Price; indeed, they need not know that Miller had come in time for the operation.

"I'm sorry, Miller," he said with apparent regret, "but we were here ahead of time, and the case took a turn which would admit of no delay, so the gentlemen went in. Dr. Burns is with the patient now, and asked me to explain why we did not wait for you."

"I'm sorry too," returned Miller, regretfully, but nothing doubting. He was well aware that in such cases danger might attend upon delay. He had lost his chance, through no fault of his own or of any one else.

"I hope that all is well?" he said, hesitatingly, not sure whether he would be asked to remain.

"All is well, so far. Step round to my office in the morning, Miller, or come in when you're passing, and I'll tell you the details."

This was tantamount to a dismissal, so Miller took his leave. Descending the doorsteps, he stood for a moment, undecided whether to return home or to go to the hotel and await the return of Dr. Burns, when he heard his name called from the house in a low tone.

"Oh, doctuh!"

He stepped back toward the door, outside of which stood the colored servant who had just let him out.

"Dat 's all a lie, doctuh," he whispered, "'bout de operation bein' already pe'fo'med. Dey-all had jes' gone in de minute befo' you come—Doctuh Price had n' even got out'n de room. Dey be'n quollin' 'bout you fer de las' ha'f hour. Majah Ca'te'et say he would n' have you, an' de No'then doctuh say he would n't do nothin' widout you, an' Doctuh Price he j'ined in on bofe sides, an' dey had it hot an' heavy, nip an' tuck, till bimeby Majah Ca'te'et up an' say it wa'n't altogether yo' color he objected to, an' wid dat de No'then doctuh give in. He's a fine man, suh, but dey wuz too much fer 'im!"

"Thank you, Sam, I'm much obliged," returned Miller mechanically. "One likes to know the truth."

Truth, it has been said, is mighty, and must prevail; but it sometimes leaves a bad taste in the mouth. In the

ordinary course of events Miller would not have anticipated such an invitation, and for that reason had appreciated it all the more. The rebuff came with a corre-
sponding shock. He had the heart of a man, the sensi-
bilities of a cultivated gentleman; the one was sore, the
other deeply wounded. He was not altogether sure, upon
reflection, whether he blamed Dr. Price very much for
the amiable lie, which had been meant to spare his feelings, or thanked Sam a great deal for the unpalatable
truth.

Janet met him at the door. "How is the baby?" she
asked excitedly.

"Dr. Price says he is doing well."

"What is the matter, Will, and why are you back so
soon?"

He would have spared her the story, but she was a
woman, and would have it. He was wounded, too, and
wanted sympathy, of which Janet was an exhaustless
fountain. So he told her what had happened. She com-
forted him after the manner of a loving woman, and felt
righteously indignant toward her sister's husband, who
had thus been instrumental in the humiliation of her
own. Her anger did not embrace her sister, and yet she
felt obscurely that their unacknowledged relationship had
been the malignant force which had given her husband
pain, and defeated his honorable ambition.

When Dr. Price entered the nursery, Dr. Burns was
leaning attentively over the operating table. The imple-
ments needed for the operation were all in readiness—
the knives, the basin, the sponge, the materials for dressing the wound—all the ghastly paraphernalia of vivisec-
tion.

Mrs. Carteret had been banished to another room, where Clara vainly attempted to soothe her. Old Mammy Jane, still burdened by her fears, fervently prayed the good Lord to spare the life of the sweet little grandson of her dear old mistress.

Dr. Burns had placed his ear to the child's chest, which had been bared for the incision. Dr. Price stood ready to administer the anæsthetic. Little Dodie looked up with a faint expression of wonder, as if dimly conscious of some unusual event. The major shivered at the thought of what the child must undergo.

"There's a change in his breathing," said Dr. Burns, lifting his head. "The whistling noise is less pronounced, and he breathes easier. The obstruction seems to have shifted."

Applying his ear again to the child's throat, he listened for a moment intently, and then picking the baby up from the table, gave it a couple of sharp claps between the shoulders. Simultaneously a small object shot out from the child's mouth, struck Dr. Price in the neighborhood of his waistband, and then rattled lightly against the floor. Whereupon the baby, as though conscious of his narrow escape, smiled and gurgled, and reaching upward clutched the doctor's whiskers with his little hand, which, according to old Jane, had a stronger grip than any other infant's in Wellington.

VIII
THE CAMPAIGN DRAGS

THE campaign for white supremacy was dragging. Carteret had set out, in the columns of the Morning Chronicle, all the reasons why this movement, inaugurated by the three men who had met, six months before, at the office of the Chronicle, should be supported by the white public. Negro citizenship was a grotesque farce—Sambo and Dinah raised from the kitchen to the cabinet were a spectacle to make the gods laugh. The laws by which it had been sought to put the negroes on a level with the whites must be swept away in theory, as they had failed in fact. If it were impossible, without a further education of public opinion, to secure the repeal of the fifteenth amendment, it was at least the solemn duty of the state to endeavor, through its own constitution, to escape from the domination of a weak and incompetent electorate and confine the negro to that inferior condition for which nature had evidently designed him.

In spite of the force and intelligence with which Carteret had expressed these and similar views, they had not met the immediate response anticipated. There were thoughtful men, willing to let well enough alone, who saw no necessity for such a movement. They believed that peace, prosperity, and popular education offered a surer remedy for social ills than the reopening of issues supposed to have been settled. There were timid men who shrank from civic strife. There were busy men, who had something else to do. There were a few fair men, prepared to admit, privately, that a class constituting half to two thirds of the population were fairly entitled to some representation in the law-making bodies. Perhaps there might have been found, somewhere in the state, a single white man ready to concede that all men were entitled to equal rights before the law.

That there were some white men who had learned little and forgotten nothing goes without saying, for knowledge and wisdom are not impartially distributed among even the most favored race. There were ignorant and vicious negroes, and they had a monopoly of neither ignorance nor crime, for there were prosperous negroes and poverty-stricken whites. Until Carteret and his committee began their baleful campaign the people of the state were living in peace and harmony. The anti-negro legislation in more southern states, with large negro majorities, had awakened scarcely an echo in this state, with a population two thirds white. Even the triumph of the Fusion party had not been regarded as a race issue. It remained for Carteret and his friends to discover, with inspiration from whatever supernatural source the discriminating reader may elect, that the darker race, docile by instinct, humble by training, patiently waiting upon its as yet uncertain destiny, was an incubus, a corpse chained to the body politic, and that the negro vote was a source of danger to the state, no matter how cast or by whom directed.

To discuss means for counteracting this apathy, a meeting of the "Big Three," as they had begun to designate themselves jocularly, was held at the office of the "Morning Chronicle," on the next day but one after little Dodie's fortunate escape from the knife.

"It seems," said General Belmont, opening the discussion, "as though we had undertaken more than we can carry through. It is clear that we must reckon on opposition, both at home and abroad. If we are to hope for success, we must extend the lines of our campaign. The North, as well as our own people, must be convinced that we have right upon our side. We are conscious of the purity of our motives, but we should avoid even the appearance of evil."

McBane was tapping the floor impatiently with his foot during this harangue.

"I don't see the use," he interrupted, "of so much beating about the bush. We may as well be honest about this thing. We are going to put the niggers down because we want to, and think we can; so why waste our time in mere pretense? I'm no hypocrite myself,—if I want a thing I take it, provided I'm strong enough."

"My dear captain," resumed the general, with biting suavity, "your frankness does you credit,—'an honest man's the noblest work of God,'—but we cannot carry on politics in these degenerate times without a certain amount of diplomacy. In the good old days when your father was alive, and perhaps nowadays in the discipline of convicts, direct and simple methods might be safely resorted to; but this is a modern age, and in dealing with so fundamental a right as the suffrage we must profess a decent regard for the opinions of even that misguided portion of mankind which may not agree with us. This is the age of crowds, and we must have the crowd with us."

The captain flushed at the allusion to his father's calling, at which he took more offense than at the mention of his own. He knew perfectly well that these old aristocrats, while reaping the profits of slavery, had despised the instruments by which they were attained—the poor-white overseer only less than the black slave. McBane was rich; he lived in Wellington, but he had never been invited to the home of either General Belmont or Major Carteret, nor asked to join the club of which they were members. His face, therefore, wore a distinct scowl, and his single eye glowed ominously. He would help these fellows carry the state for white supremacy, and then he would have his innings,—he would have more to say than they dreamed, as to who should fill the offices under the new deal. Men of no better birth or breeding than he had represented Southern states in Congress since the war. Why should he not run for governor, representative, whatever he chose? He had money enough to buy out half a dozen of these broken-down aristocrats, and money was all-powerful.

"You see, captain," the general went on, looking McBane smilingly and unflinchingly in the eye, "we need white immigration—we need Northern capital. 'A good name is better than great riches,' and we must prove our cause a righteous one."

"We must be armed at all points," added Carteret, "and prepared for defense as well as for attack,—we must make our campaign a national one."

"For instance," resumed the general, "you, Carteret, represent the Associated Press. Through your hands passes all the news of the state. What more powerful medium for the propagation of an idea? The man who would govern a nation by writing its songs was a blethering idiot beside the fellow who can edit its news dispatches. The negroes are playing into our hands,—every crime that one of them commits is reported by us. With the latitude they have had in this state they are growing more impudent and self-assertive every day. A yellow demagogue in New York made a speech only a few days ago, in which he deliberately, and in cold blood, advised negroes to defend themselves to the death when attacked by white people! I remember well the time when it was death for a negro to strike a white man."

"It's death now, if he strikes the right one," interjected McBane, restored to better humor by this mention of a congenial subject.

The general smiled a fine smile. He had heard the story of how McBane had lost his other eye.

"The local negro paper is quite outspoken, too," continued the general, "if not impudent. We must keep track of that; it may furnish us some good campaign material."

"Yes," returned Carteret, "we must see to that. I threw a copy into the waste-basket this morning, without looking at it. Here it is now!"

IX
A WHITE MAN'S "NIGGER"

CARTERET fished from the depths of the wastebasket and handed to the general an eighteen by twenty-four sheet, poorly printed on cheap paper, with a "patent" inside, a number of advertisements of proprietary medicines, quack doctors, and fortune-tellers, and two or three columns of editorial and local news. Candor compels the admission that it was not an impressive sheet in any respect, except when regarded as the first local effort of a struggling people to make public expression of their life and aspirations. From this point of view it did not speak at all badly for a class to whom, a generation before, newspapers, books, and learning had been forbidden fruit.

"It's an elegant specimen of journalism, is n't it?" laughed the general, airily. "Listen to this 'ad':—

"'Kinky, curly hair made straight by one application of our specific. Our face bleach will turn the skin of a black or brown person four or five shades lighter, and of a mulatto perfectly white. When you get the color you wish, stop using the preparation.'

"Just look at those heads!—'Before using' and 'After using.' We'd better hurry, or there'll be no negroes to disfranchise! If they don't stop till they get the color they desire, and the stuff works according to contract, they'll all be white. Ah! what have we here? This looks as though it might be serious."

Opening the sheet the general read aloud an editorial article, to which Carteret listened intently, his indignation increasing in strength from the first word to the last, while McBane's face grew darkly purple with anger.

The article was a frank and somewhat bold discussion of lynching and its causes. It denied that most lynchings were for the offense most generally charged as their justification, and declared that, even of those seemingly traced to this cause, many were not for crimes at all, but for voluntary acts which might naturally be expected to follow from the miscegenation laws by which it was sought, in all the Southern States, to destroy liberty of contract, and, for the purpose of maintaining a fanciful purity of race, to make crimes of marriages to which neither nature nor religion nor the laws of other states interposed any insurmountable barrier. Such an article in a Northern newspaper would have attracted no special attention, and might merely have furnished food to an occasional reader for serious thought upon a subject not exactly agreeable; but coming from a colored man, in a Southern city, it was an indictment of the laws and social system of the South that could not fail of creating a profound sensation.

"Infamous—infamous!" exclaimed Carteret, his voice trembling with emotion. "The paper should be suppressed immediately."

"The impudent nigger ought to be horsewhipped and run out of town," growled McBane.

"Gentlemen," said the general soothingly, after the first burst of indignation had subsided, "I believe we can find a more effective use for this article, which, by the way, will not bear too close analysis,—there's some truth in it, at least there's an argument."

"That is not the point," interrupted Carteret.

"No," interjected McBane with an oath, "that ain't at all the point. Truth or not, no damn nigger has any right to say it."

"This article," said Carteret, "violates an unwritten law of the South. If we are to tolerate this race of weaklings among us, until they are eliminated by the stress of competition, it must be upon terms which we lay down. One of our conditions is violated by this article, in which our wisdom is assailed, and our women made the subject of offensive comment. We must make known our disapproval."

"I say lynch the nigger, break up the press, and burn down the newspaper office," McBane responded promptly.

"Gentlemen," interposed the general, "would you

mind suspending the discussion for a moment, while I send Jerry across the street? I think I can then suggest a better plan."

Carteret rang the bell for Jerry, who answered promptly. He had been expecting such a call ever since the gentlemen had gone in.

"Jerry," said the general, "step across to Brown's and tell him to send me three Calhoun cocktails. Wait for them,—here's the money."

"Yas, suh," replied Jerry, taking the proffered coin.

"And make has'e, charcoal," added McBane, "for we're gettin' damn dry."

A momentary cloud of annoyance darkened Carteret's brow. McBane had always grated upon his aristocratic susceptibilities. The captain was an upstart, a product of the democratic idea operating upon the poor white man, the descendant of the indentured bondservant and the socially unfit. He had wealth and energy, however, and it was necessary to make use of him; but the example of such men was a strong incentive to Carteret in his campaign against the negro. It was distasteful enough to rub elbows with an illiterate and vulgar white man of no ancestry,—the risk of similar contact with negroes was to be avoided at any cost. He could hardly expect McBane to be a gentleman, but when among men of that class he might at least try to imitate their manners. A gentleman did not order his own servants around offensively, to say nothing of another's.

The general had observed Carteret's annoyance, and remarked pleasantly while they waited for the servant's return:—

"Jerry, now, is a very good negro. He's not one of your

new negroes, who think themselves as good as white men, and want to run the government. Jerry knows his place,—he is respectful, humble, obedient, and content with the face and place assigned to him by nature."

"Yes, he's one of the best of 'em," sneered McBane. "He'll call any man 'master' for a quarter, or 'God' for half a dollar; for a dollar he'll grovel at your feet, and for a cast-off coat you can buy an option on his immortal soul,—if he has one! I've handled niggers for ten years, and I know 'em from the ground up. They're all alike,—they're a scrub race, an affliction to the country, and the quicker we're rid of 'em all the better."

Carteret had nothing to say by way of dissent. McBane's sentiments, in their last analysis, were much the same as his, though he would have expressed them less brutally.

"The negro," observed the general, daintily flicking the ash from his cigar, "is all right in his place and very useful to the community. We lived on his labor quite a long time, and lived very well. Nevertheless we are better off without slavery, for we can get more out of the free negro, and with less responsibility. I really do not see how we could get along without the negroes. If they were all like Jerry, we'd have no trouble with them."

Having procured the drinks, Jerry, the momentary subject of the race discussion which goes on eternally in the South, was making his way back across the street, somewhat disturbed in mind.

"O Lawd!" he groaned, "I never troubles trouble till trouble troubles me; but w'en I got dem drinks befo', Gin'l Belmont gimme half a dollar an' tol' me ter keep de change. Dis time he did n' say nothin' 'bout de

84

change. I s'pose he jes' fergot erbout it, but w'at is a po' nigger gwine ter do w'en he has ter conten' wid w'ite folks's fergitfulniss? I don' see no way but ter do some fergittin' myse'f. I'll jes' stan' outside de do' here till dey gits so wrop' up in deir talk dat dey won' 'member nothin' e'se, an' den at de right minute I'll han' de glasses 'roun, an' mos' lackly de gin'l 'll fergit all 'bout de change."

While Jerry stood outside, the conversation within was plainly audible, and some inkling of its purport filtered through his mind.

"Now, gentlemen," the general was saying, "here's my plan. That editorial in the negro newspaper is good campaign matter, but we should reserve it until it will be most effective. Suppose we just stick it in a pigeon-hole, and let the editor,—what's his name?"

"The nigger's name is Barber," replied McBane. "I'd like to have him under me for a month or two; he 'd write no more editorials."

"Let Barber have all the rope he wants," resumed the general, "and he'll be sure to hang himself. In the mean time we will continue to work up public opinion,—we can use this letter privately for that purpose,—and when the state campaign opens we'll print the editorial, with suitable comment, scatter it broadcast throughout the state, fire the Southern heart, organize the white people on the color line, have a little demonstration with red shirts and shotguns, scare the negroes into fits, win the state for white supremacy, and teach our colored fellow citizens that we are tired of negro domination and have put an end to it forever. The Afro-American Banner will doubtless die about the same time."

"And so will the editor!" exclaimed McBane ferociously; "I'll see to that. But I wonder where that nigger is with them cocktails? I'm so thirsty I could swallow blue blazes."

"Here's yo' drinks, gin'l," announced Jerry, entering with the glasses on a tray.

The gentlemen exchanged compliments and imbibed—McBane at a gulp, Carteret with more deliberation, leaving about half the contents of his glass.

The general drank slowly, with every sign of appreciation. "If the illustrious statesman," he observed, "whose name this mixture bears, had done nothing more than invent it, his fame would still deserve to go thundering down the endless ages."

"It ain't bad liquor," assented McBane, smacking his lips.

Jerry received the empty glasses on the tray and left the room. He had scarcely gained the hall when the general called him back.

"O Lawd!" groaned Jerry, "he's gwine ter ax me fer de change. Yas, suh, yas, suh; comin', gin'l, comin', suh!"

"You may keep the change, Jerry," said the general.

Jerry's face grew radiant at this announcement. "Yas, suh, gin'l; thank y', suh; much obleedzed, suh. I wuz jus' gwine ter fetch it in, suh, w'en I had put de tray down. Thank y', suh, truly, suh!"

Jerry backed and bowed himself out into the hall.

"Dat wuz a close shave," he muttered, as he swallowed the remaining contents of Major Carteret's glass. "I 'lowed dem twenty cents wuz gone dat time,—an' whar I wuz gwine ter git de money ter take my gal ter de chu'ch festibal ter-night, de Lawd only knows!—'less'n I borried it off'n Mr. Ellis, an' I owes him sixty cents a'ready. But I wonduh w'at dem w'ite folks in dere is up

86

ter? Dere 's one thing sho',—dey're gwine ter git after de niggers some way er 'nuther, an' w'en dey does, whar is Jerry gwine ter be? Dat 's de mos' impo'tantes' question. I 'm gwine ter look at dat newspaper dey be'n talkin' 'bout, an' 'less'n my min' changes might'ly, I'm gwine ter keep my mouf shet an' stan' in wid de Angry-Saxon race,—ez dey calls deyse'ves nowadays,—an' keep on de right side er my bread an' meat. W'at nigger ever give me twenty cents in all my bawn days?"

"By the way, major," said the general, who lingered behind McBane as they were leaving, "is Miss Clara's marriage definitely settled upon?"

"Well, general, not exactly; but it's the understanding that they will marry when they are old enough."

"I was merely thinking," the general went on, "that if I were you I'd speak to Tom about cards and liquor. He gives more time to both than a young man can afford. I'm speaking in his interest and in Miss Clara's,—we of the old families ought to stand together."

"Thank you, general, for the hint. I'll act upon it."

This political conference was fruitful in results. Acting upon the plans there laid out, McBane traveled extensively through the state, working up sentiment in favor of the new movement. He possessed a certain forceful eloquence; and white supremacy was so obviously the divine intention that he had merely to affirm the doctrine in order to secure adherents.

General Belmont, whose business required him to spend much of the winter in Washington and New York, lost no opportunity to get the ear of lawmakers, editors, and other leaders of national opinion, and to impress upon them, with persuasive eloquence, the impossibility of maintaining existing conditions, and the tremendous blunder which had been made in conferring the franchise upon the emancipated race.

Carteret conducted the press campaign, and held out to the Republicans of the North the glittering hope that, with the elimination of the negro vote, and a proper deference to Southern feeling, a strong white Republican party might be built up in the New South. How well the bait took is a matter of history,—but the promised result is still in the future. The disfranchisement of the negro has merely changed the form of the same old problem. The negro had no vote before the rebellion, and few other rights, and yet the negro question was, for a century, the pivot of American politics. It plunged the nation into a bloody war, and it will trouble the American government and the American conscience until a sustained attempt is made to settle it upon principles of justice and equity.

The personal ambitions entertained by the leaders of this movement are but slightly involved in this story. McBane's aims have been touched upon elsewhere. The general would have accepted the nomination for governor of the state, with a vision of a senatorship in the future. Carteret hoped to vindicate the supremacy of his race, and make the state fit for his son to live in, and, incidentally, he would not refuse any office, worthy of his dignity, which a grateful people might thrust upon him.

So powerful a combination of bigot, self-seeking demagogue, and astute politician was fraught with grave menace to the peace of the state and the liberties of the people,—by which is meant the whole people, and not any one class, sought to be built up at the expense of another.

X
DELAMERE PLAYS A TRUMP

CARTERET did not forget what General Belmont had said in regard to Tom. The major himself had been young, not so very long ago, and was inclined toward indulgence for the foibles of youth. A young gentleman should have a certain knowledge of life,—but there were limits. Clara's future happiness must not be imperiled.

The opportunity to carry out this purpose was not long delayed. Old Mr. Delamere wished to sell some timber which had been cut at Belleview, and sent Tom down to the Chronicle office to leave an advertisement. The major saw him at the desk, invited him into his sanctum, and delivered him a mild lecture. The major was kind, and talked in a fatherly way about the danger of extremes, the beauty of moderation, and the value of discretion as a rule of conduct. He mentioned collaterally the unblemished honor of a fine old family, its contemplated alliance with his own, and dwelt upon the sweet simplicity of Clara's character. The major was a man of feeling and of tact, and could not have put the subject in a way less calculated to wound the *amour propre* of a very young man.

Delamere had turned red with anger while the major was speaking. He was impulsive, and an effort was required to keep back the retort that sprang once or twice to his lips; but his conscience was not clear, and he could not afford hard words with Clara's guardian and his grandfather's friend. Clara was rich, and the most beautiful girl in town; they were engaged; he loved her as well as he could love anything of which he seemed sure; and he did not mean that any one else should have her. The major's mild censure disturbed slightly his sense of security; and while the major's manner did not indicate that he knew anything definite against him, it would be best to let well enough alone.

"Thank you, major," he said, with well-simulated frankness. "I realize that I may have been a little careless, more from thoughtlessness than anything else; but my heart is all right, sir, and I am glad that my conduct has been brought to your attention, for what you have said enables me to see it in a different light. I will be more careful of my company hereafter; for I love Clara, and mean to try to be worthy of her. Do you know whether she will be at home this evening?"

"I have heard nothing to the contrary," replied the major warmly. "Call her up by telephone and ask—or come up and see. You're always welcome, my boy."

Upon leaving the office, which was on the second floor, Tom met Ellis coming up the stairs. It had several times of late occurred to Tom that Ellis had a sneaking fondness for Clara. Panoplied in his own engagement, Tom had heretofore rather enjoyed the idea of a hopeless rival. Ellis was such a solemn prig, and took life so seriously, that it was a pleasure to see him sit around sighing for the unattainable. That he should be giving pain to Ellis added a certain zest to his own enjoyment.

But this interview with the major had so disquieted him that upon meeting Ellis upon the stairs he was struck by a sudden suspicion. He knew that Major Carteret seldom went to the Clarendon Club, and that he must have got his information from some one else. Ellis was a member of the club, and a frequent visitor. Who more likely than he to try to poison Clara's mind, or the minds of her friends, against her accepted lover? Tom did not think that the world was using him well of late; bad luck had pursued him, in cards and other things, and despite his assumption of humility, Carteret's lecture had left him in an ugly mood. He nodded curtly to Ellis without relaxing the scowl that disfigured his handsome features.

"That's the damned sneak who's been giving me away," he muttered. "I'll get even with him yet for this."

Delamere's suspicions with regard to Ellis's feelings were not, as we have seen, entirely without foundation. Indeed, he had underestimated the strength of this rivalry and its chances of success. Ellis had been watching Delamere for a year. There had been nothing surreptitious about it, but his interest in Clara had led him to note things about his favored rival which might have escaped the attention of others less concerned.

Ellis was an excellent judge of character, and had formed a very decided opinion of Tom Delamere. To Ellis, unbiased by ancestral traditions, biased perhaps by jealousy, Tom Delamere was a type of the degenerate aristocrat. If, as he had often heard, it took three or four generations to make a gentleman, and as many more to complete the curve and return to the base from which it started, Tom Delamere belonged somewhere on the downward slant, with large possibilities of further decline. Old Mr. Delamere, who might be taken as the apex of an ideal aristocratic development, had been distinguished, during his active life, as Ellis had learned, for courage and strength of will, courtliness of bearing, deference to his superiors, of whom there had been few, courtesy to his equals, kindness and consideration for those less highly favored, and above all, a scrupulous sense of honor; his grandson Tom was merely the shadow without the substance, the empty husk without the grain. Of grace he had plenty. In manners he could be perfect, when he so chose. Courage and strength he had none. Ellis had seen this fellow, who boasted of his descent from a line of cavaliers, turn pale with fright and spring from a buggy to which was harnessed a fractious horse, which a negro stable-boy drove fearlessly. A valiant carpet-knight, skilled in all parlor exercises, great at whist or euchre, a dream of a dancer, unexcelled in cakewalk or "coon" impersonations, for which he was in large social demand, Ellis had seen him kick an inoffensive negro out of his path and treat a poor-white man with scant courtesy. He suspected Delamere of cheating at cards, and knew that others entertained the same suspicion. For while regular in his own habits,—his poverty would not have permitted him any considerable extravagance,—Ellis's position as a newspaper man kept him in touch with what was going on about town. He was a member, proposed by Carteret, of the Clarendon Club, where cards were indulged in within reasonable limits, and a certain set were known to bet dollars in terms of dimes.

Delamere was careless, too, about money matters. He had a habit of borrowing, right and left, small sums which might be conveniently forgotten by the borrower, and for which the lender would dislike to ask. Ellis had a strain of thrift, derived from a Scotch ancestry, and a tenacious memory for financial details. Indeed, he had never had so much money that he could lose track of it. He never saw Delamere without being distinctly conscious that Delamere owed him four dollars, which he had lent at a time when he could ill afford to spare it. It was a prerogative of aristocracy, Ellis reflected, to live upon others, and the last privilege which aristocracy in decay would willingly relinquish. Neither did the aristocratic memory seem able to retain the sordid details of a small pecuniary transaction.

No doubt the knowledge that Delamere was the favored lover of Miss Pemberton lent a touch of bitterness to Ellis's reflections upon his rival. Ellis had no grievance against the "aristocracy" of Wellington. The "best people" had received him cordially, though his father had not been of their caste; but Ellis hated a hypocrite, and despised a coward, and he felt sure that Delamere was both. Otherwise he would have struggled against his love for Clara Pemberton. His passion for her had grown with his appreciation of Delamere's unworthiness. As a friend of the family, he knew the nature and terms of the engagement, and that if the marriage took place at all, it would not be for at least a year. This was a long time,— many things might happen in a year, especially to a man like Tom Delamere. If for any reason Delamere lost his chance, Ellis meant to be next in the field. He had not made love to Clara, but he had missed no opportunity of meeting her and making himself quietly and unobtrusively agreeable.

On the day after this encounter with Delamere on the stairs of the Chronicle office, Ellis, while walking down Vine Street, met old Mrs. Ochiltree. She was seated in her own buggy, which was of ancient build and pattern, driven by her colored coachman and man of all work.

"Mr. Ellis," she called in a shrill voice, having directed her coachman to draw up at the curb as she saw the young man approaching, "come here. I want to speak to you."

Ellis came up to the buggy and stood uncovered beside it.

"People are saying," said Mrs. Ochiltree, "that Tom Delamere is drinking hard, and has to be carried home intoxicated, two or three times a week, by old Mr. Delamere's man Sandy. Is there any truth in the story?"

"My dear Mrs. Ochiltree, I am not Tom Delamere's keeper. Sandy could tell you better than I."

"You are dodging my question, Mr. Ellis. Sandy would n't tell me the truth, and I know that you would n't lie,— you don't look like a liar. They say Tom is gambling scandalously. What do you know about that?"

"You must excuse me, Mrs. Ochiltree. A great deal of what we hear is mere idle gossip, and the truth is often grossly exaggerated. I'm a member of the same club with Delamere, and gentlemen who belong to the same club are not in the habit of talking about one another. As long as a man retains his club membership, he's presumed to be a gentleman. I would n't say anything against Delamere if I could."

"You don't need to," replied the old lady, shaking her finger at him with a cunning smile. "You are a young man, Mr. Ellis, and I can read you like a book. You are much smarter than you look, but you can't fool me. Good-morning."

Mrs. Ochiltree drove immediately to her niece's, where she found Mrs. Carteret and Clara at home. Clara was very fond of the baby, and was holding him in her arms. He was a fine baby, and bade fair to realize the bright hopes built upon him.

"You hold a baby very naturally, Clara," chuckled the old lady. "I suppose you are in training. But you ought to talk to Tom. I have just learned from Mr. Ellis that Tom is carried home drunk two or three times a week, and that he is gambling in the most reckless manner imaginable."

Clara's eyes flashed indignantly. Ere she could speak, Mrs. Carteret exclaimed:—

"Why, Aunt Polly! did Mr. Ellis say that?"

"I got it from Dinah," she replied, "who heard it from her husband, who learned it from a waiter at the club. And"—

"Pshaw!" said Mrs. Carteret, "mere servants' gossip."

"No, it is n't, Olivia. I met Mr. Ellis on the street, and asked him point blank, and he didn't deny it. He's a member of the club, and ought to know."

"Well, Aunt Polly, it can't be true. Tom is here every other night, and how could he carry on so without showing the signs of it? and where would he get the money? You know he has only a moderate allowance."

"He may win it at cards,—it's better to be born lucky than rich," returned Mrs. Ochiltree. "Then he has expectations, and can get credit. There's no doubt that Tom is going on shamefully."

Clara's indignation had not yet found vent in speech; Olivia had said all that was necessary, but she had been thinking rapidly. Even if all this had been true, why should Mr. Ellis have said it? Or, if he had not stated it directly, he had left the inference to be drawn. It seemed a most unfair and ungentlemanly thing. What motive could Ellis have for such an act?

She was not long in reaching a conclusion which was

not flattering to Ellis. Mr. Ellis came often to the house, and she had enjoyed his society in a friendly way. That he had found her pleasant company had been very evident. She had never taken his attentions seriously, however, or regarded his visits as made especially to her, nor had the rest of the family treated them from that point of view. Her engagement to Tom Delamere, though not yet formally ratified, was so well understood by the world of Wellington that Mr. Ellis would scarcely have presumed to think of her as anything more than a friend.

This revelation of her aunt's, however, put a different face upon his conduct. Certain looks and sighs and enigmatical remarks of Ellis, to which she had paid but casual attention and attached no particular significance, now recurred to her memory with a new meaning. He had now evidently tried, in a roundabout way, to besmirch Tom's character and undermine him in her regard. While loving Tom, she had liked Ellis well enough as a friend; but he had abused the privileges of friendship, and she would teach him a needed lesson.

Nevertheless, Mrs. Ochiltree's story had given Clara food for thought. She was uneasily conscious, after all, that there might be a grain of truth in what had been said, enough, at least, to justify her in warning Tom to be careful, lest his enemies should distort some amiable weakness into a serious crime.

She put this view of the case to Tom at their next meeting, assuring him, at the same time, of her unbounded faith and confidence. She did not mention Ellis's name, lest Tom, in righteous indignation, might do something rash which he might thereafter regret. If any subtler or more obscure motive kept her silent as to Ellis, she was not aware of it; for Clara's views of life were still in the objective stage, and she had not yet fathomed the deepest recesses of her own consciousness.

Delamere had the cunning of weakness. He knew, too, better than any one else could know, how much truth there was in the rumors concerning him, and whether or not they could be verified too easily for him to make an indignant denial. After a little rapid reflection, he decided upon a different course.

"Clara," he said with a sigh, taking, the hand which she generously yielded to soften any suggestion of reproach which he may have read into her solicitude, "you are my guardian angel. I do not know, of course, who has told you this pack of lies,—for I can see that you have heard more than you have told me,—but I think I could guess the man they came from. I am not perfect, Clara, though I have done nothing of which a gentleman should be ashamed. There is one sure way to stop the tongue of calumny. My home life is not ideal,—grandfather is an old, weak man, and the house needs the refining and softening influence of a lady's presence. I do not love club life; its ideals are not elevating. With you by my side, dearest, I should be preserved from every influence except the purest and the best. Don't you think, dearest, that the major might be induced to shorten our weary term of waiting?"

"Oh, Tom," she demurred blushingly, "I shall be young enough at eighteen; and you are barely twenty-one."

But Tom proved an eloquent pleader, and love a still more persuasive advocate. Clara spoke to the major the same evening, who looked grave at the suggestion, and, said he would think about it. They were both very young;

but where both parties were of good family, in good health and good circumstances, an early marriage might not be undesirable. Tom was perhaps a little unsettled, but blood would tell in the long run, and marriage always exercised a steadying influence.

The only return, therefore, which Ellis received for his well-meant effort to ward off Mrs. Ochiltree's embarrassing inquiries was that he did not see Clara upon his next visit, which was made one afternoon while he was on night duty at the office. In conversation with Mrs. Carteret he learned that Clara's marriage had been definitely agreed upon, and the date fixed,—it was to take place in about six months. Meeting Miss Pemberton on the street the following day, he received the slightest of nods. When he called again at the house, after a week of misery, she treated him with a sarcastic coolness which chilled his heart.

"How have I offended you, Miss Clara?" he demanded desperately, when they were left alone for a moment.

"Offended me?" she replied, lifting her eyebrows with an air of puzzled surprise. "Why, Mr. Ellis! What could have put such a notion into your head? Oh dear, I think I hear Dodie,—I know you'll excuse me, Mr. Ellis, won't you? Sister Olivia will be back in a moment; and we're expecting Aunt Polly this afternoon,—if you'll stay awhile she'll be glad to talk to you! You can tell her all the interesting news about your friends!"

XI
THE BABY AND THE BIRD

WHEN Ellis, after this rebuff, had disconsolately taken his leave, Clara, much elated at the righteous punishment she had inflicted upon the slanderer, ran upstairs to the nursery, and, snatching Dodie from Mammy Jane's arms, began dancing gayly with him round the room.

"Look a-hyuh, honey," said Mammy Jane, "you better be keerful wid dat chile, an' don' drap 'im on de flo'. You might let him fall on his head an' break his neck. My, my! but you two does make a pretty pictur'! You'll be wantin' ole Jane ter come an' nuss yo' child'en some er dese days," she chuckled unctuously.

Mammy Jane had been very much disturbed by the recent dangers through which little Dodie had passed; and his escape from strangulation, in the first place, and then from the knife had impressed her as little less than miraculous. She was not certain whether this result had been brought about by her manipulation of the buried charm, or by the prayers which had been offered for the child, but was inclined to believe that both had coöperated to avert the threatened calamity. The favorable outcome of this particular incident had not, however, altered the general situation. Prayers and charms, after all, were merely temporary things, which must be constantly renewed, and might be forgotten or overlooked; while the mole, on the contrary, neither faded nor went away. If its malign influence might for a time seem to disappear, it was merely lying dormant, like the germs of some deadly disease, awaiting its opportunity to strike at an unguarded spot.

Clara and the baby were laughing in great glee, when a mockingbird, perched on the topmost bough of a small tree opposite the nursery window, burst suddenly into song, with many a trill and quaver. Clara, with the child in her arms, sprang to the open window.

"Sister Olivia," she cried, turning her face toward Mrs. Carteret, who at that moment entered the room, "come and look at Dodie."

The baby was listening intently to the music, meanwhile gurgling with delight, and reaching his chubby hands toward the source of this pleasing sound. It seemed as though the mockingbird were aware of his appreciative audience, for he ran through the songs of a dozen different birds, selecting, with the discrimination of a connoisseur and entire confidence in his own powers, those which were most difficult and most alluring.

Mrs. Carteret approached the window, followed by Mammy Jane, who waddled over to join the admiring party. So absorbed were the three women in the baby and the bird that neither one of them observed a neat top buggy, drawn by a sleek sorrel pony, passing slowly along the street before the house. In the buggy was seated a lady, and beside her a little boy, dressed in a child's sailor suit and a straw hat. The lady, with a wistful expression, was looking toward the party grouped in the open window.

Mrs. Carteret, chancing to lower her eyes for an instant, caught the other woman's look directed toward her and her child. With a glance of cold aversion she turned away from the window.

Old Mammy Jane had observed this movement, and had divined the reason for it. She stood beside Clara, watching the retreating buggy.

"Uhhuh!" she said to herself, "it's huh sister Janet! She ma'ied a doctuh, an' all dat, an' she lives in a big house, an' she's be'n roun' de worl' an de Lawd knows where e'se; but Mis' 'Livy don' like de sight er her, an' never will, ez long ez de sun rises an' sets. Dey ce't'nly does favor one anudder,—anybody mought 'low dey wuz twins, ef dey did n' know better. Well, well! Fo'ty years ago who'd 'a' ever expected ter see a nigger gal ridin' in her own buggy? My, my! but I don' know,—I don' know! It don' look right, an' it ain' gwine ter las'!—you can't make me b'lieve!"

Meantime Janet, stung by Mrs. Carteret's look,—the nearest approach she had ever made to a recognition of her sister's existence,—had turned away with hardening face. She had struck her pony sharply with the whip, much to the gentle creature's surprise, when the little boy, who was still looking back, caught his mother's sleeve and exclaimed excitedly:—

"Look, look, mamma! The baby,—the baby!"

Janet turned instantly, and with a mother's instinct gave an involuntary cry of alarm.

At the moment when Mrs. Carteret had turned away from the window, and while Mammy Jane was watching Janet, Clara had taken a step forward, and was leaning against the window-sill. The baby, convulsed with delight, had given a spasmodic spring and slipped from Clara's arms. Instinctively the young woman gripped the long skirt as it slipped through her hands, and held it tenaciously, though too frightened for an instant to do more. Mammy Jane, ashen with sudden dread, uttered an inarticulate scream, but retained self-possession enough to reach down and draw up the child, which hung dangerously suspended, head downward, over the brick pavement below.

"Oh, Clara, Clara, how could you!" exclaimed Mrs. Carteret reproachfully; "you might have killed my child!"

She had snatched the child from Jane's arms, and was holding him closely to her own breast. Struck by a sudden thought, she drew near the window and looked out. Twice within a few weeks her child had been in serious danger, and upon each occasion a member of the Miller family had been involved, for she had heard of Dr. Miller's presumption in trying to force himself where he must have known he would be unwelcome.

Janet was just turning her head away as the buggy moved slowly off. Olivia felt a violent wave of antipathy sweep over her toward this baseborn sister who had thus thrust herself beneath her eyes. If she had not cast her brazen glance toward the window, she herself would not have turned away and lost sight of her child. To this shameless intrusion, linked with Clara's carelessness, had been due the catastrophe, so narrowly averted, which might have darkened her own life forever. She took to her bed for several days, and for a long time was cold toward Clara, and did not permit her to touch the child.

Mammy Jane entertained a theory of her own about the accident, by which the blame was placed, in another way, exactly where Mrs. Carteret had laid it. Julia's daughter, Janet, had been looking intently toward the window just before little Dodie had sprung from Clara's arms. Might she not have cast the evil eye upon the baby, and sought thereby to draw him out of the window? One would not ordinarily expect so young a woman to possess such a power, but she might have acquired it, for this very purpose, from some more experienced person. By the same reasoning, the mockingbird might have been a familiar of the witch, and the two might have conspired to lure the infant to destruction. Whether this were so or not, the transaction at least wore a peculiar look. There was no use telling Mis' 'Livy about it, for she did n't believe, or pretended not to believe, in witchcraft and conjuration. But one could not be too careful. The child was certainly born to be exposed to great dangers,—the mole behind the left ear was an unfailing sign,—and no precaution should be omitted to counteract its baleful influence.

While adjusting the baby's crib, a few days later, Mrs. Carteret found fastened under one of the slats a small bag of cotton cloth, about half an inch long and tied with a black thread, upon opening which she found a few small roots or fibres and a pinch of dried and crumpled herbs. It was a good-luck charm which Mammy Jane had placed there to ward off the threatened evil from the grandchild of her dear old mistress. Mrs. Carteret's first impulse was to throw the bag into the fire, but on second thoughts she let it remain. To remove it would give unnecessary pain to the old nurse. Of course these old negro superstitions were absurd,—but if the charm did no good, it at least would do no harm.

XII
ANOTHER SOUTHERN PRODUCT

ONE morning shortly after the opening of the hospital, while Dr. Miller was making his early rounds, a new patient walked in with a smile on his face and a broken arm hanging limply by his side. Miller recognized in him a black giant by the name of Josh Green, who for many years had worked on the docks for Miller's father,—and simultaneously identified him as the dust-begrimed negro who had stolen a ride to Wellington on the trucks of a passenger car.

"Well, Josh," asked the doctor, as he examined the fracture, "how did you get this? Been fighting again?"

"No, suh, I don' s'pose you could ha'dly call it a fight. One er dem dagoes off'n a Souf American boat gimme some er his jaw, an' I give 'im a back answer, an' here I is wid a broken arm. He got holt er a belayin'-pin befo' I could hit 'im."

"What became of the other man?" demanded Miller suspiciously. He perceived, from the indifference with which Josh bore the manipulation of the fractured limb, that such an accident need not have interfered seriously with the use of the remaining arm, and he knew that Josh had a reputation for absolute fearlessness.

"Lemme see," said Josh reflectively, "ef I kin 'member w'at *did* become er him! Oh, yes, I 'member now! Dey tuck him ter de Marine Horspittle in de amberlance, 'cause his leg wuz broke, an' I reckon somethin' must 'a' accident'ly hit 'im in de jaw, fer he wuz scatt'rin' teeth all de way 'long de street. I did n' wan' ter kill de man, fer he might have somebody dependin' on 'im, an' I knows how dat 'd be ter dem. But no man kin call me a damn' low-down nigger and keep on enjoyin' good health right along."

"It was considerate of you to spare his life," said Miller dryly, "but you'll hit the wrong man some day. These are bad times for bad negroes. You'll get into a quarrel with a white man, and at the end of it there 'll be a lynching, or a funeral. You 'd better be peaceable and endure a little injustice, rather than run the risk of a sudden and violent death."

"I expec's ter die a vi'lent death in a quarrel wid a w'ite man," replied Josh, in a matter-of-fact tone, "an' fu'thermo', he's gwine ter die at the same time, er a little befo'. I be'n takin' my own time 'bout killin' 'im; I ain' be'n crowdin' de man, but I'll be ready after a w'ile, an' den he kin look out!"

"And I suppose you're merely keeping in practice on these other fellows who come your way. When I get your arm dressed, you 'd better leave town till that fellow's boat sails; it may save you the expense of a trial and three months in the chain-gang. But this talk about killing a man is all nonsense. What has any man in this town done to you, that you should thirst for his blood?"

"No, suh, it ain' nonsense,—it's straight, solem' fac'. I'm gwine ter kill dat man as sho' as I 'm settin' in dis cheer; an' dey ain' nobody kin say I ain' got a right ter kill 'im. Does you 'member do Ku-Klux?"

"Yes, but I was a child at the time, and recollect very little about them. It is a page of history which most people are glad to forget."

"Yas, suh; I was a chile, too, but I wuz right in it, an' so I 'members mo' erbout it'n you does. My mammy an' daddy lived 'bout ten miles f'm here, up de river. One night a crowd er w'ite men come ter ou' house an' tuck my daddy out an' shot 'im ter death, an'skeered my mammy so she ain' be'n herse'f f'm dat day ter dis. I wa'n't mo' 'n ten years ole at de time, an' w'en my mammy seed de w'ite men comin', she tol' me ter run. I hid in de bushes an' seen de whole thing, an' it wuz branded on my mem'ry, suh, like a red-hot iron bran's de skin. De w'ite folks had masks on, but one of 'em fell off,—he wuz de boss, he wuz de head man, an' tol' de res' w'at ter do,—an' I seen his face. It wuz a easy face ter 'member; an' I swo' den, 'way down deep in my hea't, little ez I wuz, dat some day er 'nother I'd kill dat man. I ain't never had no doubt erbout it; it's jus' w'at I 'm livin' fer, an' I know I ain' gwine ter die till I've done it. Some lives fer one thing an' some fer another, but dat's my job. I ain' be'n in no has'e, fer I'm not ole yit, an' dat man is in good health. I'd like ter see a little er de worl' befo' I takes chances on leavin' it sudden; an', mo'over, some-body's got ter take keer er de ole 'oman. But her time'll come some er dese days, an den *his* time'll be come— an' prob'ly mine. But I ain' keerin' 'bout myse'f: w'en I git thoo wid him, it won' make no diff'ence 'bout me."

Josh was evidently in dead earnest. Miller recalled, very vividly, the expression he had seen twice on his patient's face, during the journey to Wellington. He had often seen Josh's mother, old Aunt Milly,—"Silly Milly," the children called her,—wandering aimlessly about the street, muttering to herself incoherently. He had felt a certain childish awe at the sight of one of God's creatures who had lost the light of reason, and he had always vaguely understood that she was the victim of human cruelty, though he had dated it farther back into the past. This was his first knowledge of the real facts of the case.

He realized, too, for a moment, the continuity of life, how inseparably the present is woven with the past, how certainly the future will be but the outcome of the present. He had supposed this old wound healed. The negroes were not a vindictive people. If, swayed by passion or emotion, they sometimes gave way to gusts of rage, these were of brief duration. Absorbed in the contemplation of their doubtful present and their uncertain future, they gave little thought to the past,—it was a dark story, which they would willingly forget. He knew the timeworn explanation that the Ku-Klux movement, in the main, was merely an ebullition of boyish spirits, begun to amuse young white men by playing upon the fears and superstitions of ignorant negroes. Here, however, was its tragic side, the old wound still bleeding, the fruit of one tragedy, the seed of another. He could not approve of Josh's application of the Mosaic law of revenge, and yet the incident was not without significance. Here was a negro who could remember an injury, who could shape his life to a definite purpose, if not a high or holy one. When his race reached the point where they would resent a wrong, there was hope that they might soon attain the stage where they would try, and, if need be, die, to defend a right. This man, too, had a purpose in life, and was willing to die that he might accomplish it. Miller was willing to give up his life to a cause. Would he be equally willing, he asked himself, to die for it? Miller had no prophetic instinct to tell him how soon he would have the opportunity to answer his own question. But he could not encourage Josh to carry out this dark and revengeful purpose. Every worthy consideration required him to dissuade his patient from such a desperate course.

"You had better put away these murderous fancies, Josh," he said seriously. "The Bible says that we should 'forgive our enemies, bless them that curse us, and do good to them that despitefully use us.'"

"Yas, suh, I've l'arnt all dat in Sunday-school, an' I've heared de preachers say it time an' time ag'in. But it 'pears ter me dat dis fergitfulniss an' fergivniss is mighty one-sided. De w'ite folks don' fergive nothin' de niggers does. Dey got up de Ku-Klux, dey said, on 'count er de kyarpit-baggers. Dey be'n talkin' 'bout de kyarpit-baggers ever sence, an' dey 'pears ter fergit all 'bout de Ku-Klux. But I ain' fergot. De niggers is be'n train' ter fergiveniss; an' fer fear dey might fergit how ter fergive, de w'ite folks gives 'em somethin' new ev'y now an' den, ter practice on. A w'ite man kin do w'at he wants ter a nigger, but de minute de nigger gits back at 'im, up goes de nigger, an' don' come down tell somebody cuts 'im down. If a nigger gits a' office, er de race 'pears ter be prosperin' too much, de w'ite folks up an' kills a few, so dat de res' kin keep on fergivin' an' bein' thankful dat dey're lef' alive. Don' talk ter me 'bout dese w'ite folks,—I knows 'em, I does! Ef a nigger wants ter git down on his marrow-bones, an' eat dirt, an' call 'em 'marster,' *he's* a good nigger, dere's room, fer *him*. But I ain' no w'ite folks' nigger, I ain'. I don' call no man 'marster.' I don' wan' nothin' but w'at I wo'k fer, but I wants all er dat. I never moles's no w'ite man, 'less 'n he moles's me fus'. But w'en de ole 'oman dies, doctuh, an' I gits a good chance at dat w'ite man,—dere ain' no use talkin', suh!—dere's gwine ter be a mix-up, an' a fune'al, er two fune'als—er may be mo', ef anybody is keerliss enough to git in de way."

"Josh," said the doctor, laying a cool hand on the other's brow, "you're feverish, and don't know what you're talking about. I shouldn't let my mind dwell on such things, and you must keep quiet until this arm is well, or you may never be able to hit any one with it again."

Miller determined that when Josh got better he would talk to him seriously and dissuade him from this danger-ous design. He had not asked the name of Josh's enemy, but the look of murderous hate which the dust-begrimed tramp of the railway journey had cast at Captain George McBane rendered any such question superfluous. McBane was probably deserving of any evil fate which might be-fall him; but such a revenge would do no good, would right no wrong; while every such crime, committed by a colored man, would be imputed to the race, which was already staggering under a load of obloquy because, in the eyes of a prejudiced and undiscriminating public, it must answer as a whole for the offenses of each sepa-rate individual. To die in defense of the right was heroic. To kill another for revenge was pitifully human and weak: "Vengeance is mine, I will repay," saith the Lord.

XIII
THE CAKEWALK

OLD Mr. Delamere's servant, Sandy Campbell, was in deep trouble.

A party of Northern visitors had been staying for several days at the St. James Hotel. The gentlemen of the party were concerned in a projected cotton mill, while the ladies were much interested in the study of social conditions, and especially in the negro problem. As soon as their desire for information became known, they were taken courteously under the wing of prominent citizens and their wives, who gave them, at elaborate luncheons, the Southern white man's views of the negro, sighing sentimentally over the disappearance of the good old negro of before the war, and gravely deploring the degeneracy of his descendants. They enlarged upon the amount of money the Southern whites had spent for the education of the negro, and shook their heads over the inadequate results accruing from this unexampled generosity. It was sad, they said, to witness this spectacle of a dying race, unable to withstand the competition of a superior type. The severe reprisals taken by white people for certain crimes committed by negroes were of course not the acts of the best people, who deplored them; but still a certain charity should be extended towards those who in the intense and righteous anger of the moment should take the law into their own hands and deal out rough but still substantial justice; for no negro was ever lynched without incontestable proof of his guilt. In order to be perfectly fair, and give their visitors all opportunity to see both sides of the question, they accompanied the Northern visitors to a colored church where they might hear a colored preacher, who had won a jocular popularity throughout the whole country by an oft-repeated sermon intended to demonstrate that the earth was flat like a pancake. This celebrated divine could always draw a white audience, except on the days when his no less distinguished white rival in the field of sensationalism preached his equally famous sermon to prove that hell was exactly one half mile, linear measure, from the city limits of Wellington. Whether accidentally or not, the Northern visitors had no opportunity to meet or talk alone with any colored person in the city except the servants at the hotel. When one of the party suggested a visit to the colored mission school, a Southern friend kindly volunteered to accompany them.

The visitors were naturally much impressed by what they learned from their courteous hosts, and felt inclined to sympathize with the Southern people, for the negro is not counted as a Southerner, except to fix the basis of congressional representation. There might of course be things to criticise here and there, certain customs for which they did not exactly see the necessity, and which seemed in conflict with the highest ideals of liberty: but surely these courteous, soft-spoken ladies and gentlemen, entirely familiar with local conditions, who descanted so earnestly and at times pathetically upon the grave problems confronting them, must know more about it than people in the distant North, without their means of information. The negroes who waited on them at the hotel seemed happy enough, and the teachers whom they had met at the mission school had been well-dressed, well-mannered, and apparently content with their position in life. Surely a people who made no complaints could not be very much oppressed.

In order to give the visitors, ere they left Wellington, a pleasing impression of Southern customs, and particularly of the joyous, happy-go-lucky disposition of the Southern darky and his entire contentment with existing conditions, it was decided by the hotel management to treat them, on the last night of their visit, to a little diversion, in the shape of a genuine negro cakewalk.

On the afternoon of this same day Tom Delamere strolled into the hotel, and soon gravitated to the bar, where he was a frequent visitor. Young men of leisure spent much of their time around the hotel, and no small part of it in the bar. Delamere had been to the club, but had avoided the card-room. Time hanging heavy on his hands, he had sought the hotel in the hope that some form of distraction might present itself.

"Have you heard the latest, Mr. Delamere?" asked the bartender, as he mixed a cocktail for his customer.

"No, Billy; what is it?"

"There's to be a big cakewalk upstairs to-night. The No'the'n gentlemen an' ladies who are down here to see about the new cotton fact'ry want to study the nigger some more, and the boss has got up a cakewalk for 'em, 'mongst the waiters and chambermaids, with a little outside talent."

"Is it to be public?" asked Delamere.

"Oh, no, not generally, but friends of the house won't be barred out. The clerk 'll fix it for you. Ransom, the head waiter, will be floor manager."

Delamere was struck with a brilliant idea. The more

he considered it, the brighter it seemed. Another cock-tail imparted additional brilliancy to the conception. He had been trying, after a feeble fashion, to keep his promise to Clara, and was really suffering from lack of excitement.

He left the bar-room, found the head waiter, held with him a short conversation, and left in his intelligent and itching palm a piece of money.

The cakewalk was a great success. The most brilliant performer was a late arrival, who made his appearance just as the performance was about to commence. The newcomer was dressed strikingly, the conspicuous features of his attire being a long blue coat with brass buttons and a pair of plaid trousers. He was older, too, than the other participants, which made his agility the more remarkable. His partner was a new chambermaid, who had just come to town, and whom the head waiter introduced to the newcomer upon his arrival. The cake was awarded to this couple by a unanimous vote. The man presented it to his partner with a grandiloquent flourish, and returned thanks in a speech which sent the Northern visitors into spasms of delight at the quaintness of the darky dialect and the darky wit. To cap the climax, the winner danced a buck dance with a skill and agility that brought a shower of complimentary silver, which he gathered up and passed to the head waiter.

Ellis was off duty for the evening. Not having ventured to put in an appearance at Carteret's since his last rebuff, he found himself burdened with a superfluity of leisure, from which he essayed to find relief by dropping into the hotel office at about nine o'clock. He was invited up to see the cakewalk, which he rather enjoyed, for there was some graceful dancing and posturing. But the grotesque contortions of one participant had struck him as somewhat overdone, even for the comical type of negro. He recognized the fellow, after a few minutes' scrutiny, as the body-servant of old Mr. Delamere. The man's present occupation, or choice of diversion, seemed out of keeping with his employment as attendant upon an invalid old gentleman, and strangely inconsistent with the gravity and decorum which had been so noticeable when this agile cakewalker had served as butler at Major Carteret's table, upon the occasion of the christening dinner. There was a vague suggestion of unreality about this performance, too, which Ellis did not attempt to analyze, but which recurred vividly to his memory upon a subsequent occasion.

Ellis had never pretended to that intimate knowledge of negro thought and character by which some of his acquaintances claimed the ability to fathom every motive of a negro's conduct, and predict in advance what any one of the darker race would do under a given set of circumstances. He would not have believed that a white man could possess two so widely varying phases of character; but as to negroes, they were as yet a crude and undeveloped race, and it was not safe to make predictions concerning them. No one could tell at what moment the thin veneer of civilization might peel off and reveal the underlying savage.

The champion cakewalker, much to the surprise of his sable companions, who were about equally swayed by admiration and jealousy, disappeared immediately after the close of the performance. Any one watching him on his way home through the quiet streets to old Mr. Dela-

114

mere's would have seen him now and then shaking with laughter. It had been excellent fun. Nevertheless, as he neared home, a certain aspect of the affair, hitherto unconsidered, occurred to him, and it was in a rather serious frame of mind that he cautiously entered the house and sought his own room.

The cakewalk had results which to Sandy were very serious. The following week he was summoned before the disciplinary committee of his church and charged with unchristian conduct, in the following particulars, to wit: dancing, and participating in a sinful diversion called a cakewalk, which was calculated to bring the church into disrepute and make it the mockery of sinners.

Sandy protested his innocence vehemently, but in vain. The proof was overwhelming. He was positively identified by Sister Wanda Patterson, the hotel cook, who had watched the whole performance from the hotel corridor for the sole, single, solitary, and only purpose, she averred, of seeing how far human wickedness could be carried by a professing Christian. The whole thing had been shocking and offensive to her, and only a stern sense of duty had sustained her in looking on, that she might be qualified to bear witness against the offender. She had recognized his face, his clothes, his voice, his walk—there could be no shadow of doubt that it was Brother Sandy. This testimony was confirmed by one of the deacons, whose son, a waiter at the hotel, had also seen Sandy at the cakewalk.

Sandy stoutly insisted that he was at home the whole evening; that he had not been near the hotel for three months; that he had never in his life taken part in a cakewalk, and that he did not know how to dance. It was replied that wickedness, like every-thing else, must have a beginning; that dancing was an art that could be acquired in secret, and came natural to some people. In the face of positive proof, Sandy's protestations were of no avail; he was found guilty, and suspended from church fellowship until he should have repented and made full confession.

Sturdily refusing to confess a fault of which he claimed to be innocent, Sandy remained in contumacy, thereby falling somewhat into disrepute among the members of his church, the largest in the city. The effect of a bad reputation being subjective as well as objective, and poor human nature arguing that one may as well have the game as the name, Sandy insensibly glided into habits of which the church would not have approved, though he took care that they should not interfere with his duties to Mr. Delamere. The consolation thus afforded, however, followed as it was by remorse of conscience, did not compensate him for the loss of standing in the church, which to him was a social club as well as a religious temple. At times, in conversation with young Delamere, he would lament his hard fate.

Tom laughed until he cried at the comical idea which Sandy's plaint always brought up, of half-a-dozen negro preachers sitting in solemn judgment upon that cakewalk,—it had certainly been a good cakewalk!—and sending poor Sandy to spiritual Coventry.

"Cheer up, Sandy, cheer up!" he would say when Sandy seemed most depressed. "Go into my room and get yourself a good drink of liquor. The devil's church has a bigger congregation than theirs, and we have the consolation of knowing that when we die, we'll meet all our friends on the other side. Brace up, Sandy, and be a man, or, if you can't be a man, be as near a man as you can!"

Hoping to revive his drooping spirits, Sandy too often accepted the proffered remedy.

XIV
THE MAUNDERINGS OF
OLD MRS. OCHILTREE

WHEN Mrs. Carteret had fully recovered from the shock attendant upon the accident at the window, where little Dodie had so narrowly escaped death or serious injury, she ordered her carriage one afternoon and directed the coachman to drive her to Mrs. Ochiltree's.

Mrs. Carteret had discharged her young nurse only the day before, and had sent for Mammy Jane, who was now recovered from her rheumatism, to stay until she could find another girl. The nurse had been ordered not to take the child to negroes' houses. Yesterday, in driving past the old homestead of her husband's family, now occupied by Dr. Miller and his family, Mrs. Carteret had seen her own baby's carriage standing in the yard.

When the nurse returned home, she was immediately discharged. She offered some sort of explanation, to the effect that her sister worked for Mrs. Miller, and that some family matter had rendered it necessary for her to see her sister. The explanation only aggravated the offense: if Mrs. Carteret could have overlooked the disobedience, she would by no means have retained in her employment a servant whose sister worked for the Miller woman.

Old Mrs. Ochiltree had within a few months begun to show signs of breaking up. She was over seventy years old, and had been of late, by various afflictions, confined to the house much of the time. More than once within the year, Mrs. Carteret had asked her aunt to come and live with her; but Mrs. Ochiltree, who would have regarded such a step as an acknowledgment of weakness, preferred her lonely independence. She resided in a small, old-fashioned house, standing back in the middle of a garden on a quiet street. Two old servants made up her modest household.

This refusal to live with her niece had been lightly borne, for Mrs. Ochiltree was a woman of strong individuality, whose comments upon her acquaintance, present or absent, were marked by a frankness at times no less than startling. This characteristic caused her to be more or less avoided. Mrs. Ochiltree was aware of this sentiment on the part of her acquaintance, and rather exulted in it. She hated fools. Only fools ran away from her, and that because they were afraid she would expose their folly. If most people were fools, it was no fault of hers, and she was not obliged to indulge them by pretending to believe that they knew anything. She had once owned considerable property, but was reticent about her affairs, and told no one how much she was worth, though it was supposed that she had considerable ready money, besides her house and some other real estate. Mrs. Carteret was her nearest living relative, though her grandnephew Tom Delamere had been a great favorite with her. If she did not spare him her tongue-lashings, it was nevertheless expected in the family that she would leave him something handsome in her will.

Mrs. Ochiltree had shared in the general rejoicing upon the advent of the Carteret baby. She had been one of his godmothers, and had hinted at certain intentions held by her concerning him. During Mammy Jane's administration she had tried the old nurse's patience more or less by her dictatorial interference. Since her partial confinement to the house, she had gone, when her health and the weather would permit, to see the child, and at other times had insisted that it be sent to her in charge of the nurse at least every other day.

Mrs. Ochiltree's faculties had shared insensibly in the decline of her health. This weakness manifested itself by fits of absent-mindedness, in which she would seemingly lose connection with the present, and live over again, in imagination, the earlier years of her life. She had buried two husbands, had tried in vain to secure a third, and had never borne any children. Long ago she had petrified into a character which nothing under heaven could change, and which, if death is to take us as it finds us, and the future life to keep us as it takes us, promised anything but eternal felicity to those with whom she might associate after this life. Tom Delamere had been heard to say, profanely, that if his Aunt Polly went to heaven, he would let his mansion in the skies on a long lease, at a low figure.

When the carriage drove up with Mrs. Carteret, her aunt was seated on the little front piazza, with her wrinkled hands folded in her lap, dozing the afternoon away in fitful slumber.

"Tie the horse, William," said Mrs. Carteret, and then go in and wake Aunt Polly, and tell her I want her to come and drive with me."

Mrs. Ochiltree had not observed her niece's approach, nor did she look up when William drew near. Her eyes were closed, and she would let her head sink slowly forward, recovering it now and then with a spasmodic jerk.

"Colonel Ochiltree," she muttered, "was shot at the battle of Culpepper Court House, and left me a widow for the second time. But I would not have married any man on earth after him."

"Mis' Ochiltree!" cried William, raising his voice, "oh, Mis' Ochiltree!"

"If I had found a man,—a real man,—I might have married again. I did not care for weaklings. I could have married John Delamere if I had wanted him. But pshaw! I could have wound him round—"

"Go round to the kitchen, William," interrupted Mrs. Carteret impatiently, "and tell Aunt Dinah to come and wake her up."

William returned in a few moments with a fat, comfortable looking black woman, who curtsied to Mrs. Carteret at the gate, and then going up to her mistress seized her by the shoulder and shook her vigorously.

"Wake up dere, Mis' Polly," she screamed, as harshly as her mellow voice would permit. "Mis' 'Livy wants you ter go drivin' wid 'er!"

"Dinah," exclaimed the old lady, sitting suddenly upright with a defiant assumption of wakefulness, "why do you take so long to come when I call? Bring me my bonnet and shawl. Don't you see my niece waiting for me at the gate?"

120

"Hyuh dey is, hyuh dey is!" returned Dinah, producing the bonnet and shawl, and assisting Mrs. Ochiltree to put them on.

Leaning on William's arm, the old lady went slowly down the walk, and was handed to the rear seat with Mrs. Carteret.

"How's the baby to-day, Olivia, and why didn't you bring him?"

"He has a cold to-day, and is a little hoarse," replied Mrs. Carteret, "so I thought it best not to bring him out. Drive out the Weldon road, William, and back by Pine Street."

The drive led past an eminence crowned by a handsome brick building of modern construction, evidently an institution of some kind, surrounded on three sides by a grove of venerable oaks.

"Hugh Poindexter," Mrs. Ochiltree exclaimed explosively, after a considerable silence, "has been building a new house, in place of the old family mansion burned during the war."

"It is n't Mr. Poindexter's house, Aunt Polly. That is the new colored hospital built by the colored doctor."

"The new colored hospital, indeed, and the colored doctor! Before the war the negroes were all healthy, and when they got sick we took care of them ourselves! Hugh Poindexter has sold the graves of his ancestors to a negro,—I should have starved first!"

"He had his grandfather's grave opened, and there was nothing to remove, except a few bits of heart-pine from the coffin. All the rest had crumbled into dust."

"And he sold the dust to a negro! The world is upside down."

"He had the tombstone transferred to the white cemetery, Aunt Polly, and he has moved away."

"Esau sold his birthright for a mess of pottage. When I die, if you outlive me, Olivia, which is not likely, I shall leave my house and land to this child! He is a Carteret,—he would never sell them to a negro. I can't trust Tom Delamere, I'm afraid."

The carriage had skirted the hill, passing to the rear of the new building.

"Turn to the right, William," ordered Mrs. Carteret, addressing the coachman, "and come back past the other side of the hospital."

A turn to the right into another road soon brought them to the front of the building, which stood slightly back from the street, with no intervening fence or inclosure. A sorrel pony in a light buggy was fastened to a hitching-post near the entrance. As they drove past, a lady came out of the front door and descended the steps, holding by the hand a very pretty child about six years old.

"Who is that woman, Olivia?" asked Mrs. Ochiltree abruptly, with signs of agitation.

The lady coming down the steps darted at the approaching carriage a look which lingered involuntarily.

Mrs. Carteret, perceiving this glance, turned away coldly.

With a sudden hardening of her own features the other woman lifted the little boy into the buggy and drove sharply away in the direction opposite to that taken by Mrs. Carteret's carriage.

"Who is that woman, Olivia?" repeated Mrs. Ochiltree, with marked emotion.

"I have not the honor of her acquaintance," returned Mrs. Carteret sharply. "Drive faster, William."

"I want to know who that woman is," persisted Mrs.

Ochiltree querulously. "William," she cried shrilly, poking the coachman in the back with the end of her cane, "who is that woman?"

"Dat 's Mis' Miller, ma'am," returned the coachman, touching his hat; "Doctuh Miller's wife."

"What was her mother's name?"

"Her mother's name wuz Julia Brown. She's be'n dead dese twenty years er mo'. Why, you knowed Julia, Mis' Polly!—she used ter b'long ter yo' own father befo' de wah; an' after de wah she kep' house fer"—

"Look to your horses, William!" exclaimed Mrs. Carteret sharply.

"It 's that hussy's child," said Mrs. Ochiltree, turning to her niece with great excitement. "When your father died, I turned the mother and the child out into the street. The mother died and went to—the place provided for such as she. If I had n't been just in time, Olivia, they would have turned you out. I saved the property for you and your son! You can thank me for it all!"

"Hush, Aunt Polly, for goodness' sake! William will hear you. Tell me about it when you get home."

Mrs. Ochiltree was silent, except for a few incoherent mumblings. What she might say, what distressing family secret she might repeat in William's hearing, should she take another talkative turn, was beyond conjecture.

Olivia looked anxiously around for something to distract her aunt's attention, and caught sight of a colored man, dressed in sober gray, who was coming toward the carriage.

"There's Mr. Delamere's Sandy!" exclaimed Mrs. Carteret, touching her aunt on the arm. "I wonder how his master is? Sandy, oh, Sandy!"

Sandy approached the carriage, lifting his hat with a slight exaggeration of Chesterfieldian elegance. Sandy, no less than his master, was a survival of an interesting type. He had inherited the feudal deference for his superiors in position, joined to a certain self-respect which saved him from sycophancy. His manners had been formed upon those of old Mr. Delamere, and were not a bad imitation; for in the man, as in the master, they were the harmonious reflection of a mental state.

"How is Mr. Delamere, Sandy?" asked Mrs. Carteret, acknowledging Sandy's salutation with a nod and a smile.

"He ain't ez peart ez he has be'n, ma'am," replied Sandy, "but he's doin' tol'able well. De doctuh say he's good fer a dozen years yit, ef he 'll jes' take good keer of hisse'f an' keep f'm gittin' excited; fer sence dat secon' stroke, excitement is dange'ous fer 'im."

"I'm sure you take the best care of him," returned Mrs. Carteret kindly.

"You can't do anything for him, Sandy," interposed old Mrs. Ochiltree, shaking her head slowly to emphasize her dissent. "All the doctors in creation couldn't keep him alive another year. I shall outlive him by twenty years, though we are not far from the same age."

"Lawd, ma'am!" exclaimed Sandy, lifting his hands in affected amazement,—his study of gentle manners had been more than superficial,—"whoever would 'a' s'picion' dat you an' Mars John wuz nigh de same age? I 'd 'a' 'lowed you wuz ten years younger'n him, easy, ef you wuz a day!"

"Give my compliments to the poor old gentleman," returned Mrs. Ochiltree, with a simper of senile vanity, though her back was weakening under the strain of the effort to sit erect that she might maintain this illusion of comparative youthfulness. "Bring him to see me some day when he is able to walk."

"Yas 'm, I will," rejoined Sandy. "He's gwine out ter Belleview nex' week, fer ter stay a mont' er so, but I'll fetch him' roun' w'en he comes back. I'll tell 'im dat you ladies 'quired fer 'im."

Sandy made another deep bow, and held his hat in his hand until the carriage had moved away. He had not condescended to notice the coachman at all, who was one of the young negroes of the new generation; while Sandy regarded himself as belonging to the quality, and seldom stooped to notice those beneath him. It would not have been becoming in him, either, while conversing with white ladies, to have noticed a colored servant. Moreover, the coachman was a Baptist, while Sandy was a Methodist, though under a cloud, and considered a Methodist in poor standing as better than a Baptist of any degree of sanctity.

"Lawd, Lawd!" chuckled Sandy, after the carriage had departed, "I never seed nothin' lack de way dat ole lady do keep up her temper! Wid one foot in de grave, an' de other hov'rin' on de edge, she talks 'bout my ole marster lack he wuz in his secon' chil'hood. But I'm jes' willin' ter bet dat he'll outlas' her! She ain't half de woman she wuz dat night I waited on de table at de christenin' pa'ty, w'en she 'lowed she wuz n' feared er no man livin'."

XV
MRS. CARTERET SEEKS AN EXPLANATION

As a stone dropped into a pool of water sets in motion a series of concentric circles which disturb the whole mass in varying degree, so Mrs. Ochiltree's enigmatical remark had started in her niece's mind a disturbing train of thought. Had her words, Mrs. Carteret asked herself, any serious meaning, or were they the mere empty babblings of a clouded intellect?

"William," she said to the coachman when they reached Mrs. Ochiltree's house, "you may tie the horse and help us out. I shall be here a little while."

William helped the ladies down, assisted Mrs. Ochiltree into the house, and then went round to the kitchen. Dinah was an excellent hand at potato-pone and other culinary delicacies dear to the Southern heart, and William was a welcome visitor in her domain.

"Now, Aunt Polly," said Mrs. Carteret resolutely, as soon as they were alone, "I want to know what you meant by what you said about my father and Julia, and this— this child of hers?"

The old woman smiled cunningly, but her expression soon changed to one more grave.

"Why do you want to know?" she asked suspiciously. "You've got the land, the houses, and the money. You've nothing to complain of. Enjoy yourself, and be thankful!"

"I'm thankful to God," returned Olivia, "for all his good gifts, and he has blessed me abundantly,—but why should I be thankful to *you* for the property my father left me?"

"Why should you be thankful to me?" rejoined Mrs. Ochiltree with querulous indignation. "You'd better ask why *should n't* you be thankful to me. What have I not done for you?"

"Yes, Aunt Polly, I know you've done a great deal. You reared me in your own house when I had been cast out of my father's; you have been a second mother to me, and I am very grateful,—you can never say that I have not shown my gratitude. But if you have done anything else for me, I wish to know it. Why should I thank you for my inheritance?"

"Why should you thank me? Well, because I drove that woman and her brat away."

"But she had no right to stay, Aunt Polly, after father died. Of course she had no moral right before, but it was his house, and he could keep her there if he chose. But after his death she surely had no right."

"Perhaps not so surely as you think,—if she had not been a negro. Had she been white, there might have been a difference. When I told her to go, she said"—

"What did she say, Aunt Polly," demanded Olivia eagerly.

It seemed for a moment as though Mrs. Ochiltree would speak no further: but her once strong will, now weakened by her bodily infirmities, yielded to the influence of her niece's imperious demand.

"I'll tell you the whole story," she said, "and then you'll know what I did for you and yours."

Mrs. Ochiltree's eyes assumed an introspective expression, and her story, as it advanced, became as keenly dramatic as though memory had thrown aside the veil of intervening years and carried her back directly to the events which she now described.

"Your father," she said, "while living with that woman, left home one morning the picture of health. Five minutes later he tottered into the house groaning with pain, stricken unto death by the hand of a just God, as a punishment for his sins."

Olivia gave a start of indignation, but restrained herself.

"I was at once informed of what had happened, for I had means of knowing all that took place in the household. Old Jane—she was younger then—had come with you to my house; but her daughter remained, and through her I learned all that went on.

"I hastened immediately to the house, entered without knocking, and approached Mr. Merkell's bedroom, which was on the lower floor and opened into the hall. The door was ajar, and as I stood there for a moment I heard your father's voice.

"'Listen, Julia,' he was saying. 'I shall not live until the doctor comes. But I wish you to know, *dear* Julia!'—he called her 'dear Julia!'—'before I die, that I have kept my promise. You did me one great service, Julia,—you saved me from Polly Ochiltree!' Yes, Olivia, that is what he said! 'You have served me faithfully and well, and I owe you a great deal, which I have tried to pay.'

"'Oh, Mr. Merkell, dear Mr. Merkell,' cried the hypocritical hussy, falling to her knees by his bedside, and shedding her crocodile tears, 'you owe me nothing. You have done more for me than I could ever repay. You will not die and leave me,—no, no, it cannot be!'

"'Yes, I am going to die,—I am dying now, Julia. But listen,—compose yourself and listen, for this is a more important matter. Take the keys from under my pillow, open the desk in the next room, look in the second drawer on the right, and you will find an envelope containing three papers: one of them is yours, one is the paper I promised to make, and the third is a letter which I wrote last night. As soon as the breath has left my body, deliver the envelope to the address indorsed upon it. Do not delay one moment, or you may live to regret it. Say nothing until you have delivered the package, and then be guided by the advice which you receive,—it will come from a friend of mine who will not see you wronged.'

"I slipped away from the door without making my presence known and entered, by a door from the hall, the room adjoining the one where Mr. Merkell lay. A moment later there was a loud scream. Returning quickly to the hall, I entered Mr. Merkell's room as though just arrived.

"'How is Mr. Merkell?' I demanded, as I crossed the threshold.

"'He is dead,' sobbed the woman, without lifting her head,—she had fallen on her knees by the bedside. She had good cause to weep, for my time had come.

"'Get up,' I said. 'You have no right here. You pollute Mr. Merkell's dead body by your touch. Leave the house immediately,—your day is over!'

"'I will not!' she cried, rising to her feet and facing me with brazen-faced impudence. 'I have a right to stay,—he has given me the right!'

"'Ha, ha!' I laughed. 'Mr. Merkell is dead, and I am mistress here henceforth. Go, and go at once,—do you hear?'

"'I hear, but I shall not heed. I can prove my rights! I shall not leave!'

"'Very well,' I replied, 'we shall see. The law will decide.'

"I left the room, but did not leave the house. On the contrary, I concealed myself where I could see what took place in the room adjoining the death-chamber.

"She entered the room a moment later, with her child on one arm and the keys in the other hand. Placing the child on the floor, she put the key in the lock, and seemed surprised to find the desk already unfastened. She opened the desk, picked up a roll of money and a ladies' watch, which first caught her eye, and was reaching toward the drawer upon the right, when I interrupted her:—

"'Well, thief, are you trying to strip the house before you leave it?'

"She gave an involuntary cry, clasped one hand to her bosom and with the other caught up her child, and stood like a wild beast at bay.

"'I am not a thief,' she panted. 'The things are mine!'

"'You lie,' I replied. 'You have no right to them,—no more right than you have to remain in this house!'

"'I have a right,' she persisted, 'and I can prove it!'

"She turned toward the desk, seized the drawer, and drew it open. Never shall I forget her look,—never shall I forget that moment; it was the happiest of my life. The drawer was empty!

"Pale as death she turned and faced me.

"'The papers!' she shrieked, 'the papers! *You* have stolen them!'

"'Papers?' I laughed, 'what papers? Do you take me for a thief, like yourself?'

"'There were papers here,' she cried, 'only a minute since. They are mine,—give them back to me!'

130

"'Listen, woman,' I said sternly, 'you are lying or dreaming. My brother-in-law's papers are doubtless in his safe at his office, where they ought to be. As for the rest,—you are a thief.'

"'I am not,' she screamed; 'I am his wife. He married me, and the papers that were in the desk will prove it.'

"'Listen,' I exclaimed, when she had finished, 'listen carefully, and take heed to what I say. You are a liar. You have no proofs,—there never were any proofs of what you say, because it never happened,—it is absurd upon the face of it. Not one person in Wellington would believe it. Why should he marry you? He did not need to! You are merely lying—you are not even self-deceived. If he had really married you, you would have made it known long ago. That you did not is proof that your story is false.'

"She was hit so hard that she trembled and sank into a chair. But I had no mercy—she had saved your father from *me*—'dear Julia,' indeed!

"'Stand up,' I ordered. 'Do not dare to sit down in my presence. I have you on the hip, my lady, and will teach you your place.'

"She struggled to her feet, and stood supporting herself with one hand on the chair. I could have killed her, Olivia! She had been my father's slave; if it had been before the war, I would have had her whipped to death.

"'You are a thief,' I said, 'and of that there *are* proofs. I have caught you in the act. The watch in your bosom is my own, the money belongs to Mr. Merkell's estate, which belongs to my niece, his daughter Olivia. I saw you steal them. My word is worth yours a hundred times over, for I am a lady, and you are—what? And now hear me:

if ever you breathe to a living soul one word of this preposterous story, I will charge you with the theft, and have you sent to the penitentiary. Your child will be taken from you, and you shall never see it again. I will give you now just ten minutes to take your brat and your rags out of this house forever. But before you go, put down your plunder there upon the desk!'

"She laid down the money and the watch, and a few minutes later left the house with the child in her arms.

"And now, Olivia, you know how I saved your estate, and why you should be grateful to me."

Olivia had listened to her aunt's story with intense interest. Having perceived the old woman's mood, and fearful lest any interruption might break the flow of her narrative, she had with an effort kept back the one question which had been hovering upon her lips, but which could now no longer be withheld.

"What became of the papers, Aunt Polly?"

"Ha, ha!" chuckled Mrs. Ochiltree with a cunning look, "did I not tell you that she found no papers?"

A change had come over Mrs. Ochiltree's face, marking the reaction from her burst of energy. Her eyes were half closed, and she was muttering incoherently. Olivia made some slight effort to arouse her but in vain, and realizing the futility of any further attempt to extract information from her aunt at this time, she called William and drove homeward.

XVI
ELLIS TAKES A TRICK

LATE one afternoon a handsome trap, drawn by two spirited bays, drove up to Carteret's gate. Three places were taken by Mrs. Carteret, Clara, and the major, leaving the fourth seat vacant.

"I've asked Ellis to drive out with us," said the major, as he took the lines from the colored man who had the trap in charge. "We'll go by the office and pick him up."

Clara frowned, but perceiving Mrs. Carteret's eye fixed upon her, restrained any further expression of annoyance.

The major's liking for Ellis had increased within the year. The young man was not only a good journalist, but possessed sufficient cleverness and tact to make him excellent company. The major was fond of argument, but extremely tenacious of his own opinions. Ellis handled the foils of discussion with just the requisite skill to draw out the major, permitting himself to be vanquished, not too easily, but, as it were, inevitably, by the major's incontrovertible arguments.

Olivia had long suspected Ellis of feeling a more than friendly interest in Clara. Herself partial to Tom, she had more than once thought it hardly fair to Delamere, or even to Clara, who was young and impressionable, to have another young man constantly about the house. True, there had seemed to be no great danger, for Ellis had neither the family nor the means to make him a suitable match for the major's sister; nor had Clara made any secret of her dislike for Ellis, or of her resentment for his supposed depreciation of Delamere. Mrs. Carteret was inclined to a more just and reasonable view of Ellis's conduct in this matter, but nevertheless did not deem it wise to undeceive Clara. Dislike was a stout barrier, which remorse might have broken down. The major, absorbed in schemes of empire and dreams of his child's future, had not become cognizant of the affair. His wife, out of friendship for Tom, had refrained from mentioning it; while the major, with a delicate regard for Clara's feelings, had said nothing at home in regard to his interview with her lover.

At the Chronicle office Ellis took the front seat beside the major. After leaving the city pavements, they bowled along merrily over an excellent toll-road, built of oyster shells from the neighboring sound, stopping at intervals to pay toll to the gate-keepers, most of whom were white women with tallow complexions and snuff-stained lips,—the traditional "poor-white." For part of the way the road was bordered with a growth of scrub oak and pine, interspersed with stretches of cleared land, white with the opening cotton or yellow with ripening corn. To the right, along the distant river-bank, were visible here and there groups of turpentine pines, though most of this growth had for some years been exhausted. Twenty years before, Wellington had been the world's greatest shipping port for naval stores. But as the turpentine industry had moved southward, leaving a trail of devastated forests in its rear, the city had fallen to a poor fifth or sixth place in this trade, relying now almost entirely upon cotton for its export business.

Occasionally our party passed a person, or a group of persons,—mostly negroes approximating the pure type, for those of lighter color grew noticeably scarcer as the town was left behind. Now and then one of these would salute the party respectfully, while others glanced at them indifferently or turned away. There would have seemed, to a stranger, a lack of spontaneous friendliness between the people of these two races, as though each felt that it had no part or lot in the other's life. At one point the carriage drew near a party of colored folks who were laughing and jesting among themselves with great glee. Paying no attention to the white people, they continued to laugh and shout boisterously as the carriage swept by.

Major Carteret's countenance wore an angry look.

"The negroes around this town are becoming absolutely insufferable," he averred. "They are sadly in need of a lesson in manners."

Half an hour later they neared another group, who were also making merry. As the carriage approached, they became mute and silent as the grave until the major's party had passed.

"The negroes are a sullen race," remarked the major thoughtfully. "They will learn their lesson in a rude school, and perhaps much sooner than they dream. By the way," he added, turning to the ladies, "what was the arrangement with Tom? Was he to come out this evening?"

"He came out early in the afternoon," replied Clara, "to go a-fishing. He is to join us at the hotel."

After an hour's drive they reached the hotel, in front of which stretched the beach, white and inviting along the shallow sound. Mrs. Carteret and Clara found seats on the veranda. Having turned the trap over to a hostler, the major joined a group of gentlemen, among whom was General Belmont, and was soon deep in the discussion of the standing problem of how best to keep the negroes down.

Ellis remained by the ladies. Clara seemed restless and ill at ease. Half an hour elapsed and Delamere had not appeared.

"I wonder where Tom is," said Mrs. Carteret.

"I guess he has n't come in yet from fishing," said Clara. "I wish he would come. It's lonesome here. Mr. Ellis, would you mind looking about the hotel and seeing if there's any one here that we know?"

For Ellis the party was already one too large. He had accepted this invitation eagerly, hoping to make friends with Clara during the evening. He had never been able to learn definitely the reason of her coldness, but had dated it from his meeting with old Mrs. Ochiltree, with which he felt it was obscurely connected. He had noticed Delamere's scowling look, too, at their last meeting. Clara's injustice, whatever its cause, he felt keenly. To Delamere's scowl he had paid little attention,—he despised Tom so much that, but for his engagement to Clara, he would have held his opinions in utter contempt.

He had even wished that Clara might make some charge against him,—he would have preferred that to her attitude of studied indifference, the only redeeming feature about which was that it *was* studied, showing that she, at least, had him in mind. The next best thing, he reasoned, to having a woman love you, is to have her dislike you violently,—the main point is that you should be kept in mind, and made the subject of strong emotions. He thought of the story of Hall Caine's, where the woman, after years of persecution at the hands of an unwelcome suitor, is on the point of yielding, out of sheer irresistible admiration for the man's strength and persistency,

136

when the lover, unaware of his victory and despairing of success, seizes her in his arms and, springing into the sea, finds a watery grave for both. The analogy of this case with his own was, of course, not strong. He did not anticipate any tragedy in their relations; but he was glad to be thought of upon almost any terms. He would not have done a mean thing to make her think of him; but if she did so because of a misconception, which he was given no opportunity to clear up, while at the same time his conscience absolved him from evil and gave him the compensating glow of martyrdom, it was at least better than nothing.

He would, of course, have preferred to be upon a different footing. It had been a pleasure to have her speak to him during the drive,—they had exchanged a few trivial remarks in the general conversation. It was a greater pleasure to have her ask a favor of him,—a pleasure which, in this instance, was partly offset when he interpreted her request to mean that he was to look for Tom Delamere. He accepted the situation gracefully, however, and left the ladies alone.

Knowing Delamere's habits, he first went directly to the bar-room,—the atmosphere would be congenial, even if he were not drinking. Delamere was not there. Stepping next into the office, he asked the clerk if young Mr. Delamere had been at the hotel.

"Yes, sir," returned the man at the desk, "he was here at luncheon, and then went out fishing in a boat with several other gentlemen. I think they came back about three o'clock. I'll find out for you."

He rang the bell, to which a colored boy responded.

"Front," said the clerk, "see if young Mr. Delamere's

upstairs. Look in 255 or 256, and let me know at once."

The bell-boy returned in a moment.

"Yas, suh," he reported, with a suppressed grin, "he's in 256, suh. De do' was open, an' I seed 'im from de hall, suh."

"I wish you'd go up and tell him," said Ellis, "that— What are you grinning about?" he asked suddenly, noticing the waiter's expression.

"Nothin' suh, nothin' at all, suh," responded the negro, lapsing into the stolidity of a wooden Indian. "What shall I tell Mr. Delamere, suh?"

"Tell him," resumed Ellis, still watching the boy suspiciously,—"no, I'll tell him myself."

He ascended the broad stair to the second floor. There was an upper balcony and a parlor, with a piano for the musically inclined. To reach these one had to pass along the hall upon which the room mentioned by the bell-boy opened. Ellis was quite familiar with the hotel. He could imagine circumstances under which he would not care to speak to Delamere; he would merely pass through the hall and glance into the room casually, as any one else might do, and see what the darky downstairs might have meant by his impudence.

It required but a moment to reach the room. The door was not wide open, but far enough ajar for him to see what was going on within.

Two young men, members of the fast set at the Clarendon Club, were playing cards at a small table, near which stood another, decorated with an array of empty bottles and glasses. Sprawling on a lounge, with flushed face and disheveled hair, his collar unfastened, his vest buttoned awry, lay Tom Delamere, breathing stertorously,

138

in what seemed a drunken sleep. Lest there should be any doubt of the cause of his condition, the fingers of his right hand had remained clasped mechanically around the neck of a bottle which lay across his bosom.

Ellis turned away in disgust, and went slowly back to the ladies.

"There seems to be no one here yet," he reported. "We came a little early for the evening crowd. The clerk says Tom Delamere was here to luncheon, but he has n't seen him for several hours."

"He 's not a very gallant cavalier," said Mrs. Carteret severely. "He ought to have been waiting for us."

Clara was clearly disappointed, and made no effort to conceal her displeasure, leaving Ellis in doubt as to whether or not he were its object. Perhaps she suspected him of not having made a very thorough search. Her next remark might have borne such a construction.

"Sister Olivia," she said pettishly, "let's go up to the parlor. I can play the piano anyway, if there's no one to talk to."

"I find it very comfortable here, Clara," replied her sister placidly. "Mr. Ellis will go with you. You'll probably find some one in the parlor, or they'll come when you begin to play."

Clara's expression was not cordial, but she rose as if to go. Ellis was in a quandary. If she went through the hall, the chances were at least even that she would see Delamere. He did not care a rap for Delamere,—if he chose to make a public exhibition of himself, it was his own affair; but to see him would surely spoil Miss Pemberton's evening, and, in her frame of mind, might lead to the suspicion that Ellis had prearranged the exposure.

Even if she should not harbor this unjust thought, she would not love the witness of her discomfiture. We had rather not meet the persons who have seen, even though they never mention, the skeletons in our closets. Delamere had disposed of himself for the evening. Ellis would have a fairer field with Delamere out of sight and unaccounted for, than with Delamere in evidence in his present condition.

"Wouldn't you rather take a stroll on the beach, Miss Clara?" he asked, in the hope of creating a diversion.

"No, I'm going to the parlor. *You* need n't come, Mr. Ellis, if you 'd rather go down to the beach. I can quite as well go alone."

"I'd rather go with you," he said meekly.

They were moving toward the door opening into the hall, from which the broad staircase ascended. Ellis, whose thoughts did not always respond quickly to a sudden emergency, was puzzling his brain as to how he should save her from any risk of seeing Delamere. Through the side door leading from the hall into the office, he saw the bell-boy to whom he had spoken seated on the bench provided for the servants.

"Won't you wait for me just a moment, Miss Clara, "while I step into the office? I'll be with you in an instant."

Clara hesitated.

"Oh, certainly," she replied nonchalantly.

Ellis went direct to the bell-boy. "Sit right where you are," he said, "and don't move a hair. What is the lady in the hall doing?"

"She's got her back tu'ned this way, suh. I 'spec' she's lookin' at the picture on the opposite wall, suh."

"All right," whispered Ellis, pressing a coin into the servant's hand. "I'm going up to the parlor with the lady. You go up ahead of us, and keep in front of us along the hall. Don't dare to look back. I shall keep on talking to the lady, so that you can tell by my voice where we are. When you get to room 256, go in and shut the door behind you: pretend that you were called,—ask the gentlemen what they want,—tell any kind of a lie you like,—but keep the door shut until you're sure we've got by. Do you hear?"

"Yes, suh," replied the negro intelligently.

The plan worked without a hitch. Ellis talked steadily, about the hotel, the furnishings, all sorts of irrelevant subjects, to which Miss Pemberton paid little attention. She was angry with Delamere, and took no pains to conceal her feelings. The bell-boy entered room 256 just before they reached the door. Ellis had heard loud talking as they approached, and as they were passing there was a crash of broken glass, as though some object had been thrown at the door.

"What is the matter there?" exclaimed Clara, quickening her footsteps and instinctively drawing closer to Ellis.

"Some one dropped a glass, I presume," replied Ellis calmly.

Miss Pemberton glanced at him suspiciously. She was in a decidedly perverse mood. Seating herself at the piano, she played brilliantly for a quarter of an hour. Quite a number of couples strolled up to the parlor, but Delamere was not among them.

"Oh dear!" exclaimed Miss Pemberton, as she let her fingers fall upon the keys with a discordant crash, after the last note, "I don't see why we came out here to-night. Let's go back downstairs."

Ellis felt despondent. He had done his utmost to serve and to please Miss Pemberton, but was not likely, he foresaw, to derive much benefit from his opportunity. Delamere was evidently as much or more in her thoughts by reason of his absence than if he had been present. If the door should have been opened, and she should see him from the hall upon their return, Ellis could not help it. He took the side next to the door, however, meaning to hurry past the room so that she might not recognize Delamere.

Fortunately the door was closed and all quiet within the room. On the stairway they met the bellboy, rubbing his head with one hand and holding a bottle of seltzer upon a tray in the other. The boy was well enough trained to give no sign of recognition, though Ellis guessed the destination of the bottle.

Ellis hardly knew whether to feel pleased or disappointed at the success of his manœuvres. He had spared Miss Pemberton some mortification, but he had saved Tom Delamere from merited exposure. Clara ought to know the truth, for her own sake.

On the beach, a few rods away, fires were burning, around which several merry groups had gathered. The smoke went mostly to one side, but a slight whiff came now and then to where Mrs. Carteret sat awaiting them.

"They're roasting oysters," said Mrs. Carteret. "I wish you'd bring me some, Mr. Ellis."

Ellis strolled down to the beach. A large iron plate, with a turned-up rim like a great baking-pan, supported by legs which held it off the ground, was set over a fire built upon the sand. This primitive oven was heaped with small oysters in the shell, taken from the neighboring sound, and hauled up to the hotel by a negro whose pony cart stood near by. A wet coffee-sack of burlaps was spread over the oysters, which, when steamed sufficiently, were opened by a colored man and served gratis to all who cared for them.

Ellis secured a couple of plates of oysters, which he brought to Mrs. Carteret and Clara; they were small, but finely flavored.

Meanwhile Delamere, who possessed a remarkable faculty of recuperation from the effects of drink, had waked from his sleep, and remembering his engagement, had exerted himself to overcome the ravages of the afternoon's debauch. A dash of cold water braced him up somewhat. A bottle of seltzer and a big cup of strong coffee still further strengthened his nerves.

When Ellis returned to the veranda, after having taken away the plates, Delamere had joined the ladies and was explaining the cause of his absence.

He had been overcome by the heat, he said, while out fishing, and had been lying down ever since. Perhaps he ought to have sent for a doctor, but the fellows had looked after him. He had n't sent word to his friends because he had n't wished to spoil their evening.

"That was very considerate of you, Tom," said Mrs. Carteret dryly, "but you ought to have let us know. We have been worrying about you very much. Clara has found the evening dreadfully dull."

"Indeed, no, sister Olivia," said the young lady cheerfully, "I've been having a lovely time. Mr. Ellis and I have been up in the parlor; I played the piano; and we've been eating oysters and having a most delightful time. Won't you take me down there to the beach, Mr. Ellis? I want to see the fires. Come on."

"Can't I go?" asked Tom jealously.

"No, indeed, you must n't stir a foot! You must not overtax yourself so soon; it might do you serious injury. Stay here with sister Olivia."

She took Ellis's arm with exaggerated cordiality. Delamere glared after them angrily. Ellis did not stop to question her motives, but took the goods the gods provided. With no very great apparent effort, Miss Pemberton became quite friendly, and they strolled along the beach, in sight of the hotel, for nearly half an hour. As they were coming up she asked him abruptly,—

"Mr. Ellis, did you know Tom was in the hotel?"

Ellis was looking across the sound, at the lights of a distant steamer which was making her way toward the harbor.

"I wonder," he said musingly, as though he had not heard her question, "if that is the Ocean Belle?"

"And was he really sick? " she demanded.

"She's later than usual this trip," continued Ellis, pursuing his thought. "She was due about five o'clock."

Miss Pemberton, under cover of the darkness, smiled a fine smile, which foreboded ill for some one. When they joined the party on the piazza, the major had come up and was saying that it was time to go. He had been engaged in conversation, for most of the evening, with General Belmont and several other gentlemen.

"Here comes the general now. Let me see. There are five of us. The general has offered me a seat in his buggy, and Tom can go with you-all."

The general came up and spoke to the ladies. Tom

murmured his thanks; it would enable him to make up a part of the delightful evening be had missed.

When Mrs. Carteret had taken the rear seat, Clara promptly took the place beside her. Ellis and Delamere sat in front. When Delamere, who had offered to drive, took the reins, Ellis saw that his hands were shaking.

"Give me the lines," he whispered. "Your nerves are unsteady and the road is not well lighted."

Delamere prudently yielded the reins. He did not like Ellis's tone, which seemed sneering rather than expressive of sympathy with one who had been suffering. He wondered if the beggar knew anything about his illness. Clara had been acting strangely. It would have been just like Ellis to have slandered him. The upstart had no business with Clara anyway. He would cheerfully have strangled Ellis, if he could have done so with safety to himself and no chance of discovery.

The drive homeward through the night was almost a silent journey. Mrs. Carteret was anxious about her baby. Clara did not speak, except now and then to Ellis with reference to some object in or near the road. Occasionally they passed a vehicle in the darkness, sometimes barely avoiding a collision. Far to the north the sky was lit up with the glow of a forest fire. The breeze from the Sound was deliciously cool. Soon the last toll-gate was passed and the lights of the town appeared.

Ellis threw the lines to William, who was waiting, and hastened to help the ladies out.

"Good-night, Mr. Ellis," said Clara sweetly, as she gave Ellis her hand. "Thank you for a very pleasant evening Come up and see us soon."

She ran into the house without a word to Tom.

XVII
THE SOCIAL ASPIRATIONS
OF CAPTAIN McBANE

It was only eleven o'clock, and Delamere, not being at all sleepy, and feeling somewhat out of sorts as the combined results of his afternoon's debauch and the snubbing he had received at Clara's hands, directed the major's coachman, who had taken charge of the trap upon its arrival, to drive him to the St. James Hotel before returning the horses to the stable. First, however, the coachman left Ellis at his boarding-house, which was near by. The two young men parted with as scant courtesy as was possible without an open rupture.

Delamere hoped to find at the hotel some form of distraction to fill in an hour or two before going home. Ill fortune favored him by placing in his way the burly form of Captain George McBane, who was sitting in an arm-chair alone, smoking a midnight cigar, under the hotel balcony. Upon Delamere's making known his desire for amusement, the captain proposed a small game of poker in his own room.

McBane had been waiting for some such convenient opportunity. We have already seen that the captain was desirous of social recognition, which he had not yet obtained beyond the superficial acquaintance acquired by association with men about town. He had determined to assault society in its citadel by seeking membership in the Clarendon Club, of which most gentlemen of the best families of the city were members.

The Clarendon Club was a historic institution, and its membership a social cult, the temple of which was located just off the main street of the city, in a dignified old colonial mansion which had housed it for the nearly one hundred years during which it had maintained its existence unbroken. There had grown up around it many traditions and special usages. Membership in the Clarendon was the *sine qua non* of high social standing, and was conditional upon two of three things,—birth, wealth, and breeding. Breeding was the prime essential, but, with rare exceptions, must be backed by either birth or money.

Having decided, therefore, to seek admission into this social arcanum, the captain, who had either not quite appreciated the standard of the Clarendon's membership, or had failed to see that he fell beneath it, looked about for an intermediary through whom to approach the object of his desire. He had already thought of Tom Delamere in this connection, having with him such an acquaintance as one forms around a hotel, and having long ago discovered that Delamere was a young man of superficially amiable disposition, vicious instincts, lax principles, and a weak will, and, which was quite as much to the purpose, a member of the Clarendon Club. Possessing mental characteristics almost entirely opposite, Delamere and the captain had certain tastes in common, and had smoked, drunk, and played cards together more than once.

Still more to his purpose, McBane had detected Delamere trying to cheat him at cards. He had said nothing about this discovery, but had merely noted it as something which at some future time might prove useful. The captain had not suffered by Delamere's deviation from the straight line of honor, for while Tom was as clever with the cards as might be expected of a young man who had devoted most of his leisure for several years to handling them, McBane was past master in their manipulation. During a stormy career he had touched more or less pitch, and had escaped few sorts of defilement.

The appearance of Delamere at a late hour, unaccompanied, and wearing upon his countenance an expression in which the captain read aright the craving for mental and physical excitement, gave him the opportunity for which he had been looking. McBane was not the man to lose an opportunity, nor did Delamere require a second invitation. Neither was it necessary, during the progress of the game, for the captain to press upon his guest the contents of the decanter which stood upon the table within convenient reach.

The captain permitted Delamere to win from him several small amounts, after which he gradually increased the stakes and turned the tables.

Delamere, with every instinct of a gamester, was no more a match for McBane in self-control than in skill. When the young man had lost all his money, the captain expressed his entire willingness to accept notes of hand, for which he happened to have convenient blanks in his apartment.

When Delamere, flushed with excitement and wine, rose from the gaming table at two o'clock, he was vaguely conscious that he owed McBane a considerable sum, but could not have stated how much. His opponent, who was entirely cool and collected, ran his eye carelessly over the bits of paper to which Delamere had attached his signature.

"Just one thousand dollars even," he remarked.

The announcement of this total had as sobering an effect upon Delamere as though he had been suddenly deluged with a shower of cold water. For a moment he caught his breath. He had not a dollar in the world with which to pay this sum. His only source of income was an allowance from his grandfather, the monthly installment of which, drawn that very day, he had just lost to McBane, before starting in upon the notes of hand.

"I'll give you your revenge another time," said McBane, as they rose. "Luck is against you to-night, and I'm unwilling to take advantage of a clever young fellow like you. Meantime," he added, tossing the notes of hand carelessly on a bureau, "don't worry about these bits of paper. Such small matters should n't cut any figure between friends; but if you are around the hotel to-morrow, I should like to speak to you upon another subject."

"Very well, captain," returned Tom somewhat ungraciously.

Delamere had been completely beaten with his own weapons. He had tried desperately to cheat McBane. He knew perfectly well that McBane had discovered his efforts and had cheated him in turn, for the captain's play had clearly been gauged to meet his own. The biter had been bit, and could not complain of the outcome.

The following afternoon McBane met Delamere at the hotel, and bluntly requested the latter to propose him for membership in the Clarendon Club.

Delamere was annoyed at this request. His aristocratic gorge rose at the presumption of this son of an overseer and ex-driver of convicts. McBane was good enough to win money from, or even to lose money to, but not good enough to be recognized as a social equal. He would instinctively have blackballed McBane had he been proposed by some one else; with what grace could he put himself forward as the sponsor for this impossible social aspirant? Moreover, it was clearly a vulgar, cold-blooded attempt on McBane's part to use his power over him for a personal advantage.

"Well, now, Captain McBane," returned Delamere diplomatically, "I've never put any one up yet, and it's not regarded as good form for so young a member as myself to propose candidates. I 'd much rather you'd ask some older man."

"Oh, well," replied McBane, "just as you say, only I thought you had cut your eye teeth."

Delamere was not pleased with McBane's tone. His remark was not acquiescent, though couched in terms of assent. There was a sneering savagery about it, too, that left Delamere uneasy. He was, in a measure, in McBane's power. He could not pay the thousand dollars, unless it fell from heaven, or he could win it from some one else. He would not dare go to his grandfather for help. Mr. Delamere did not even know that his grandson gambled. He might not have objected, perhaps, to a gentleman's game, with moderate stakes, but he would certainly, Tom knew very well, have looked upon a thousand dollars as a preposterous sum to be lost at cards by a man who had nothing with which to pay it. It was part of Mr. Delamere's creed that a gentleman should not make debts that he was not reasonably able to pay.

There was still another difficulty. If he had lost the money to a gentleman, and it had been his first serious departure from Mr. Delamere's perfectly well understood standard of honor, Tom might have risked a confession and thrown himself on his grandfather's mercy; but he owed other sums here and there, which, to his just now much disturbed imagination, loomed up in alarming number and amount. He had recently observed signs of coldness, too, on the part of certain members of the club. Moreover, like most men with one commanding vice, he was addicted to several subsidiary forms of iniquity, which in case of a scandal were more than likely to come to light. He was clearly and most disagreeably caught in the net of his own hypocrisy. His grandfather believed him a model of integrity, a pattern of honor; he could not afford to have his grandfather undeceived.

He thought of old Mrs. Ochiltree. If she were a liberal soul, she could give him a thousand dollars now, when he needed it, instead of making him wait until she died, which might not be for ten years or more, for a legacy which was steadily growing less and might be entirely exhausted if she lived long enough,—some old people were very tenacious of life! She was a careless old woman, too, he reflected, and very foolishly kept her money in the house. Latterly she had been growing weak and childish. Some day she might be robbed, and then his prospective inheritance from that source would vanish into thin air!

With regard to this debt to McBane, if he could not pay it, he could at least gain a long respite by proposing the captain at the club. True, he would undoubtedly be blackballed, but before this inevitable event his name must remain posted for several weeks, during which interval McBane would be conciliatory. On the other hand, to propose McBane would arouse suspicion of his own motives; it might reach his grandfather's ears, and lead to a demand for an explanation, which it would be difficult to make. Clearly, the better plan would be to temporize with McBane, with the hope that something might intervene to remove this cursed obligation.

"Suppose, captain," he said affably, "we leave the matter open for a few days. This is a thing that can't be rushed. I'll feel the pulse of my friends and yours, and when we get the lay of the land, the affair can be accomplished much more easily."

"Well, that 's better," returned McBane, somewhat mollified,—"*if* you'll do that."

"To be sure I will," replied Tom easily, too much relieved to resent, if not too preoccupied to perceive, the implied doubt of his veracity.

McBane ordered and paid for more drinks, and they parted on amicable terms.

"We'll let these notes stand for the time being, Tom," said McBane, with significant emphasis, when they separated.

Delamere winced at the familiarity. He had reached that degree of moral deterioration where, while principles were of little moment, the externals of social intercourse possessed an exaggerated importance. McBane had never before been so personal. He had addressed the young aristocrat first as "Mr. Delamere," then, as their acquaintance advanced, as "Delamere." He had now reached the abbreviated Christian name stage of familiarity. There was no lower depth to which Tom could sink, unless McBane should invent a nickname by which to address him.

He did not like McBane's manner,—it was characterized by a veiled insolence which was exceedingly offensive. He would go over to the club and try his luck with

152

some honest player,—perhaps something might turn up to relieve him from his embarrassment.

He put his hand in his pocket mechanically,—and found it empty! In the present state of his credit, he could hardly play without money.

A thought struck him. Leaving the hotel, he hastened home, where he found Sandy dusting his famous suit of clothes on the back piazza. Mr. Delamere was not at home, having departed for Belleview about two o'clock, leaving, Sandy to follow him in the morning.

"Hello, Sandy," exclaimed Tom, with an assumed jocularity which he was very far from feeling, "what are you doing with those gorgeous garments?"

"I'm a-dustin' of 'em, Mistuh Tom, dat's w'at I'm a-doin'. Dere 's somethin' wrong 'bout dese clo's er mine—I don' never seem ter be able ter keep 'em clean no mo'. Ef I b'lieved in dem ole-timey sayin's, I'd 'low dere wuz a witch come here eve'y night an' tuk 'em out an' wo' 'em, er tuk me out an' rid me in' 'em. Dere wuz somethin' wrong 'bout dat cakewalk business, too, dat I ain' never unde'stood an' don' know how ter 'count fer, 'less dere wuz some kin' er dev'lishness goin' on dat don' show on de su'face."

"Sandy," asked Tom irrelevantly, "have you any money in the house?"

"Yas, suh, I got de money Mars John give me ter git dem things ter take out ter Belleview in de mawnin'."

"I mean money of your own."

"I got a qua'ter ter buy terbacker wid," returned Sandy cautiously.

"Is that all? Have n't you some saved up?"

"Well, yas, Mistuh Tom," returned Sandy, with evident

reluctance, "dere's a few dollahs put away in my bureau drawer fer a rainy day,—not much, suh."

"I'm a little short this afternoon, Sandy, and need some money right away. Grandfather is n't here, so I can't get any from him. Let me take what you have for a day or two, Sandy, and I'll return it with good interest."

"Now, Mistuh Tom," said Sandy seriously, "I don' min' lettin' you take my money, but I hopes you ain' gwine ter use it for none er dem rakehelly gwines-on er yo'n,—gamblin' an' bettin' an' so fo'th. Yo' grandaddy 'll fin' out 'bout you yit, ef you don' min'yo 'P's an 'Q's. I does my bes'ter keep yo' misdoin's f'm 'im, an' sense I b'en tu'ned out er de chu'ch—thoo no fault er my own, God knows!—I've tol' lies 'nuff 'bout you ter sink a ship. But it ain't right, Mistuh Tom, it ain't right! an' I only does it for do sake er de fam'ly honuh, dat Mars John sets so much sto' by, an' ter save his feelin's; for de doctuh says he mus' n' git ixcited 'bout nothin', er it mought bring on another stroke."

"That's right, Sandy," replied Tom approvingly; "but the family honor is as safe in my hands as in grandfather's own, and I'm going to use the money for an excellent purpose, in fact to relieve a case of genuine distress; and I'll hand it back to you in a day or two,—perhaps to-morrow. Fetch me the money, Sandy,—that's a good darky!"

"All right, Mistuh Tom, you shill have de money; but I wants ter tell you, suh, dat in all de yeahs I has wo'ked for yo' gran'daddy, he has never called me a 'darky' ter my face, suh. Co'se I knows dere's w'ite folks an' black folks,—but dere's manners, suh, dere's manners, an' gent'emen oughter be de ones ter use 'em, suh, ef dey ain't ter be fergot enti'ely!"

154

"There, there, Sandy," returned Tom in a conciliatory tone, "I beg your pardon! I've been associating with some Northern white folks at the hotel, and picked up the word from them. You're a high-toned colored gentleman, Sandy,—the finest one on the footstool."

Still muttering to himself, Sandy retired to his own room, which was in the house, so that he might be always near his master. He soon returned with a time-stained leather pocket-book and a coarse-knit cotton sock, from which two receptacles he painfully extracted a number of bills and coins.

"You count dat, Mistuh Tom, so I'll know how much I'm lettin' you have."

"This is n't worth anything," said Tom, pushing aside one roll of bills. "It's Confederate money."

"So it is, suh. It ain't wuth nothin' now; but it has be'n money, an' who kin tell but what it mought be money agin? De rest er dem bills is greenbacks,—dey'll pass all right, I reckon."

The good money amounted to about fifty dollars, which Delamere thrust eagerly into his pocket.

"You won't say anything to grandfather about this, will you, Sandy," he said, as he turned away.

"No, suh, co'se I won't! Does I ever tell 'im 'bout yo' gwines-on? Ef I did," he added to himself, as the young man disappeared down the street, "I would n' have time ter do nothin' e'se ha'dly. I don' know whether I 'll ever see dat money agin er no, do' I 'magine de ole gent'eman would n' lemme lose it ef he knowed. But I ain' gwine ter tell him, whether I git my money back er no, fer he is jes' so wrop' up in dat boy dat I b'lieve it'd jes' break his hea't ter fin' out how he's be'n gwine on. Doctuh Price has tol' me not ter let de ole gent'eman git ixeited, er e'se dere's no tellin' w'at mought happen. He's be'n good ter me, he has, an' I'm gwine ter take keer er him,—dat 's w'at I is, ez long ez I has de chance."

Delamere went directly to the club, and soon lounged into the card-room, where several of the members were engaged in play. He sauntered here and there, too much absorbed in his own thoughts to notice that the greetings he received were less cordial than those usually exchanged between the members of a small and select social club. Finally, when Augustus, commonly and more appropriately called "Gus," Davidson came into the room, Tom stepped toward him.

"Will you take a hand in a game, Gus?"

"Don't care if I do," said the other. "Let's sit over here."

Davidson led the way to a table near the fireplace, near which stood a tall screen, which at times occupied various places in the room. Davidson took the seat opposite the fireplace, leaving Delamere with his back to the screen.

Delamere staked half of Sandy's money, and lost. He staked the rest, and determined to win, because he could not afford to lose. He had just reached out his hand to gather in the stakes, when he was charged with cheating at cards, of which two members, who had quietly entered the room and posted themselves behind the screen, had secured specific proof.

A meeting of the membership committee was hastily summoned, it being an hour at which most of them might be found at the club. To avoid a scandal, and to save the feelings of a prominent family, Delamere was given an opportunity to resign quietly from the club, on condition that he paid all his gambling debts within three days, and took an oath never to play cards again for money. This latter condition was made at the suggestion of an elderly member, who apparently believed that a man who would cheat at cards would stick at perjury.

Delamere acquiesced very promptly. The taking of the oath was easy. The payment of some fifteen hundred dollars of debts was a different matter. He went away from the club thoughtfully, and it may be said, in full justice to a past which was far from immaculate, that in his present thoughts he touched a depth of scoundrelism far beyond anything of which he had as yet deemed himself capable. When a man of good position, of whom much is expected, takes to evil courses, his progress is apt to resemble that of a well-bred woman who has started on the downward path,—the pace is all the swifter because of the distance which must be traversed to reach the bottom. Delamere had made rapid headway; having hitherto played with sin, his servant had now become his master, and held him in an iron grip.

XVIII
SANDY SEES HIS OWN HA'NT

HAVING finished cleaning his clothes, Sandy went out to the kitchen for supper, after which he found himself with nothing to do. Mr. Delamere's absence relieved him from attendance at the house during the evening. He might have smoked his pipe tranquilly in the kitchen until bed-time, had not the cook intimated, rather pointedly, that she expected other company. To a man of Sandy's tact a word was sufficient, and he resigned himself to seeking companionship elsewhere.

Under normal circumstances, Sandy would have attended prayer-meeting on this particular evening of the week; but being still in contumacy, and cherishing what he considered the just resentment of a man falsely accused, he stifled the inclination which by long habit led him toward the church, and set out for the house of a friend with whom it occurred to him that he might spend the evening pleasantly. Unfortunately, his friend proved to be not at home, so Sandy turned his footsteps toward the lower part of the town, where the streets were well lighted, and on pleasant evenings quite animated. On the way he met Josh Green, whom he had known for many years, though their paths did not often cross. In his loneliness Sandy accepted an invitation to go with Josh and have a drink,—a single drink.

When Sandy was going home about eleven o'clock, three sheets in the wind, such was the potent effect of the single drink and those which had followed it, he was seared almost into soberness by a remarkable apparition. As it seemed to Sandy, he saw himself hurrying along in front of himself toward the house. Possibly the muddled condition of Sandy's intellect had so affected his judgment as to vitiate any conclusion he might draw, but Sandy was quite sober enough to perceive that the figure ahead of him wore his best clothes and looked exactly like him, but seemed to be in something more of a hurry, a discrepancy which Sandy at once corrected by quickening his own pace so as to maintain as nearly as possible an equal distance between himself and his double. The situation was certainly an incomprehensible one, and savored of the supernatural.

"Ef dat's me gwine 'long in front," mused Sandy, in vinous perplexity, "den who is dis behin' here? Dere ain' but one er me, an' my ha'nt would n' leave my body 'tel I wuz dead. Ef dat's me in front, den I mus' be my own ha'nt; an' whichever one of us is de ha'nt, de yuther must be dead an' don' know it. I don' know what ter make er no sech gwines-on, I don't. Maybe it ain' me after all, but it certainly do look lack me."

When the apparition disappeared in the house by the side door, Sandy stood in the yard for several minutes, under the shade of an elm-tree, before he could make up his mind to enter the house. He took courage, however, upon the reflection that perhaps, after all, it was only the bad liquor he had drunk. Bad liquor often made people see double.

He entered the house. It was dark, except for a light in Tom Delamere's room. Sandy tapped softly at the door.

"Who's there?" came Delamere's voice, in a somewhat startled tone, after a momentary silence.

"It's me, suh; Sandy."

They both spoke softly. It was the rule of the house when Mr. Delamere had retired, and though he was not at home, habit held its wonted sway.

"Just a moment, Sandy."

Sandy waited patiently in the hall until the door was opened. If the room showed any signs of haste or disorder, Sandy was too full of his own thoughts—and other things—to notice them.

"What do you want, Sandy," asked Tom.

"Mistuh Tom," asked Sandy solemnly, "ef I wuz in yo' place, an' you wuz in my place, an' we wuz bofe in de same place, whar would I be?"

Tom looked at Sandy keenly, with a touch of apprehension. Did Sandy mean anything in particular by this enigmatical inquiry, and if so, what? But Sandy's face clearly indicated a state of mind in which consecutive thought was improbable; and after a brief glance Delamere breathed more freely.

"I give it up, Sandy," he responded lightly. "That's too deep for me."

"'Scuse me, Mistuh Tom, but is you heared er seed anybody er anything come in de house fer de las' ten minutes?"

"Why, no, Sandy, I have n't heard any one. I came from the club an hour ago. I had forgotten my key, and Sally got up and let me in, and then went back to bed. I've been sitting here reading ever since. I should have heard any one who came in."

"Mistuh Tom," inquired Sandy anxiously, "would you 'low dat I'd be'n drinkin' too much?"

"No, Sandy, I should say you were sober enough, though of course you may have had a few drinks. Perhaps you'd like another? I've got something good here."

"No, suh, Mistuh Tom, no, suh! No mo' liquor fer me, suh, never! When liquor kin make a man see his own ha'nt, it's 'bout time fer dat man ter quit drinkin', it sho' is! Good-night, Mistuh Tom."

As Sandy turned to go, Delamere was struck by a sudden and daring thought. The creature of impulse, he acted upon it immediately.

160

"By the way, Sandy," he exclaimed carelessly, "I can pay you back that money you were good enough to lend me this afternoon. I think I'll sleep better if I have the debt off my mind, and I should n't wonder if you would. You don't mind having it in gold, do you?"

"No, indeed, suh," replied Sandy. "I ain' seen no gol' fer so long dat de sight er it'd be good fer my eyes."

Tom counted out ten five-dollar gold pieces upon the table at his elbow.

"And here's another, Sandy," he said, adding an eleventh, "as interest for the use of it."

"Thank y', Mistuh Tom. I did n't spec' no intrus', but I don' never 'fuse gol' w'en I kin git it."

"And here," added Delamere, reaching carelessly into a bureau drawer, "is a little old silk purse that I've had since I was a boy. I'll put the gold in it, Sandy; it will hold it very nicely."

"Thank y', Mistuh Tom. You're a gentleman, suh, an' wo'thy er de fam'ly name. Good-night, suh, an' I hope yo' dreams'll be pleasanter'n' mine. Ef it wa'n't fer dis gol' kinder takin' my min' off'n dat ha'nt, I don' s'pose I 'd be able to do much sleepin' ter-night. Good-night suh."

"Good-night, Sandy."

Whether or not Delamere slept soundly, or was troubled by dreams, pleasant or unpleasant, it is nevertheless true that he locked his door, and sat up an hour later, looking through the drawers of his bureau, and burning several articles in the little iron stove which constituted part of the bedroom furniture.

It is also true that he rose very early, before the household was stirring. The cook slept in a room off the kitchen, which was in an outhouse in the back yard. She was just stretching herself, preparatory to getting up, when Tom came to her window and said that he was going off fishing, to be gone all day, and that he would not wait for breakfast.

XIX
A MIDNIGHT WALK

ELLIS left the office of the Morning Chronicle about eleven o'clock the same evening and set out to walk home. His boarding-house was only a short distance beyond old Mr. Delamere's residence, and while he might have saved time and labor by a slightly shorter route, he generally selected this one because it led also by Major Carteret's house. Sometimes there would be a ray of light from Clara's room, which was on one of the front corners; and at any rate he would have the pleasure of gazing at the outside of the casket that enshrined the jewel of his heart. It was true that this purely sentimental pleasure was sometimes dashed with bitterness at the thought of his rival; but one in love must take the bitter with the sweet, and who would say that a spice of jealousy does not add a certain zest to love? On this particular evening, however, he was in a hopeful mood. At the Clarendon Club, where he had gone, a couple of hours before, to verify a certain news item for the morning paper, he had heard a story about Tom Delamere which, he imagined, would spike that gentleman's guns for all time, so far as Miss Pemberton was concerned. So grave an affair as cheating at cards could never be kept secret,—it was certain to reach her ears; and Ellis was morally certain that Clara would never marry a man who had been proved dishonorable. In all probability there would be no great sensation about the matter. Delamere was too well connected; too many prominent people would be involved,—even Clara, and the editor himself, of whom Delamere was a distant cousin. The reputation of the club was also to be considered. Ellis was not the man to feel a malicious delight in the misfortunes of another, nor was he a pessimist who welcomed scandal and disgrace with open arms, as confirming a gloomy theory of human life. But, with the best intentions in the world, it was no more than human nature that he should feel a certain elation in the thought that his rival had been practically disposed of, and the field left clear; especially since this good situation had been brought about merely by the unmasking of a hypocrite, who had held him at an unfair disadvantage in the race for Clara's favor.

The night was quiet, except for the faint sound of distant music now and then, or the mellow laughter of some group of revelers. Ellis met but few pedestrians, but as he neared old Mr. Delamere's, he saw two men walking in the same direction as his own, on the opposite side of the street. He had observed that they kept at about an equal distance apart, and that the second, from the stealthy manner in which he was making his way, was anxious to keep the first in sight, without disclosing his own presence. This aroused Ellis's curiosity, which was satisfied in some degree when the man in advance stopped beneath a lamp-post and stood for a moment looking across the street, with his face plainly visible in the yellow circle of light. It was a dark face, and Ellis recognized it instantly as that of old Mr. Delamere's body servant, whose personal appearance had been very vividly impressed upon Ellis at the christening dinner at Major Carteret's. He had seen Sandy once since, too, at the hotel cakewalk. The negro had a small bundle in his hand, the nature of which Ellis could not make out.

When Sandy had stopped beneath the lamp-post, the man who was following him had dodged behind a tree-trunk. When Sandy moved on, Ellis, who had stopped in turn, saw the man in hiding come out and follow Sandy. When this second man came in range of the light, Ellis wondered that there should be two men so much alike. The first of the two had undoubtedly been Sandy. Ellis had recognized the peculiar, old-fashioned coat that Sandy had worn upon the two occasions when he had noticed him. Barring this difference, and the somewhat unsteady gait of the second man, the two were as much alike as twin brothers.

When they had entered Mr. Delamere's house, one after the other,—in the stillness of the night Ellis could perceive that each of them tried to make as little noise as possible,—Ellis supposed that they were probably relatives, both employed as servants, or that some younger negro, taking Sandy for a model, was trying to pattern himself after his superior. Why all this mystery, of course he could not imagine, unless the younger man had been out without permission and was trying to avoid the accusing eye of Sandy. Ellis was vaguely conscious that he had seen the other negro somewhere, but he could not for the moment place him,—there were so many negroes, nearly three negroes to one white man in the city of Wellington!

The subject, however, while curious, was not important as compared with the thoughts of his sweetheart which drove it from his mind. Clara had been kind to him the night before,—whatever her motive, she had been kind, and could not consistently return to her attitude of coldness. With Delamere hopelessly discredited, Ellis hoped to have at least fair play,—with fair play, he would take his chances of the outcome.

XX
A SHOCKING CRIME

On Friday morning, when old Mrs. Ochiltree's cook Dinah went to wake her mistress, she was confronted with a sight that well-nigh blanched her ebony cheek and caused her eyes almost to start from her head with horror. As soon as she could command her trembling limbs sufficiently to make them carry her, she rushed out of the house and down the street, bareheaded, covering in an incredibly short time the few blocks that separated Mrs. Ochiltree's residence from that of her niece.

She hastened around the house, and finding the back door open and the servants stirring, ran into the house and up the stairs with the familiarity of an old servant, not stopping until she reached the door of Mrs. Carteret's chamber, at which she knocked in great agitation.

Entering in response to Mrs. Carteret's invitation, she found the lady, dressed in a simple wrapper, superintending the morning toilet of little Dodie, who was a wakeful child, and insisted upon rising with the birds, for whose music he still showed a great fondness, in spite of his narrow escape while listening to the mockingbird.

"What is it, Dinah?" asked Mrs. Carteret, alarmed at the frightened face of her aunt's old servitor.

"O my Lawd, Mis' 'Livy, my Lawd, my Lawd! My legs is trim'lin' so dat I can't ha'dly hol' my han's stiddy 'nough ter say w'at I got ter say! O Lawd have mussy on us po' sinners! W'atever is gwine ter happen in dis worl' er sin an' sorrer!"

"What in the world is the matter, Dinah?" demanded Mrs. Carteret, whose own excitement had increased with the length of this preamble. "Has anything happened to Aunt Polly?"

"Somebody done broke in de house las' night, Mis, 'Livy, an' kill' Mis' Polly, an' lef' her layin' dead on de flo', in her own blood, wid her cedar chis' broke' open, an' eve'thing scattered roun' de flo'! O my Lawd, my Lawd, my Lawd, my Lawd!"

Mrs. Carteret was shocked beyond expression. Perhaps the spectacle of Dinah's unrestrained terror aided her to retain a greater measure of self-control than she might otherwise have been capable of. Giving the nurse some directions in regard to the child, she hastily descended the stairs, and seizing a hat and jacket from the rack in the hall, ran immediately with Dinah to the scene of the tragedy. Before the thought of this violent death all her aunt's faults faded into insignificance, and only her good qualities were remembered. She had reared Olivia; she had stood up for the memory of Olivia's mother when others had seemed to forget what was due to it. To her niece she had been a second mother, and had never been lacking in affection.

More than one motive, however, lent wings to Mrs. Carteret's feet. Her aunt's incomplete disclosures on the day of the drive past the hospital had been weighing upon Mrs. Carteret's mind, and she had intended to make another effort this very day, to get an answer to her question about the papers which the woman had claimed were in existence. Suppose her aunt had really found such papers,—papers which would seem to prove the preposterous claim made by her father's mulatto mistress? Suppose that, with the fatuity which generally leads human beings to keep compromising documents, her aunt had preserved these papers? If they should be found there in the house, there might be a scandal, if nothing worse, and this was to be avoided at all hazards.

Guided by some fortunate instinct, Dinah had as yet informed no one but Mrs. Carteret of her discovery. If they could reach the house before the murder became known to any third person, she might be the first to secure access to the remaining contents of the cedar chest, which would be likely to be held as evidence in case the officers of the law forestalled her own arrival.

They found the house wrapped in the silence of death. Mrs. Carteret entered the chamber of the dead woman. Upon the floor, where it had fallen, lay the body in a pool of blood, the strongly marked countenance scarcely more grim in the rigidity of death than it had been in life. A gaping wound in the head accounted easily for the death. The cedar chest stood open, its strong fastenings having been broken by a steel bar which still lay beside it. Near it were scattered pieces of old lace, antiquated jewelry, tarnished silverware, the various mute souvenirs of the joys and sorrows of a long and active life.

Kneeling by the open chest, Mrs. Carteret glanced hurriedly through its contents. There were no papers there except a few old deeds and letters. She had risen with a sigh of relief, when she perceived the end of a paper projecting from beneath the edge of a rug which had been carelessly rumpled, probably by the burglar in his hasty search for plunder. This paper, or sealed envelope as it proved to be, which evidently contained some inclosure, she seized, and at the sound of approaching footsteps thrust hastily into her own bosom.

The sight of two agitated women rushing through the quiet streets at so early an hour in the morning had attracted attention and aroused curiosity, and the story of the murder, having once become known, spread with the customary rapidity of bad news. Very soon a policeman, and a little later a sheriff's officer, arrived at the house and took charge of the remains to await the arrival of the coroner.

By nine o'clock a coroner's jury had been summoned, who, after brief deliberation, returned a verdict of willful murder at the hands of some person or persons unknown, while engaged in the commission of a burglary.

No sooner was the verdict announced than the community, or at least the white third of it, resolved itself spontaneously into a committee of the whole to discover the perpetrator of this dastardly crime, which, at this stage of the affair, seemed merely one of robbery and murder.

Suspicion was at once directed toward the negroes, as it always is when an unexplained crime is committed in a Southern community. The suspicion was not entirely an illogical one. Having been, for generations, trained up

168

to thriftlessness, theft, and immorality, against which only thirty years of very limited opportunity can be offset, during which brief period they have been denied in large measure the healthful social stimulus and sympathy which holds most men in the path of rectitude, colored people might reasonably be expected to commit at least a share of crime proportionate to their numbers. The population of the town was at least two thirds colored. The chances were, therefore, in the absence of evidence, at least two to one that a man of color had committed the crime. The Southern tendency to charge the negroes with all the crime and immorality of that region, unjust and exaggerated as the claim may be, was therefore not without a logical basis to the extent above indicated.

It must not be imagined that any logic was needed, or any reasoning consciously worked out. The mere suggestion that the crime had been committed by a negro was equivalent to proof against any negro that might be suspected and could not prove his innocence. A committee of white men was hastily formed. Acting independently of the police force, which was practically ignored as likely to favor the negroes, this committee set to work to discover the murderer.

The spontaneous activity of the whites was accompanied by a visible shrinkage of the colored population. This could not be taken as any indication of guilt, but was merely a recognition of the palpable fact that the American habit of lynching had so whetted the thirst for black blood that a negro suspected of crime had to face at least the possibility of a short shrift and a long rope, not to mention more gruesome horrors, without the intervention of judge or jury. Since to have a black face at such a time was to challenge suspicion, and since there was neither the martyr's glory nor the saint's renown in being killed for some one else's crime, and very little hope of successful resistance in case of an attempt at lynching, it was obviously the part of prudence for those thus marked to seek immunity in a temporary disappearance from public view.

XXI
THE NECESSITY OF AN EXAMPLE

ABOUT ten o'clock on the morning of the discovery of the murder, Captain McBane and General Belmont, as though moved by a common impulse, found themselves at the office of the Morning Chronicle. Carteret was expecting them, though there had been no appointment made. These three resourceful and energetic minds, representing no organized body, and clothed with no legal authority, had so completely arrogated to themselves the leadership of white public sentiment as to come together instinctively when an event happened which concerned the public, and, as this murder presumably did, involved the matter of race.

"Well, gentlemen," demanded McBane impatiently, "what are we going to do with the scoundrel when we catch him?"

"They've got the murderer," announced a reporter, entering the room.

"Who is he?" they demanded in a breath.

"A nigger by the name of Sandy Campbell, a servant of old Mr. Delamere."

"How did they catch him?"

"Our Jerry saw him last night, going toward Mrs. Ochiltree's house, and a white man saw him coming away, half an hour later."

"Has he confessed?"

"No, but he might as well. When the posse went to arrest him, they found him cleaning the clothes he had worn last night, and discovered in his room a part of the plunder. He denies it strenuously, but it seems a clear case."

"There can be no doubt," said Ellis, who had come into the room behind the reporter. "I saw the negro last night, at twelve o'clock, going into Mr. Delamere's yard, with a bundle in his hand."

"He is the last negro I should have suspected," said Carteret. "Mr. Delamere had implicit confidence in him."

"All niggers are alike," remarked McBane sententiously. "The only way to keep them from stealing is not to give them the chance. A nigger will steal a cent off a dead man's eye. He has assaulted and murdered a white woman,—an example should be made of him."

Carteret recalled very distinctly the presence of this negro at his own residence on the occasion of little Theodore's christening dinner. He remembered having questioned the prudence of letting a servant know that Mrs. Ochiltree kept money in the house. Mr. Delamere had insisted strenuously upon the honesty of this particular negro. The whole race, in the major's opinion, was morally undeveloped, and only held within bounds by the restraining influence of the white people. Under Mr. Delamere's thumb this Sandy had been a model servant,—faithful, docile, respectful, and self-respecting; but Mr. Delamere had grown old, and had probably lost in a measure his moral influence over his servant. Left to his own degraded ancestral instincts, Sandy had begun to deteriorate, and a rapid decline had culminated in this robbery and murder,—and who knew what other horror? The criminal was a negro, the victim a white woman;— it was only reasonable to expect the worst.

"He'll swing for it," observed the general.

Ellis went into another room, where his duty called him.

"He should burn for it," averred McBane. "I say, burn the nigger."

"This," said Carteret, "is something more than an or- dinary crime, to be dealt with by the ordinary processes of law. It is a murderous and fatal assault upon a woman of our race,—upon our race in the person of its woman- hood, its crown and flower. If such crimes are not pun- ished with swift and terrible directness, the whole white womanhood of the South is in danger."

"Burn the nigger," repeated McBane automatically.

"Neither is this a mere sporadic crime," Carteret went on. "It is symptomatic; it is the logical and inevitable re- sult of the conditions which have prevailed in this town for the past year. It is the last straw."

"Burn the nigger," reiterated McBane. We seem to have the right nigger, but whether we have or not, burn *a* nigger. It is an assault upon the white race, in the per- son of old Mrs. Ochiltree, committed by the black race, in the person of some nigger. It would justify the white people in burning *any* nigger. The example would be all the more powerful if we got the wrong one. It would serve notice on the niggers that we shall hold the whole race responsible for the misdeeds of each individual."

"In ancient Rome," said the general, "when a master was killed by a slave, all his slaves were put to the sword."

"We could n't afford that before the war," said McBane, "but the niggers don't belong to anybody now, and there 's nothing to prevent our doing as we please with them. A dead nigger is no loss to any white man. I say, burn the nigger."

"I do not believe," said Carteret, who had gone to the window and was looking out,—"I do not believe that we need trouble ourselves personally about his punishment. I should judge, from the commotion in the street, that the public will take the matter into it own hands. I, for one, would prefer that any violence, however justifiable, should take place without my active intervention."

"It won't take place without mine, if I know it," exclaimed McBane, starting for the door.

"Hold on a minute, captain," exclaimed Carteret. "There's more at stake in this matter than the life of a black scoundrel. Wellington is in the hands of negroes and scalawags. What better time to rescue it?"

"It's a trifle premature," replied the general. "I should have preferred to have this take place, if it was to happen, say three months hence, on the eve of the election,—but discussion always provokes thirst with me; I wonder if I could get Jerry to bring us some drinks?"

Carteret summoned the porter. Jerry's usual manner had taken on an element of self-importance, resulting in what one might describe as a sort of condescending obsequiousness. Though still a porter, he was also a hero, and wore his aureole.

173

"Jerry," said the general kindly, "the white people are very much pleased with the assistance you have given them in apprehending this scoundrel Campbell. You have rendered a great public service, Jerry, and we wish you to know that it is appreciated."

"Thank y', gin'l, thank y', suh! I alluz tries ter do my duty, suh, an' stan' by dem dat stan's by me. Dat low-down nigger oughter be lynch', suh, don't you think, er e'se bu'nt? Dere ain' nothin' too bad ter happen ter 'im."

"No doubt he will be punished as he deserves, Jerry," returned the general, "and we will see that you are suitably rewarded. Go across the street and get me three Calhoun cocktails. I seem to have nothing less than a two-dollar bill, but you may keep the change, Jerry,—all the change."

Jerry was very happy. He had distinguished himself in the public view, for to Jerry, as to the white people themselves, the white people were the public. He had won the goodwill of the best people, and had already begun to reap a tangible reward. It is true that several strange white men looked at him with lowering brows as he crossed the street, which was curiously empty of colored people; but he nevertheless went firmly forward, panoplied in the consciousness of his own rectitude, and serenely confident of the protection of the major and the major's friends.

"Jerry is about the only negro I have seen since nine o'clock," observed the general when the porter had gone. "If this were election day, where would the negro vote be?"

"In hiding, where most of the negro population is to-day," answered McBane. "It's a pity, if old Mrs. Ochiltree had to go this way, that it could n't have been deferred a mouth or six weeks."

Carteret frowned at this remark, which, coming from McBane, seemed lacking in human feeling, as well as in respect to his wife's dead relative.

"But," resumed the general, "if this negro is lynched, as he well deserves to be, it will not be without its effect. We still have in reserve for the election a weapon which this affair will only render more effective. What became of the piece in the negro paper?"

"I have it here," answered Carteret. "I was just about to use it as the text for an editorial."

"Save it awhile longer," responded the general. "This crime itself will give you text enough for a four-volume work."

When this conference ended, Carteret immediately put into press an extra edition of the Morning Chronicle, which was soon upon the streets, giving details of the crime, which was characterized as an atrocious assault upon a defenseless old lady, whose age and sex would have protected her from harm at the hands of any one but a brute in the lowest human form. This event, the Chronicle suggested, had only confirmed the opinion, which had been of late growing upon the white people, that drastic efforts were necessary to protect the white women of the South against brutal, lascivious, and murderous assaults at the hands of negro men. It was only another significant example of the results which might have been foreseen from the application of a false and pernicious political theory, by which ignorance, clothed in a little brief authority, was sought to be exalted over knowledge, vice over virtue, an inferior and degraded race above the heaven-crowned Anglo-Saxon. If an outraged people, justly infuriated, and impatient of the slow processes of the courts, should assert their inherent sovereignty, which the law after all was merely intended to embody, and should choose, in obedience to the higher law, to set aside, temporarily, the ordinary judicial procedure, it would serve as a warning and an example to the vicious elements of the community, of the swift and terrible punishment which would fall, like the judgment of God, upon any one who laid sacrilegious hands upon white womanhood.

XXII
HOW NOT TO PREVENT A LYNCHING

DR. MILLER, who had sat up late the night before with a difficult case at the hospital, was roused, about eleven o'clock, from a deep and dreamless sleep. Struggling back into consciousness, he was informed by his wife, who stood by his bedside, that Mr. Watson, the colored lawyer, wished to see him upon a matter of great importance.

"Nothing but a matter of life and death would make me get up just now," he said with a portentous yawn.

"This *is* a matter of life and death," replied Janet. "Old Mrs. Polly Ochiltree was robbed and murdered last night, and Sandy Campbell has been arrested for the crime,—and they are going to lynch him!"

"Tell Watson to come right up," exclaimed Miller, springing out of bed. "We can talk while I'm dressing."

While Miller made a hasty toilet Watson explained the situation. Campbell had been arrested on the charge of murder. He had been seen, during the night, in the neighborhood of the scene of the crime, by two different persons, a negro, and a white man, and had been identified later while entering Mr. Delamere's house, where he lived, and where damning proofs of his guilt had been discovered; the most important item of which was an old-fashioned knit silk purse, recognized as Mrs. Ochiltree's, and several gold pieces of early coinage, of which the murdered woman was known to have a number. Watson brought with him one of the first copies procurable of the extra edition of the Chronicle, which contained these facts and further information.

They were still talking when Mrs. Miller, knocking at the door, announced that big Josh Green wished to see the doctor about Sandy Campbell. Miller took his collar and necktie in his hand and went downstairs, where Josh sat waiting.

"Doctuh," said Green, "de w'ite folks is talkin' 'bout lynchin' Sandy Campbell fer killin' ole Mis' Ochiltree. He never done it, an' dey ought n' ter be 'lowed ter lynch 'im."

"They ought not to lynch him, even if he committed the crime," returned Miller, "but still less if he didn't. What do you know about it?"

"I know he was wid me, suh, las' night, at de time when dey say ole Mis' Ochiltree wuz killed. We wuz down ter Sam Taylor's place, havin' a little game of kyards an' a little liquor. Den we lef dere an' went up ez fur ez de corner er Main an' Vine Streets, where we pa'ted, an' Sandy went 'long to'ds home. Mo'over, dey say he had on check' britches an' a blue coat. When Sandy wuz wid

177

me he had on gray clo's, an' when we sep'rated he wa'n't in no shape ter be changin' his clo's, let 'lone robbin' er killin' anybody."

"Your testimony ought to prove an alibi for him," declared Miller.

"Dere ain' gwine ter be no chance ter prove nothin', 'iess'n we kin do it mighty quick! Dey say dey 're gwine ter lynch 'im ter-night,—some on 'em, is talkin' 'bout burnin' 'im. My idee is ter hunt up de niggers an' git 'em ter stan' tergether an' gyard de jail."

"Why should n't we go to the principal white people of the town and tell them Josh's story, and appeal to them to stop this thing until Campbell can have a hearing?"

"It would n't do any good," said Watson despondently; "their blood is up. It seems that some colored man attacked Mrs. Ochiltree,—and he was a murderous villain, whoever he may be. To quote Josh would destroy the effect of his story,—we know he never harmed any one but himself"—

"An' a few keerliss people w'at got in my way," corrected Josh.

"He has been in court several times for fighting,—and that's against him. To have been at Sam Taylor's place is against Sandy, too, rather than in his favor. No, Josh, the white people would believe that you were trying to shield Sandy, and you would probably be arrested as an accomplice."

"But look a-here, Mr. Watson,—Dr. Miller, is we-all jes' got ter set down here, widout openin' ou' mouths, an' let dese w'ite folks hang er bu'n a man w'at we *know* ain' guilty? Dat ain't no law, ner jestice, ner nothin'! Ef you-all won't he'p, I'll do somethin' myse'f! Dere's two niggers ter one white man in dis town, an' I'm sho' I kin fin' fifty of 'em, w'at 'll fight, ef dey kin fin' anybody ter lead 'em."

"Now hold on, Josh," argued Miller; "what is to be gained by fighting? Suppose you got your crowd together and surrounded the jail,—what then?"

"There'd be a clash," declared Watson, "and instead of one dead negro there'd be fifty. The white people are claiming now that Campbell did n't stop with robbery and murder. A special edition of the Morning Chronicle, just out, suggests a further purpose, and has all the old shop-worn cant about race purity and supremacy and imperative necessity, which always comes to the front whenever it is sought to justify some outrage on the colored folks. The blood of the whites is up, I tell you!"

"Is there anything to that suggestion?" asked Miller incredulously.

"It does n't matter whether there is or not," returned Watson. "Merely to suggest it proves it. Nothing was said about this feature until the paper came out,—and even its statement is vague and indefinite,—but now the claim is in every mouth. I met only black looks as I came down the street. White men with whom I have long been on friendly terms passed me without a word. A negro has been arrested on suspicion,—the entire race is condemned on general principles."

"The whole thing is profoundly discouraging," said Miller sadly. "Try as we may to build up the race in the essentials of good citizenship and win the good opinion of the best people, some black scoundrel comes along, and by a single criminal act, committed in the twinkling of an eye, neutralizes the effect of a whole year's work."

"It's mighty easy neut'alize', er whatever you call it," said Josh sullenly. "De w'ite folks don' want too good an opinion er de niggers,—ef dey had a good opinion of 'em, dey would n' have no excuse fer 'busin' an' hangin an' burnin' 'em. But ef dey can't keep from doin' it, let 'em git de right man! Dis way er pickin' up de fus' nigger dey comes across, an' stringin' 'im up rega'dliss, ought ter be stop', an' stop' right now!"

"Yes, that's the worst of lynch law," said Watson; "but we are wasting valuable time,—it's hardly worth while for us to discuss a subject we are all agreed upon. One of our race, accused of certain acts, is about to be put to death without judge or jury, ostensibly because he committed a crime,—really because he is a negro, for if he were white he would not be lynched. It is thus made a race issue, on the one side as well as on the other. What can we do to protect him?"

"We kin fight, ef we haf ter," replied Josh resolutely.

"Well, now, let us see. Suppose the colored people armed themselves? Messages would at once be sent to every town and county in the neighborhood. White men from all over the state, armed to the teeth, would at the slightest word pour into town on every railroad train, and extras would be run for their benefit."

"They're already coming in," said Watson.

"We might go to the sheriff," suggested Miller, "and demand that he telegraph the governor to call out the militia."

"I spoke to the sheriff an hour ago," replied Watson. "He has a white face and a whiter liver. He does not dare call out the militia to protect a negro charged with such a brutal crime;—and if he did, the militia are white men, and who can say that their efforts would not be directed to keeping the negroes out of the way, in order that the white devils might do their worst? The whole machinery of the state is in the hands of white men, elected partly by our votes. When the color line is drawn, if they choose to stand together with the rest of their race against us, or to remain passive and let the others work their will, we are helpless,—our cause is hopeless."

"We might call on the general government," said Miller, "Surely the President would intervene."

"Such a demand would be of no avail, returned Watson. "The government can only intervene under certain conditions, of which it must be informed through designated channels. It never sees anything that is not officially called to its attention. The whole negro population of the South might be slaughtered before the necessary red tape could be spun out to inform the President that a state of anarchy prevailed. There's no hope there."

"Den w'at we gwine ter do?" demanded Josh indignantly; "jes' set here an' let 'em hang Sandy, er bu'n 'im?"

"God knows!" exclaimed Miller. "The outlook is dark, but we should at least try to do something. There must be *some* white men in the town who would stand for law and order,—there 's no possible chance for Sandy to escape hanging by due process of law, if he is guilty. We might at least try half a dozen gentlemen."

"We'd better leave Josh here," said Watson. "He's too truculent. If he went on the street he'd make trouble, and if he accompanied us he'd do more harm than good. Wait for us here, Josh, until we've seen what we can do. We'll be back in half an hour."

In half an hour they had both returned.

"It's no use," reported Watson gloomily. "I called at

the mayor's office and found it locked. He is doubtless afraid on his own account, and would not dream of asserting his authority. I then looked up Judge Everton, who has always seemed to be fair. My reception was cold. He admitted that lynching was, as a rule, unjustifiable, but maintained that there were exceptions to all rules,— that laws were made, after all, to express the will of the people in regard to the ordinary administration of justice, but that in an emergency the sovereign people might assert itself and take the law into its own hands,—the creature was not greater than the creator. He laughed at my suggestion that Sandy was innocent. 'If he is innocent,' he said, 'then produce the real criminal. You negroes are standing in your own light when you try to protect such dastardly scoundrels as this Campbell, who is an enemy of society and not fit to live. I shall not move in the matter. If a negro wants the protection of the law, let him obey the law.' A wise judge,—a second Daniel come to judgment! If this were the law, there would be no need of judges or juries."

"I called on Dr. Price," said Miller, "my good friend Dr. Price, who would rather lie than hurt my feelings. 'Miller,' he declared, 'this is no affair of mine, or yours. I have too much respect for myself and my profession to interfere in such a matter, and you will accomplish nothing, and only lessen your own influence, by having anything to say.' 'But the man may be innocent,' I replied; 'there is every reason to believe that he is.' He shook his head pityingly. 'You are self-deceived, Miller; your prejudice has warped your judgment. The proof is overwhelming that he robbed this old lady, laid violent hands upon her, and left her dead. If he did no more, he has violated the written and unwritten law of the Southern States. I could not save him if I would, Miller, and frankly, I would not if I could. If he is innocent, his people can console themselves with the reflection that Mrs. Ochiltree was also innocent, and balance one crime against the other, the white against the black. Of course I shall take no part in whatever may be done,—but it is not my affair, nor yours. Take my advice, Miller, and keep out of it.'

"That is the situation," added Miller, summing up. "Their friendship for us, a slender stream at the best, dries up entirely when it strikes their prejudices. There is seemingly not one white man in Wellington who will speak a word for law, order, decency, or humanity. Those who do not participate will stand idly by and see an untried man deliberately and brutally murdered. Race prejudice is the devil unchained."

"Well, den, suh," said Josh, "where does we stan' now? W'at is we gwine ter do? I would n' min' fightin', fer my time ain't come yit,—I feels dat in my bones. W'at we gwine ter do, dat's w'at I wanter know."

"What does old Mr. Delamere have to say about the matter?" asked Miller suddenly. "Why have n't we thought of him before? Has he been seen?"

"No," replied Watson gloomily, "and for a good reason,—he is not in town. I came by the house just now, and learned that he went out to his country place yesterday afternoon, to remain a week. Sandy was to have followed him out there this morning,—it's a pity he did n't go yesterday. The old gentleman has probably heard nothing about the matter."

"How about young Delamere?"

"He went away early this morning, down the river, to

fish. He'll probably not hear of it before night, and he's only a boy anyway, and could very likely do nothing," said Watson.

Miller looked at his watch.

"Belleview is ten miles away," he said. "It is now eleven o'clock. I can drive out there in an hour and a half at the farthest. I'll go and see Mr. Delamere,—he can do more than any living man, if he is able to do any thing at all. There's never been a lynching here, and one good white man, if he choose, may stem the flood long enough to give justice a chance. Keep track of the white people while I'm gone, Watson; and you, Josh, learn what the colored folks are saying, and do nothing rash until I return. In the meantime, do all that you can to find out who did commit this most atrocious murder."

XXIII
BELLEVIEW

MILLER did not reach his destination without interruption. At one point a considerable stretch of the road was under repair, which made it necessary for him to travel slowly. His horse cast a shoe, and threatened to go lame; but in the course of time he arrived at the entrance gate of Belleview, entering which he struck into a private road, bordered by massive oaks, whose multitudinous branches, hung with long streamers of trailing moss, formed for much of the way a thick canopy above his head. It took him only a few minutes to traverse the quarter of a mile that lay between the entrance gate and the house itself.

This old colonial plantation, rich in legendary lore and replete with historic distinction, had been in the Delamere family for nearly two hundred years. Along the bank of the river which skirted its domain the famous pirate Blackbeard had held high carnival, and was reputed to have buried much treasure, vague traditions of which still lingered among the negroes and poor-whites of the country roundabout. The beautiful residence, rising white and stately in a grove of ancient oaks, dated from 1750, and was built of brick which had been brought from England. Enlarged and improved from generation to generation, it stood, like a baronial castle, upon a slight eminence from which could be surveyed the large demesne still belonging to the estate, which had shrunk greatly from its colonial dimensions. While still embracing several thousand acres, part forest and part cleared land, it had not of late years been profitable; in spite of which Mr. Delamere, with the conservatism of his age and caste, had never been able to make up his mind to part with any considerable portion of it. His grandson, he imagined, could make the estate pay and yet preserve it in its integrity. Here, in pleasant weather, surrounded by the scenes which he loved, old Mr. Delamere spent much of the time during his declining years.

Dr. Miller had once passed a day at Belleview, upon Mr. Delamere's invitation. For this old-fashioned gentleman, whose ideals not even slavery had been able to spoil, regarded himself as a trustee for the great public, which ought, in his opinion, to take as much pride as he in the contemplation of this historic landmark. In earlier years Mr. Delamere had been a practicing lawyer, and had numbered Miller's father among his clients. He had always been regarded as friendly to the colored people, and, until age and ill health had driven him from active life, had taken a lively interest in their advancement since the abolition of slavery. Upon the public opening of Miller's new hospital, he had made an effort to be present, and had made a little speech of approval and encouragement which had manifested his kindliness and given Miller much pleasure.

It was with the consciousness, therefore, that he was approaching a friend, as well as Sandy's master, that Miller's mind was chiefly occupied as his tired horse, scenting the end of his efforts, bore him with a final burst of speed along the last few rods of the journey; for the urgency of Miller's errand, involving as it did the issues of life and death, did not permit him to enjoy the charm of mossy oak or forest reaches, or even to appreciate the noble front of Belleview House when it at last loomed up before him.

"Well, William," said Mr. Delamere, as he gave his hand to Miller from the armchair in which he was seated under the broad and stately portico, "I did n't expect to see you out here. You'll excuse my not rising—I'm none too firm on my legs. Did you see anything of my man Sandy back there on the road? He ought to have been here by nine o'clock, and it's now one. Sandy is punctuality itself, and I don't know how to account for his delay."

Clearly there need be no time wasted in preliminaries. Mr. Delamere had gone directly to the subject in hand.

"He will not be here to-day, sir," replied Miller. "I have come to you on his account."

186

In a few words Miller stated the situation.

"Preposterous!" exclaimed the old gentleman, with more vigor than Miller had supposed him to possess. "Sandy is absolutely incapable of such a crime as robbery, to say nothing of murder; and as for the rest, that is absurd upon the face of it! And so the poor old woman is dead! Well, well, well! she could not have lived much longer anyway; but Sandy did not kill her,—it's simply impossible! Why, *I* raised that boy! He was born on my place. I'd as soon believe such a thing of my own grandson as of Sandy! No negro raised by a Delamere would ever commit such a crime. I really believe, William, that Sandy has the family honor of the Delameres quite as much at heart as I have. Just tell them I say Sandy is innocent, and it will be all right."

"I'm afraid, sir," rejoined Miller, who kept his voice up so that the old gentleman could understand without having it suggested that Miller knew he was hard of hearing, "that you don't quite appreciate the situation. *I* believe Sandy innocent; *you* believe him innocent; but there are suspicious circumstances which do not explain themselves, and the white people of the city believe him guilty, and are going to lynch him before he has a chance to clear himself."

"Why does n't he explain the suspicious circumstances?" asked Mr. Delamere. "Sandy is truthful and can be believed. I would take Sandy's word as quickly as another man's oath."

"He has no chance to explain," said Miller. "The case is prejudged. A crime has been committed. Sandy is charged with it. He is black, and therefore he is guilty. No colored lawyer would be allowed in the jail, if one should dare to go there. No white lawyer will intervene. He'll be lynched to-night, without judge, jury, or preacher, unless we can stave the thing off for a day or two."

"Have you seen my grandson?" asked the old gentleman. "Is he not looking after Sandy?"

"No, sir. It seems he went down the river this morning to fish, before the murder was discovered; no one knows just where he has gone, or at what hour he will return."

"Well, then," said Mr. Delamere, rising from his chair with surprising vigor, "I shall have to go myself. No faithful servant of mine shall be hanged for a crime he did n't commit, so long as I have a voice to speak or a dollar to spend. There'll be no trouble after I get there, William. The people are naturally wrought up at such a crime. A fine old woman,—she had some detestable traits, and I was always afraid she wanted to marry me, but she was of an excellent family and had many good points,—an old woman of one of the best families, struck down by the hand of a murderer! You must remember, William, that blood is thicker than water, and that the provocation is extreme, and that a few hotheads might easily lose sight of the great principles involved and seek immediate vengeance, without too much discrimination. But they are good people, William, and when I have spoken, and they have an opportunity for the sober second thought, they will do nothing rashly, but will wait for the operation of the law, which will, of course, clear Sandy."

"I'm sure I hope so," returned Miller. "Shall I try to drive you back, sir, or will you order your own carriage?"

"My horses are fresher, William, and I'll have them brought around. You can take the reins, if you will,—I'm rather old to drive,—and my man will come behind with your buggy."

In a few minutes they set out along the sandy road. Having two fresh horses, they made better headway than Miller had made coming out, and reached Wellington easily by three o'clock.

"I think, William," said Mr. Delamere, as they drove into the town, "that I had first better talk with Sandy. He may be able to explain away the things that seem to connect him with this atrocious affair; and that will put me in a better position to talk to other people about it."

Miller drove directly to the county jail. Thirty or forty white men, who seemed to be casually gathered near the door, closed up when the carriage approached. The sheriff, who had seen them from the inside, came to the outer door and spoke to the visitor through grated wicket.

"Mr. Wemyss," said Mr. Delamere, when he had made his way to the entrance with the aid of his cane, "I wish to see my servant, Sandy Campbell, who is said to be in your custody."

The sheriff hesitated. Meantime there was some parleying in low tones among the crowd outside. No one interfered, however, and in a moment the door opened sufficiently to give entrance to the old gentleman, after which it closed quickly and clangorously behind him.

Feeling no desire to linger in the locality, Miller, having seen his companion enter the jail, drove the carriage round to Mr. Delamere's house, and leaving it in charge of a servant with instructions to return for his master in a quarter of an hour, hastened to his own home to meet Watson and Josh and report the result of his efforts.

XXIV
TWO SOUTHERN GENTLEMEN

THE iron bolt rattled in the lock, the door of a cell swung open, and when Mr. Delamere had entered was quickly closed again.

"Well, Sandy!"

"Oh, Mars John! Is you fell from hebben ter he'p me out er here? I prayed de Lawd ter sen' you, an' He answered my prayer, an' here you is, Mars John,—here you is! Oh, Mars John, git me out er dis place!"

"Tut, tut, Sandy!" answered his master; "of course I'll get you out. That's what I've come for. How in the world did such a mistake ever happen? You would no more commit such a crime than I would!"

"No, suh, 'deed I would n', an' you know I would n'! I would n' want ter bring no disgrace on de fam'ly dat raise' me, ner ter make no trouble fer you, suh; but here I is, suh, lock' up in jail, an' folks talkin' 'bout hangin' me fer somethin' dat never entered my min', suh. I swea' ter God I never thought er sech a thing!"

"Of course you did n't, Sandy," returned Mr. Delamere soothingly; "and now the next thing, and the simplest thing, is to get you out of this. I 'll speak to the officers, and at the preliminary hearing to-morrow I'll tell them all about you, and they will let you go. You won't mind spending one night in jail for your sins."

"No, suh, ef I wuz sho' I'd be lowed ter spen' it here. But dey say dey're gwine ter lynch me ter-night,—I kin hear 'em talkin' f'm de winders er de cell, suh."

"Well, *I* say, Sandy, that they shall do no such thing! Lynch a man brought up by a Delamere, for a crime of which he is innocent? Preposterous! I'll speak to the authorities and see that you are properly protected until this mystery is unraveled. If Tom had been here, he would have had you out before now, Sandy. My grandson is a genuine Delamere, is he not, Sandy?"

"Yas, suh, yas, suh," returned Sandy, with a lack of enthusiasm which he tried to conceal from his master. "An' I s'pose ef he had n' gone fishin' so soon dis mawnin', he'd 'a' be'n lookin' after me, suh."

"It has been my love for him and your care of me, Sandy," said the old gentleman tremulously, "that have kept me alive so long; but now explain to me everything concerning this distressing matter, and I shall then be able to state your case to better advantage."

"Well, suh," returned Sandy, "I mought's well tell do whole tale an' not hol' nothin' back. I wuz kind er lonesome las' night, an' sence I be'n tu'ned outen de chu'ch on account er dat cakewalk I did n' go ter, so he'p me God! I did n' feel like gwine ter prayer-meetin', so I went roun' ter see Solomon Williams, an' he wa'n't home, an' den I walk' down street an' met Josh Green, an' he ax' me inter Sam Taylor's place, an' I sot roun' dere wid Josh till 'bout 'leven o'clock, w'en I sta'ted back home. I went straight ter de house, suh, an' went ter bed an' ter sleep widout sayin' a wo'd ter a single soul excep' Mistuh Tom, who wuz settin' up readin' a book w'en I come in. I wish I may drap dead in my tracks, suh, ef dat ain't de God's truf, suh, eve'y wo'd of it!"

"I believe every word of it, Sandy; now tell me about the clothes that you are said to have been found cleaning, and the suspicious articles that were found in your room?"

"Dat's w'at beats me, Mars John," replied Sandy, shaking his head mournfully. "W'en I lef' home las' night after supper, my clo's wuz all put erway in de closet in my room, folded up on de she'f ter keep de moths out. Dey wuz my good clo's,—de blue coat dat you wo' ter de weddin' fo'ty years ago, an' dem dere plaid pants I gun Mistuh Cohen fo' dollars fer three years ago; an' w'en I looked in my closet dis mawnin' suh, befo' I got ready ter sta't fer Belleview, dere wuz my clo's layin' on de flo', all muddy an' crumple' up, des lack somebody had wo' 'em in a fight! Somebody e'se had wo' my clo's,—er e'se dere'd be'n some witchcraf', er some sort er devilment gwine on dat I can't make out, suh, ter save my soul!"

"There was no witchcraft, Sandy, but that there was some deviltry might well be. Now, what other negro, who might have been mistaken for you, could have taken your clothes? Surely no one about the house?"

"No, suh, no, suh. It could n't 'a' be'n Jeff, fer he wuz at Belleview wid you; an' it could n't 'a' be'n Billy, fer he wuz too little ter wear my clo's; an' it could n't 'a' be'n Sally, fer she's a 'oman. It's a myst'ry ter me, suh!"

"Have you no enemies? Is there any one in Wellington whom you imagine would like to do you an injury?"

"Not a livin' soul dat I knows of, suh. I've be'n tu'ned out'n de chu'ch, but I don' know who my enemy is dere, er ef it wuz all a mistake, like dis yer jailin' is; but de Debbil is in dis somewhar, Mars John,—an' I got my reasons fer sayin' so."

"What do you mean, Sandy?"

Sandy related his experience of the preceding evening: how he had seen the apparition preceding him to the house, and how he had questioned Tom upon the subject.

"There's some mystery here, Sandy," said Mr. Delamere reflectively. "Have you told me all, now, upon your honor? I am trying to save your life, Sandy, and I must be able to trust your word implicitly. You must tell me every circumstance; a very little and seemingly unimportant bit of evidence may sometimes determine the issue of a great lawsuit. There is one thing especially, Sandy: where did you get the gold which was found in your trunk?"

Sandy's face lit up with hopefulness.

"Why, Mars John, I kin 'splain dat part easy. Dat wuz money I had lent out, an' I got back f'm—But no, suh, I promise' not ter tell."

"Circumstances absolve you from your promise, Sandy. Your life is of more value to you than any other thing. If you will explain where you got the gold, and the silk purse that contained it, which is said to be Mrs. Ochiltree's, you will be back home before night."

Old Mr. Delamere's faculties, which had been waning somewhat in sympathy with his health, were stirred to unusual acuteness by his servant's danger. He was watching Sandy with all the awakened instincts of the trial lawyer. He could see clearly enough that, in beginning to account for the possession of the gold, Sandy had started off with his explanation in all sincerity. At the mention of the silk purse, however, his face had blanched to an ashen gray, and the words had frozen upon his lips.

A less discerning observer might have taken these things as signs of guilt, but not so Mr. Delamere.

"Well, Sandy," said his master encouragingly, "go on. You got the gold from"—

Sandy remained silent. He had had a great shock, and had taken a great resolution.

"Mars John," he asked dreamily, "you don' b'lieve dat I done dis thing?"

"Certainly not, Sandy, else why should I be here?"

"An' nothin' would n' make you b'lieve it, suh?"

"No, Sandy,—I could not believe it of you. I've known you too long and too well."

"An' you would n' b'lieve it, not even ef I would n' say one wo'd mo' about it?"

"No, Sandy, I believe you no more capable of this crime than I would be,—or my grandson, Tom. I wish Tom were here, that he might help me overcome your stubbornness; but you'll not be so foolish, so absurdly foolish, Sandy, as to keep silent and risk your life merely to shield some one else, when by speaking you might clear up this mystery and be restored at once to liberty. Just tell me where you got the gold," added the old gentleman persuasively. "Come, now, Sandy, that's a good fellow!"

"Mars John," asked Sandy softly, "w'en my daddy, 'way back yander befo' de wah, wuz about ter be sol' away f'm his wife an' child'en, you bought him an' dem, an' kep' us all on yo' place tergether, did n't you, suh?"

"Yes, Sandy, and he was a faithful servant, and proved worthy of all I did for him."

"And w'en he had wo'ked fer you ten years, suh, you sot 'im free?"

"Yes, Sandy, he had earned his freedom."

"An' w'en de wah broke out, an' my folks wuz scattered, an' I did n' have nothin' ter do ner nowhar ter go, you kep' me on yo' place, and tuck me ter wait on you, suh, did n't you?"

194

"Yes, Sandy, and you have been a good servant and a good friend; but tell me now about this gold, and I'll go and get you out of this, right away, for I need you, Sandy, and you'll not be of any use to me shut up here!"

"Jes' hol' on a minute befo' you go, Mars John; fer ef dem people outside should git holt er me befo' you *does* git me out er here, I may never see you no mo', suh, in dis worl'. W'en Mars Billy McLean shot me by mistake, w'ile we wuz out huntin' dat day, who wuz it boun' up my woun's an' kep' me from bleedin' ter def, an' kyar'ed me two miles on his own shoulders ter a doctuh?"

"Yes, Sandy, and when black Sally ran away with your young mistress and Tom, when Tom was a baby, who stopped the runaway, and saved their lives at the risk of his own?"

"Dat wa'n't nothin', suh; anybody could 'a' done dat, w'at wuz strong ernuff an' swif' ernuff. You is be'n good ter me, suh, all dese years, an' I've tried ter do my duty by you, suh, an' by Mistuh Tom, who wuz yo' own gran'son, an' de las' one er de fam'ly."

"Yes, you have, Sandy, and when I am gone, which will not be very long, Tom will take care of you, and see that you never want. But we are wasting valuable time, Sandy, in these old reminiscences. Let us get back to the present. Tell me about the gold, now, so that I may at once look after your safety. It may not even be necessary for you to remain here all night."

"Jes' one wo'd mo', Mars John, befo' you go! I know you're gwine ter do de bes' you kin fer me, an' I'm sorry I can't he'p you no mo' wid it; but ef dere should be any accident, er ef you *can't* git me out er here, don' bother yo' min' 'bout it no mo', suh, an' don' git yo'se'f ixcited, fer you know de doctuh says, suh, dat you can't stan' ixcitement; but jes' leave me in de han's er de Lawd, suh,—*He'll* look after me, here er hereafter. I know I've fell f'm grace mo' d'n once, but I've done made my peace wid Him in dis here jail-house, suh, an' I ain't 'feared ter die—ef I haf ter. I ain' got no wife ner child'n ter mo'n fer me, an' I'll die knowin' dat I've done my duty ter dem dat hi'ed me, an' trusted me, an' had claims on me. Fer I wuz raise' by a Delamere, suh, an' all de ole Delameres wuz gent'emen, an' deir principles spread ter de niggers 'round 'em, suh; an' ef I has ter die fer somethin' I did n' do,—I kin die, suh, like a gent'eman! But ez fer dat gol', suh, I ain' gwine ter say one wo'd mo' 'bout it ter nobody in dis worl'!"

Nothing could shake Sandy's determination. Mr. Delamere argued, expostulated, but all in vain. Sandy would not speak.

More and more confident of some mystery, which would come out in time, if properly investigated, Mr. Delamere, strangely beset by a vague sense of discomfort over and beyond that occasioned by his servant's danger, hurried away upon his errand of mercy. He felt less confident of the outcome than when he had entered the jail, but was quite as much resolved that no effort should be spared to secure protection for Sandy until there had been full opportunity for the truth to become known.

"Take good care of your prisoner, sheriff," he said sternly, as he was conducted to the door. "He will not be long in your custody, and I shall see that you are held strictly accountable for his safety."

"I'll do what I can, sir," replied the sheriff in an even tone and seemingly not greatly impressed by this warning. "If the prisoner is taken from me, it will be because the force that comes for him is too strong for resistance."

"There should be no force too strong for an honest man in your position to resist,—whether successfully or not is beyond the question. The officer who is intimidated by threats, or by his own fears, is recreant to his duty, and no better than the mob which threatens him. But you will have no such test, Mr. Wemyss! I shall see to it myself that there is no violence!"

XXV
THE HONOR OF A FAMILY

MR. DELAMERE'S coachman, who, in accordance with instructions left by Miller, had brought the carriage around to the jail and was waiting anxiously at the nearest corner, drove up with some trepidation as he saw his master emerge from the prison. The old gentleman entered the carriage, and gave the order to be driven to the office of the Morning Chronicle. According to Jerry, the porter, whom he encountered at the door, Carteret was in his office, and Mr. Delamere, with the aid of his servant, climbed the stairs painfully and found the editor at his desk.

"Carteret," exclaimed Mr. Delamere, "what is all this talk about lynching my man for murder and robbery and criminal assault? It's perfectly absurd! The man was raised by me; he has lived in my house forty years. He has been honest, faithful, and trustworthy. He would no more be capable of this crime than you would, or my grandson Tom. Sandy has too much respect for the family to do anything that would reflect disgrace upon it."

"My dear Mr. Delamere," asked Carteret, with an indulgent smile, "how could a negro possibly reflect discredit upon a white family? I should really like to know."

"How, sir? A white family raised him. Like all the negroes, he has been clay in the hands of the white people. They are what we have made them, or permitted them to become."

"We are not God, Mr. Delamere! We do not claim to have created these—masterpieces."

"No; but we thought to overrule God's laws, and we enslaved these people for our greed, and sought to escape the manstealer's curse by laying to our souls the flattering unction that we were making of barbarous negroes civilized and Christian men. If we did not, if instead of making them Christians we have made some of them brutes, we have only ourselves to blame, and if these prey upon society, it is our just punishment! But my negroes, Carteret, were well raised and well behaved. This man is innocent of this offense, I solemnly affirm, and I want your aid to secure his safety until a fair trial can be had."

"On your bare word, sir?" asked Carteret, not at all moved by this outburst.

Old Mr. Delamere trembled with anger, and his withered cheek flushed darkly, but he restrained his feelings, and answered with an attempt at calmness:—

"Time was, sir, when the word of a Delamere was held as good as his bond, and those who questioned it were forced to maintain their skepticism upon the field of honor. Time was, sir, when the law was enforced in this state in a manner to command the respect of the world! Our lawyers, our judges, our courts, were a credit to humanity and civilization. I fear I have outlasted my epoch,—I have lived to hear of white men, the most favored of races, the heirs of civilization, the conservators of liberty, howling like red Indians around a human being slowly roasting at the stake."

"My dear sir," said Carteret soothingly, "you should undeceive yourself. This man is no longer your property. The negroes are no longer under our control, and with their emancipation ceased our responsibility. Their insolence and disregard for law have reached a point where they must be sternly rebuked."

"The law," retorted Mr. Delamere, "furnishes a sufficient penalty for any crime, however heinous, and our code is by no means lenient. To my old-fashioned notions, death would seem an adequate punishment for any crime, and torture has been abolished in civilized countries for a hundred years. It would be better to let a crime go entirely unpunished, than to use it as a pretext for turning the whole white population into a mob of primitive savages, dancing in hellish glee around the mangled body of a man who has never been tried for a crime. All this, however, is apart from my errand, which is to secure your assistance in heading off this mob until Sandy can have a fair hearing and an opportunity to prove his innocence."

"How can I do that, Mr. Delamere?"

"You are editor of the Morning Chronicle. The Chronicle is the leading newspaper of the city. This morning's issue practically suggested the mob; the same means will stop it. I will pay the expense of an extra edition, calling off the mob, on the ground that newly discovered evidence has shown the prisoner's innocence."

"But where is the evidence?" asked Carteret.

Again Mr. Delamere flushed and trembled." "*My* evidence, sir! I say the negro was morally incapable of the crime. A man of forty-five does not change his nature over-night. He is no more capable of a disgraceful deed than my grandson would be!"

Carteret smiled sadly.

"I am sorry, Mr. Delamere," he said, "that you should permit yourself to be so exercised about a worthless scoundrel who has forfeited his right to live. The proof against him is overwhelming. As to his capability of crime, we will apply your own test. You have been kept in the dark too long, Mr. Delamere,—indeed, we all have,—about others as well as this negro. Listen, sir: last night, at the Clarendon Club, Tom Delamere was caught cheating outrageously at cards. He had been suspected for some time; a trap was laid for him, and he fell into it. Out of regard for you and for my family, he has been permitted to resign quietly, with the understanding that he first pay off his debts, which are considerable."

Mr. Delamere's face, which had taken on some color in the excitement of the interview, had gradually paled to a chalky white while Carteret was speaking. His head sunk forward; already an old man, he seemed to have aged ten years in but little more than as many seconds.

"Can this be true?" he demanded in a hoarse whisper. "Is it—entirely authentic?"

"True as gospel; true as it is that Mrs. Ochiltree has been murdered, and that this negro killed her. Ellis was at the club a few minutes after the affair happened, and learned the facts from one of the participants. Tom made no attempt at denial. We have kept the matter out of the other papers, and I would have spared your feelings,—I surely would not wish to wound them,—but the temptation proved too strong for me, and it seemed the only way to convince you: it was your own test. If a gentleman of a distinguished name and an honorable ancestry, with all the restraining forces of social position surrounding him, to hold him in check, can stoop to dishonor, what is the improbability of an illiterate negro's being at least *capable* of crime?"

"Enough, sir," said the old gentleman. "You have proved enough. My grandson may be a scoundrel,—I can see, in the light of this revelation, how he might be; and he seems not to have denied it. I maintain, nevertheless, that my man Sandy is innocent of the charge against him. He *has* denied it, and it has not been proved. Carteret, I owe that negro my life; he, and his father before him, have served me and mine faithfully and well. I cannot see him killed like a dog, without judge or jury,—no, not even if he were guilty, which I do not believe!"

Carteret felt a twinge of remorse for the pain he had inflicted upon this fine old man, this ideal gentleman of the ideal past,—the past which be himself so much admired and regretted. He would like to spare his old friend any further agitation; he was in a state of health where too great excitement might prove fatal. But how could he? The negro was guilty, and sure to die sooner or later. He had not meant to interfere, and his intervention might be fruitless.

"Mr. Delamere," he said gently, "there is but one way to gain time. You say the negro is innocent. Appearances are against him. The only way to clear him is to produce the real criminal, or prove an alibi. If you, or some other white man of equal standing, could swear that the negro was in your presence last night at any hour when this crime could have taken place, it might be barely possible to prevent the lynching for the present; and when he is tried, which will probably be not later than next week, he will have every opportunity to defend himself, with you to see that he gets no less than justice. I think it can be managed, though there is still a doubt. I will do my best, for your sake, Mr. Delamere,—solely for your sake, be it understood, and not for that of the negro, in whom you are entirely deceived."

"I shall not examine your motives, Carteret," replied the other, "if you can bring about what I desire."

"Whatever is done," added Carteret, "must be done quickly. It is now four o'clock; no one can answer for what may happen after seven. If he can prove an alibi, there may yet be time to save him. White men might lynch a negro on suspicion; they would not kill a man who was proven, by the word of white men, to be entirely innocent."

"I do not know," returned Mr. Delamere, shaking his head sadly. "After what you have told me, it is no longer safe to assume what white men will or will not do;—what I have learned here has shaken my faith in humanity. I am going away, but shall return in a short time. Shall I find you here?"

"I will await your return," said Carteret.

He watched Mr. Delamere pityingly as the old man moved away on the arm of the coachman waiting in the hall. He did not believe that Mr. Delamere could prove an alibi for his servant, and without some positive proof the negro would surely die,—as he well deserved to die.

XXVI
THE DISCOMFORT OF ELLIS

Mr. Ellis was vaguely uncomfortable. In the first excitement following the discovery of the crime, he had given his bit of evidence, and had shared the universal indignation against the murderer. When public feeling took definite shape in the intention to lynch the prisoner, Ellis felt a sudden sense of responsibility growing upon himself. When he learned, an hour later, that it was proposed to burn the negro, his part in the affair assumed a still graver aspect; for his had been the final word to fix the prisoner's guilt.

Ellis did not believe in lynch law. He had argued against it, more than once, in private conversation, and had written several editorials against the practice, while in charge of the Morning Chronicle during Major Carteret's absence. A young man, however, and merely representing another, he had not set up as a reformer, taking rather the view that this summary method of punishing crime, with all its possibilities of error, to say nothing of the resulting disrespect of the law and contempt for the time-honored methods of establishing guilt, was a mere temporary symptom of the unrest caused by the unsettled relations of the two races at the South. There had never before been any special need for any vigorous opposition to lynch law, so far as the community was concerned, for there had not been a lynching in Wellington since Ellis had come there, eight years before, from a smaller town, to seek a place for himself in the world of action. Twenty years before, indeed, there had been wild doings, during the brief Ku-Klux outbreak, but that was before Ellis's time,—or at least when he was but a child. He had come of a Quaker family,—the modified Quakers of the South,—and while sharing in a general way the Southern prejudice against the negro, his prejudices had been tempered by the peaceful tenets of his father's sect. His father had been a Whig, and a non-slaveholder; and while he had gone with the South in the civil war so far as a man of peace could go, he had not done so for love of slavery.

As the day wore on, Ellis's personal responsibility for the intended *auto-da-fé* bore more heavily upon him. Suppose he had been wrong? He had seen the accused negro; he had recognized him by his clothes, his whiskers, his spectacles, and his walk; but he had also seen another man, who resembled Sandy so closely that but for the difference in their clothes, he was forced to acknowledge, he could not have told them apart. Had he not seen the first man, he would have sworn with even greater confidence that the second was Sandy. There had been, he recalled, about one of the men—he had not been then nor was he now able to tell which—something vaguely familiar, and yet seemingly discordant to whichever of the two it was, or, as it seemed to him now, to any man of that race. His mind reverted to the place where he had last seen Sandy, and then a sudden wave of illumination swept over him, and filled him with a thrill of horror. The cakewalk,—the dancing—the speech,—they were not Sandy's at all, nor any negro's! It was a white man who had stood in the light of the street lamp, so that the casual passer-by might see and recognize in him old Mr. Delamere's servant. The scheme was a dastardly one, and worthy of a heart that was something worse than weak and vicious.

Ellis resolved that the negro should not, if he could prevent it, die for another's crime; but what proof had he himself to offer in support of his theory? Then again, if he denounced Tom Delamere as the murderer, it would involve, in all probability, the destruction of his own hopes with regard to Clara. Of course she could not marry Delamere after the disclosure,—the disgraceful episode at the club would have been enough to make that reasonably certain; it had put a nail in Delamere's coffin, but this crime had driven it in to the head and clinched it. On the other hand, would Miss Pemberton ever speak again to the man who had been the instrument of bringing disgrace upon the family? Spies, detectives, police officers, may be useful citizens, but they are rarely pleasant company for other people. We fee the executioner, but we do not touch his bloody hand. We might feel a certain tragic admiration for Brutus condemning his sons to death, but we would scarcely invite Brutus to dinner after the event. It would harrow our feelings too much.

Perhaps, thought Ellis, there might be a way out of the dilemma. It might be possible to save this innocent negro without, for the time being, involving Delamere. He believed that murder will out, but it need not be through his initiative. He determined to go to the jail and interview the prisoner, who might give such an account of himself as would establish his innocence beyond a doubt. If so, Ellis would exert himself to stem the tide of popular fury. If, as a last resort, he could save Sandy only by denouncing Delamere, he would do his duty, let it cost him what it might.

The gravity of his errand was not lessened by what he

saw and heard on the way to the jail. The anger of the people was at a white heat. A white woman had been assaulted and murdered by a brutal negro. Neither advanced age, nor high social standing, had been able to protect her from the ferocity of a black savage. Her sex, which should have been her shield and buckler, had made her an easy mark for the villainy of a black brute. To take the time to try him would be a criminal waste of public money. To hang him would be too slight a punishment for so dastardly a crime. An example must be made.

Already the preparations were under way for the impending execution. A T-rail from the railroad yard had been procured, and men were burying it in the square before the jail. Others were bringing chains, and a load of pine wood was piled in convenient proximity. Some enterprising individual had begun the erection of seats from which, for a pecuniary consideration, the spectacle might be the more easily and comfortably viewed.

Ellis was stopped once or twice by persons of his acquaintance. From one he learned that the railroads would run excursions from the neighboring towns in order to bring spectators to the scene; from another that the burning was to take place early in the evening, so that the children might not be kept up beyond their usual bedtime. In one group that he passed he heard several young men discussing the question of which portions of the negro's body they would prefer for souvenirs. Ellis shuddered and hastened forward. Whatever was to be done must be done quickly, or it would be too late. He saw that already it would require a strong case in favor of the accused to overcome the popular verdict.

Going up the steps of the jail, he met Mr. Delamere, who was just coming out, after a fruitless interview with Sandy.

"Mr. Ellis," said the old gentleman, who seemed greatly agitated, "this is monstrous!"

"It is indeed, sir!" returned the younger man. "I mean to stop it if I can. The negro did not kill Mrs. Ochiltree."

Mr. Delamere looked at Ellis keenly, and, as Ellis recalled afterwards, there was death in his eyes. Unable to draw a syllable from Sandy, he had found his servant's silence more eloquent than words. Ellis felt a presentiment that this affair, however it might terminate, would be fatal to this fine old man, whom the city could ill spare, in spite of his age and infirmities.

"Mr. Ellis," asked Mr. Delamere, in a voice which trembled with ill-suppressed emotion, "do you know who killed her?"

Ellis felt a surging pity for his old friend; but every step that he had taken toward the jail had confirmed and strengthened his own resolution that this contemplated crime, which he dimly felt to be far more atrocious than that of which Sandy was accused, in that it involved a whole community rather than one vicious man, should be stopped at any cost. Deplorable enough had the negro been guilty, it became, in view of his certain innocence, an unspeakable horror, which for all time would cover the city with infamy.

"Mr. Delamere," he replied, looking the elder man squarely in the eyes, "I think I do,—and I am very sorry."

"And who was it, Mr. Ellis?"

He put the question hopelessly, as though the answer were a foregone conclusion.

"I do not wish to say at present," replied Ellis, with a remorseful pang, "unless it becomes absolutely necessary, to save the negro's life. Accusations are dangerous,—as this case proves,—unless the proof be certain."

For a moment it seemed as though Mr. Delamere would collapse upon the spot. Rallying almost instantly, however, he took the arm which Ellis involuntarily offered, and said with an effort:—

"Mr. Ellis, you are a gentleman whom it is an honor to know. If you have time, I wish you would go with me to my house,—I can hardly trust myself alone,—and thence to the Chronicle office. This thing shall be stopped, and you will help me stop it."

It required but a few minutes to cover the half mile that lay between the prison and Mr. Delamere's residence.

XXVII
THE VAGARIES OF THE HIGHER LAW

Mr. Delamere went immediately to his grandson's room, which he entered alone, closing and locking the door behind him. He had requested Ellis to wait in the carriage.

The bed had been made, and the room was apparently in perfect order. There was a bureau in the room, through which Mr. Delamere proceeded to look thoroughly. Finding one of the drawers locked, he tried it with a key of his own, and being unable to unlock it, took a poker from beside the stove and broke it ruthlessly open.

The contents served to confirm what he had heard concerning his grandson's character. Thrown together in disorderly confusion were bottles of wine and whiskey; soiled packs of cards; a dice-box with dice; a box of poker chips, several revolvers, and a number of photographs and paper-covered books at which the old gentleman merely glanced to ascertain their nature.

So far, while his suspicion had been strengthened, he had found nothing to confirm it. He searched the room more carefully, and found, in the wood-box by the small heating-stove which stood in the room, a torn and crumpled bit of paper. Stooping to pick this up, his eye caught a gleam of something yellow beneath the bureau, which lay directly in his line of vision.

First he smoothed out the paper. It was apparently the lower half of a label, or part of the cover of a small box, torn diagonally from corner to corner. From the business card at the bottom, which gave the name of a firm of manufacturers of theatrical supplies in a Northern city, and from the letters remaining upon the upper and nar-rower half, the bit of paper had plainly formed part of the wrapper of a package of burnt cork.

Closing his fingers spasmodically over this damning piece of evidence, Mr. Delamere knelt painfully, and with the aid of his cane drew out from under the bureau the yellow object which had attracted his attention. It was a five-dollar gold piece of a date back toward the begin-ning of the century.

To make assurance doubly sure, Mr. Delamere sum-moned the cook from the kitchen in the back yard. In answer to her master's questions, Sally averred that Mr. Tom had got up very early, had knocked at her window,—she slept in a room off the kitchen in the yard,—and had told her that she need not bother about breakfast for him, as he had had a cold bite from the pantry; that he was going hunting and fishing, and would be gone all day. According to Sally, Mr. Tom had come in about ten o'clock the night before. He had forgotten his night-key, Sandy was out, and she had admitted him with her own key. He had said that he was very tired and was going immediately to bed.

Mr. Delamere seemed perplexed; the crime had been committed later in the evening than ten o'clock. The cook cleared up the mystery.

"I reckon he must 'a' be'n dead ti'ed, suh, fer I went back ter his room fifteen er twenty minutes after he come in fer ter fin' out w'at he wanted fer breakfus'; an' I knock' two or three times, rale ha'd, an' Mistuh Tom did n' wake up no mo' d'n de dead. He sho'ly had a good sleep, er he'd never 'a' got up so ea'ly."

"Thank you, Sally," said Mr. Delamere, when the woman had finished, "that will do."

"Will you be home ter suppah, suh?" asked the cook.

"Yes."

It was a matter of the supremest indifference to Mr. Delamere whether he should ever eat again, but he would not betray his feelings to a servant. In a few minutes he was driving rapidly with Ellis toward the office of the Morning Chronicle. Ellis could see that Mr. Delamere had discovered something of tragic import. Neither spoke. Ellis gave all his attention to the horses, and Mr. Delamere remained wrapped in his own sombre reflections.

When they reached the office, they were informed by Jerry that Major Carteret was engaged with General Belmont and Captain McBane. Mr. Delamere knocked peremptorily at the door of the inner office, which was opened by Carteret in person.

"Oh, it is you, Mr. Delamere."

"Carteret," exclaimed Mr. Delamere, "I must speak to you immediately, and alone."

"Excuse me a moment, gentlemen," said Carteret, turning to those within the room. "I'll be back in a moment—don't go away."

Ellis had left the room, closing the door behind him. Mr. Delamere and Carteret were quite alone.

"Carteret," declared the old gentleman, "this murder must not take place."

"'Murder' is a hard word," replied the editor, frowning slightly.

"It is the right word," rejoined Mr. Delamere, decidedly. "It would be a foul and most unnatural murder, for Sandy did not kill Mrs. Ochiltree."

Carteret with difficulty restrained a smile of pity. His old friend was very much excited, as the tremor in his voice gave proof. The criminal was his trusted servant, who had proved unworthy of confidence. No one could question Mr. Delamere's motives; but he was old, his judgment was no longer to be relied upon. It was a great pity that he should so excite and over-strain himself about a worthless negro, who had forfeited his life for a dastardly crime. Mr. Delamere had had two paralytic strokes, and a third might prove fatal. He must be dealt with gently.

"Mr. Delamere," he said, with patient tolerance, "I

think you are deceived. There is but one sure way to stop this execution. If your servant is innocent, you must produce the real criminal. If the negro, with such overwhelming proofs against him, is not guilty, who is?"

"I will tell you who is," replied Mr. Delamere. "The murderer is,"—the words came with a note of anguish, as though torn from his very heart,—"the murderer is Tom Delamere, my own grandson!"

"Impossible, sir!" exclaimed Carteret, starting back involuntarily. "That could not be! The man was seen leaving the house, and he was black!"

"All cats are gray in the dark, Carteret; and, moreover, nothing is easier than for a white man to black his face. God alone knows how many crimes have been done in this guise! Tom Delamere, to get the money to pay his gambling debts, committed this foul murder, and then tried to fasten it upon as honest and faithful a soul as ever trod the earth."

Carteret, though at first overwhelmed by this announcement, perceived with quick intuition that it might easily be true. It was but a step from fraud to crime, and in Delamere's need of money there lay a palpable motive for robbery,—the murder may have been an afterthought. Delamere knew as much about the cedar chest as the negro could have known, and more.

But a white man must not be condemned without proof positive.

"What foundation is there, sir," he asked, "for this astounding charge?"

Mr. Delamere related all that had taken place since he had left Belleview a couple of hours before, and as he proceeded, step by step, every word carried conviction to Carteret. Tom Delamere's skill as a mimic and a negro impersonator was well known; he had himself laughed at more than one of his performances. There had been a powerful motive, and Mr. Delamere's discoveries had made clear the means. Tom's unusual departure, before breakfast, on a fishing expedition was a suspicious circumstance. There was a certain devilish ingenuity about the affair which he would hardly have expected of Tom Delamere, but for which the reason was clear enough. One might have thought that Tom would have been satisfied with merely blacking his face, and leaving to chance the identification of the negro who might be apprehended. He would hardly have implicated, out of pure malignity, his grandfather's old servant, who had been his own care-taker for many years. Here, however, Carteret could see where Tom's own desperate position operated to furnish a probable motive for the crime. The surest way to head off suspicion from himself was to direct it strongly toward some particular person, and this he had been able to do conclusively by his access to Sandy's clothes, his skill in making up to resemble him, and by the episode of the silk purse. By placing himself beyond reach during the next day, he would not be called upon to corroborate or deny any inculpating statements which Sandy might make, and in the very probable case that the crime should be summarily avenged, any such statements on Sandy's part would be regarded as mere desperate subterfuges of the murderer to save his own life. It was a bad affair.

"The case seems clear," said Carteret reluctantly but conclusively. "And now, what shall we do about it?"

"I want you to print a handbill," said Mr. Delamere,

and circulate it through the town, stating that Sandy Campbell is innocent and Tom Delamere guilty of this crime. If this is not done, I will go myself and declare it to all who will listen, and I will publicly disown the villain who is no more grandson of mine. There is no deeper sink of iniquity into which he could fall."

Carteret's thoughts were chasing one another tumultuously. There could be no doubt that the negro was innocent, from the present aspect of affairs, and he must not be lynched; but in what sort of position would the white people be placed, if Mr. Delamere carried out his Spartan purpose of making the true facts known? The white people of the city had raised the issue of their own superior morality, and had themselves made this crime a race question. The success of the impending "revolution," for which he and his *confrères* had labored so long, depended in large measure upon the maintenance of their race prestige, which would be injured in the eyes of the world by such a fiasco. While they might yet win by sheer force, their cause would suffer in the court of morals, where they might stand convicted as pirates, instead of being applauded as patriots. Even the negroes would have the laugh on them,—the people whom they hoped to make approve and justify their own despoilment. To be laughed at by the negroes was a calamity only less terrible than failure or death.

Such an outcome of an event which had already been heralded to the four corners of the earth would throw a cloud of suspicion upon the stories of outrage which had gone up from the South for so many years, and had done so much to win the sympathy of the North for the white South and to alienate it from the colored people. The reputation of the race was threatened. They must not lynch the negro, and yet, for the credit of the town, its aristocracy, and the race, the truth of this ghastly story must not see the light,—at least not yet.

"Mr. Delamere," he exclaimed, "I am shocked and humiliated. The negro, must be saved, of course, but—consider the family honor."

"Tom is no longer a member of my family. I disown him. He has covered the family name—my name, sir—with infamy. We have no longer a family honor. I wish never to hear his name spoken again!"

For several minutes Carteret argued with his old friend. Then he went into the other room and consulted with General Belmont.

As a result of these conferences, and of certain urgent messages sent out, within half an hour thirty or forty of the leading citizens of Wellington were gathered in the Morning Chronicle office. Several other curious persons, observing that there was something in the wind, and supposing correctly that it referred to the projected event of the evening, crowded in with those who had been invited.

Carteret was in another room, still arguing with Mr. Delamere. "It's a mere formality, sir," he was saying suavely, "accompanied by a mental reservation. We know the facts; but this must be done to justify us, in the eyes of the mob, in calling them off before they accomplish their purpose."

"Carteret," said the old man, in a voice eloquent of the struggle through which he had passed, "I would not perjure myself to prolong my own miserable existence another day, but God will forgive a sin committed to save another's life. Upon your head be it, Carteret, and not on mine!"

"Gentlemen," said Carteret, entering with Mr. Delamere the room where the men were gathered, and raising his hand for silence, "the people of Wellington were on the point of wreaking vengeance upon a negro who was supposed to have been guilty of a terrible crime. The white men of this city, impelled by the highest and holiest sentiments, were about to take steps to defend their hearthstones and maintain the purity and ascendency of their race. Your purpose sprung from hearts wounded in their tenderest susceptibilities."

"'Rah, 'rah!" shouted a tipsy sailor, who had edged in with the crowd.

"But this same sense of justice," continued Carteret oratorically, "which would lead you to visit swift and terrible punishment upon the guilty, would not permit you to slay an innocent man. Even a negro, as long as he behaves himself and keeps in his place, is entitled to the protection of the law. We may be stern and unbending in the punishment of crime, as befits our masterful race, but we hold the scales of justice with even and impartial hand."

"'Rah f' 'mpa'tial han'!" cried the tipsy sailor, who was immediately ejected with slight ceremony.

"We have discovered, beyond a doubt, that the negro Sandy Campbell, now in custody, did not commit this robbery and murder, but that it was perpetrated by some unknown man, who has fled from the city. Our venerable and distinguished fellow townsman, Mr. Delamere, in whose employment this Campbell has been for many years, will vouch for his character, and states, furthermore, that Campbell was with him all last night, covering any hour at which this crime could have been committed."

"If Mr. Delamere will swear to that," said some one in the crowd, "the negro should not be lynched."

There were murmurs of dissent. The preparations had all been made. There would be great disappointment if the lynching did not occur.

"Let Mr. Delamere swear, if he wants to save the nigger," came again from the crowd.

"Certainly," assented Carteret. "Mr. Delamere can have no possible objection to taking the oath. Is there a notary public present, or a justice of the peace?"

A man stepped forward. "I am a justice of the peace," he announced.

"Very well, Mr. Smith," said Carteret, recognizing the speaker. "With your permission, I will formulate the oath, and Mr. Delamere may repeat it after me, if he will. I solemnly swear,"—

"I solemnly swear,"—

Mr. Delamere's voice might have come from the tomb, so hollow and unnatural did it sound.

"So help me God,"—

"So help me God,"—

"That the negro Sandy Campbell, now in jail on the charge of murder, robbery, and assault, was in my presence last night between the hours of eight and two o'clock."

Mr. Delamere repeated this statement in a firm voice; but to Ellis, who was in the secret, his words fell upon the ear like clods dropping upon the coffin in an open grave.

"I wish to add," said General Belmont, stepping forward, "that it is not our intention to interfere, by anything which may be done at this meeting, with the orderly process of the law, or to advise the prisoner's immediate release. The prisoner will remain in custody, Mr. Delamere, Major Carteret, and I guaranteeing that he will be proved entirely innocent at the preliminary hearing to-morrow morning."

Several of those present looked relieved; others were plainly disappointed; but when the meeting ended, the news went out that the lynching had been given up. Carteret immediately wrote and had struck off a handbill giving a brief statement of the proceedings, and sent out a dozen boys to distribute copies among the people in the streets. That no precaution might be omitted, a call was issued to the Wellington Grays, the crack independent military company of the city, who in an incredibly short time were on guard at the jail.

Thus a slight change in the point of view had demonstrated the entire ability of the leading citizens to maintain the dignified and orderly processes of the law whenever they saw fit to do so.

The night passed without disorder, beyond the somewhat rough handling of two or three careless negroes that came in the way of small parties of the disappointed who had sought alcoholic consolation.

At ten o'clock the next morning, a preliminary hearing of the charge against Campbell was had before a magistrate. Mr. Delamere, perceptibly older and more wizened than he had seemed the day before, and leaning heavily on the arm of a servant, repeated his state-

218

ment of the evening before. Only one or two witnesses were called, among whom was Mr. Ellis, who swore positively that in his opinion the prisoner was not the man whom he had seen and at first supposed to be Campbell. The most sensational piece of testimony was that of Dr. Price, who had examined the body, and who swore that the wound in the head was not necessarily fatal, and might have been due to a fall,—that she had more than likely died of shock attendant upon the robbery, she being of advanced age and feeble health. There was no evidence, he said, of any other personal violence.

Sandy was not even bound over to the grand jury, but was discharged upon the ground that there was not sufficient evidence upon which to hold him. Upon his release he received the congratulations of many present, some of whom would cheerfully have done him to death a few hours before. With the childish fickleness of a mob, they now experienced a satisfaction almost as great as, though less exciting than, that attendant upon taking life. We speak of the mysteries of inanimate nature. The workings of the human heart are the profoundest mystery of the universe. One moment they make us despair of our kind, and the next we see in them the reflection of the divine image. Sandy, having thus escaped from the Mr. Hyde of the mob, now received the benediction of its Dr. Jekyll. Being no cynical philosopher, and realizing how nearly the jaws of death had closed upon him, he was profoundly grateful for his escape, and felt not the slightest desire to investigate or criticise any man's motives.

With the testimony of Dr. Price, the worst feature of the affair came to an end. The murder eliminated or rendered doubtful, the crime became a mere vulgar robbery, the extent of which no one could estimate, since no living soul knew how much money Mrs. Ochiltree had had in the cedar chest. The absurdity of the remaining charge became more fully apparent in the light of the reaction from the excitement of the day before.

Nothing further was ever done about the case; but though the crime went unpunished, it carried evil in its train. As we have seen, the charge against Campbell had been made against the whole colored race. All over the United States the Associated Press had flashed the report of another dastardly outrage by a burly black brute,—all black brutes it seems are burly,—and of the impending lynching with its prospective horrors. This news, being highly sensational in its character, had been displayed in large black type on the front pages of the daily papers. The dispatch that followed, to the effect that the accused had been found innocent and the lynching frustrated, received slight attention, if any, in a fine-print paragraph on an inside page. The facts of the case never came out at all. The family honor of the Delameres was preserved, and the prestige of the white race in Wellington was not seriously impaired.

Upon leaving the preliminary hearing, old Mr. Delamere had requested General Belmont to call at his house during the day upon professional business. This the general did in the course of the afternoon.

"Belmont," said Mr. Delamere, "I wish to make my will. I should have drawn it with my own hand; but you know my motives, and can testify to my soundness of mind and memory."

He thereupon dictated a will, by the terms of which he left to his servant, Sandy Campbell, three thousand dollars, as a mark of the testator's appreciation of services rendered and sufferings endured by Sandy on behalf of his master. After some minor dispositions, the whole remainder of the estate was devised to Dr. William Miller, in trust for the uses of his hospital and training-school for nurses, on condition that the institution be incorporated and placed under the management of competent trustees. Tom Delamere was not mentioned in the will.

"There, Belmont," he said, "that load is off my mind. Now, if you will call in some witnesses,—most of my people can write,—I shall feel entirely at ease."

The will was signed by Mr. Delamere, and witnessed by Jeff and Billy, two servants in the house, neither of whom received any information as to its contents, beyond the statement that they were witnessing their master's will.

"I wish to leave that with you for safe keeping, Belmont," said Mr. Delamere, after the witnesses had retired. "Lock it up in your safe until I die, which will not be very long, since I have no further desire to live."

An hour later Mr. Delamere suffered a third paralytic stroke, from which he died two days afterwards, without having in the meantime recovered the power of speech.

The will was never produced. The servants stated, and General Belmont admitted, that Mr. Delamere had made a will a few days before his death; but since it was not discoverable, it seemed probable that the testator had destroyed it. This was all the more likely, the general was inclined to think, because the will had been of a most unusual character. What the contents of the will were, he of course did not state, it having been made under the seal of professional secrecy.

This suppression was justified by the usual race argument: Miller's hospital was already well established, and, like most negro institutions, could no doubt rely upon Northern philanthropy for any further support it might need. Mr. Delamere's property belonged of right to the white race, and by the higher law should remain in the possession of white people. Loyalty to one's race was a more sacred principle than deference to a weak old man's whims.

Having reached this conclusion, General Belmont's first impulse was to destroy the will; on second thoughts he locked it carefully away in his safe. He would hold it awhile. It might some time be advisable to talk the matter over with young Delamere, who was of a fickle disposition and might wish to change his legal adviser.

XXVIII
IN SEASON AND OUT

WELLINGTON soon resumed its wonted calm, and in a few weeks the intended lynching was only a memory. The robbery and assault, however, still remained a mystery to all but a chosen few. The affair had been dropped as absolutely as though it had never occurred. No colored man ever learned the reason of this sudden change of front, and Sandy Campbell's loyalty to his old employer's memory kept him silent. Tom Delamere did not offer to retain Sandy in his service, though he presented him with most of the old gentleman's wardrobe. It is only justice to Tom to state that up to this time he had not been informed of the contents of his grandfather's latest will. Major Carteret gave Sandy employment as butler, thus making a sort of vicarious atonement, on the part of the white race, of which the major felt himself in a way the embodiment, for the risk to which Sandy had been subjected.

Shortly after these events Sandy was restored to the bosom of the church, and, enfolded by its sheltering arms, was no longer tempted to stray from the path of rectitude, but became even a more rigid Methodist than before his recent troubles.

Tom Delamere did not call upon Clara again in the character of a lover. Of course they could not help meeting, from time to time, but he never dared presume upon their former relations. Indeed, the social atmosphere of Wellington remained so frigid toward Delamere that he left town, and did not return for several months.

Ellis was aware that Delamere had been thrown over, but a certain delicacy restrained him from following up immediately the advantage which the absence of his former rival gave him. It seemed to him, with the quixotry of a clean, pure mind, that Clara would pass through a period of mourning for her lost illusion, and that it would be indelicate, for the time being, to approach her with a lover's attentions. The work of the office had been unusually heavy of late. The major, deeply absorbed in politics, left the detail work of the paper to Ellis. Into the intimate counsels of the revolutionary committee Ellis had not been admitted, nor would he have desired to be. He knew, of course, in a general way, the results that it was sought to achieve; and while he did not see their necessity, he deferred to the views of older men, and was satisfied to remain in ignorance of anything which he might disapprove. Moreover, his own personal affairs occupied his mind to an extent that made politics or any other subject a matter of minor importance.

As for Dr. Miller, he never learned of Mr. Delamere's good intentions toward his institution, but regretted the old gentleman's death as the loss of a sincere friend and well-wisher of his race in their unequal struggle.

Despite the untiring zeal of Carteret and his associates, the campaign for the restriction of the suffrage, which was to form the basis of a permanent white supremacy, had seemed to languish for a while after the Ochiltree affair. The lull, however, was only temporary, and more apparent than real, for the forces adverse to the negro were merely gathering strength for a more vigorous assault. While little was said in Wellington, public sentiment all over the country became every day more favorable to the views of the conspirators. The nation was rushing forward with giant strides toward colossal wealth and world-dominion, before the exigencies of which mere abstract ethical theories must not be permitted to stand. The same argument that justified the conquest of an inferior nation could not be denied to those who sought the suppression of an inferior race. In the South, all obscure jealousy of the negro's progress, an obscure fear of the very equality so contemptuously denied, furnished a rich soil for successful agitation. Statistics of crime, ingeniously manipulated, were made to present a fearful showing against the negro. Vital statistics were made to prove that he had degenerated from an imaginary standard of physical excellence which had existed under the benign influence of slavery. Constant lynchings emphasized his impotence, and bred everywhere a growing contempt for his rights.

At the North, a new Pharaoh had risen, who knew not Israel,—a new generation, who knew little of the fierce passions which had played around the negro in a past epoch, and derived their opinions of him from the "coon song" and the police reports. Those of his old friends who survived were disappointed that he had not flown with clipped wings; that he had not in one generation of limited opportunity attained the level of the whites. The whole race question seemed to have reached a sort of *impasse*, a blind alley, of which no one could see the outlet. The negro had become a target at which any one might try a shot. Schoolboys gravely debated the question as to whether or not the negro should exercise the franchise. The pessimist gave him up in despair; while the optimist, smilingly confident that everything would come out all right in the end, also turned aside and went his buoyant way to more pleasing themes.

For a time there were white men in the state who opposed any reactionary step unless it were of general application. They were conscientious men, who had learned the ten commandments and wished to do right; but this class was a small minority, and their objections were soon silenced by the all-powerful race argument. Selfishness is the most constant of human motives. Patriotism, humanity, or the love of God may lead to sporadic outbursts which sweep away the heaped-up wrongs of centuries; but they languish at times, while the love of self works

225

on ceaselessly, unwearyingly, burrowing always at the very roots of life, and heaping up fresh wrongs for other centuries to sweep away. The state was at the mercy of venal and self-seeking politicians, bent upon regaining their ascendency at any cost, stultifying their own minds by vague sophistries and high-sounding phrases, which deceived none but those who wished to be deceived, and these but imperfectly; and dulling the public conscience by a loud clamor in which the calm voice of truth was for the moment silenced. So the cause went on.

Carteret, as spokesman of the campaign, and sincerest of all its leaders, performed prodigies of labor. The Morning Chronicle proclaimed, in season and out, the doctrine of "White Supremacy." Leaving the paper in charge of Ellis, the major made a tour of the state, rousing the white people of the better class to an appreciation of the terrible danger which confronted them in the possibility that a few negroes might hold a few offices or dictate the terms upon which white men should fill them. Difficulties were explained away. The provisions of the Federal Constitution, it was maintained, must yield to the "higher law," and if the Constitution could neither be altered nor bent to this end, means must be found to circumvent it.

The device finally hit upon for disfranchising the colored people in this particular state was the notorious "grandfather clause." After providing various restrictions of the suffrage, based upon education, character, and property, which it was deemed would in effect disfranchise the colored race, an exception was made in favor of all citizens whose fathers or grandfathers had been entitled to vote prior to 1867. Since none but white men could vote prior to 1867, this exception obviously took in the poor and ignorant whites, while the same class of negroes were excluded.

It was ingenious, but it was not fair. In due time a constitutional convention was called, in which the above scheme was adopted and submitted to a vote of the people for ratification. The campaign was fought on the color line. Many white Republicans, deluded with the hope that by the elimination of the negro vote their party might receive accessions from the Democratic ranks, went over to the white party. By fraud in one place, by terrorism in another, and everywhere by the resistless moral force of the united whites, the negroes were reduced to the apathy of despair, their few white allies demoralized, and the amendment adopted by a large majority. The negroes were taught that this is a white man's country, and that the sooner they made up their minds to this fact, the better for all concerned. The white people would be good to them so long as they behaved themselves and kept their place. As theoretical equals,—practical equality being forever out of the question, either by nature or by law,—there could have been nothing but strife between them, in which the weaker party would invariably have suffered most.

Some colored men accepted the situation thus outlined, if not as desirable, at least as inevitable. Most of them, however, had little faith in this condescending friendliness which was to take the place of constitutional rights. They knew they had been treated unfairly; that their enemies had prevailed against them; that their whilom friends had stood passively by and seen them undone. Many of the most enterprising and progressive left the state, and those who remain still labor under a sense of wrong and outrage which renders them distinctly less valuable as citizens.

The great steal was made, but the thieves did not turn honest,—the scheme still shows the mark of the burglar's tools. Sins, like chickens, come home to roost. The South paid a fearful price for the wrong of negro slavery; in some form or other it will doubtless reap the fruits of this later iniquity.

Drastic as were these "reforms," the results of which we have anticipated somewhat, since the new Constitution was not to take effect immediately, they moved all too slowly for the little coterie of Wellington conspirators, whose ambitions and needs urged them to prompt action. Under the new Constitution it would be two full years before the "nigger amendment " became effective, and meanwhile the Wellington district would remain hopelessly Republican. The committee decided, about two months before the fall election, that an active local campaign must be carried on, with a view to discourage the negroes from attending the polls on election day.

The question came up for discussion one forenoon in a meeting at the office of the Morning Chronicle, at which all of the "Big Three" were present.

"Something must be done," declared McBane, "and that damn quick. Too many white people are saying that it will be better to wait until the amendment goes into effect. That would mean to leave the niggers in charge of this town for two years after the state has declared for white supremacy! I'm opposed to leaving it in their hands one hour,—them 's my sentiments!"

This proved to be the general opinion, and the discussion turned to the subject of ways and means.

"What became of that editorial in the nigger paper?" inquired the general in his blandest tones, cleverly directing a smoke ring toward the ceiling. "It lost some of its point back there, when we came near lynching that nigger; but now that that has blown over, why wouldn't it be a good thing to bring into play at the present juncture? Let's read it over again."

Carteret extracted the paper from the pigeon-hole where he had placed it some months before. The article was read aloud with emphasis and discussed phrase by phrase. Of its wording there could be little criticism,— it was temperately and even cautiously phrased. As suggested by the general, the Ochiltree affair had proved that it was not devoid of truth. Its great offensiveness lay in its boldness: that a negro should publish in a newspaper what white people would scarcely acknowledge to themselves in secret was much as though a Russian *moujik* or a German peasant should rush into print to question the divine right of the Lord's Anointed. The article was racial *lèse-majesté* in the most aggravated form. A peg was needed upon which to hang a *coup d'état*, and this editorial offered the requisite opportunity. It was unanimously decided to republish the obnoxious article, with comment adapted to fire the inflammable Southern heart and rouse it against any further self-assertion of the negroes in politics or elsewhere.

"The time is ripe!" exclaimed McBane. "In a month we can have the niggers so scared that they won't dare stick their heads out of doors on 'lection day."

"I wonder," observed the general thoughtfully, after

this conclusion had been reached, "if we could n't have Jerry fetch us some liquor?"

Jerry appeared in response to the usual summons. The general gave him the money, and ordered three Calhoun cocktails. When Jerry returned with the glasses on a tray, the general observed him with pointed curiosity.

"What in h——ll is the matter with you, Jerry? Your black face is splotched with brown and yellow patches, and your hair shines as though you had fallen head-foremost into a firkin of butter. What 's the matter with you?"

Jerry seemed much embarrassed by this inquiry.

"Nothin', suh, nothin'," he stammered. "It's—it's jes' somethin' I be'n puttin' on my hair, suh, ter improve de quality, suh."

"Jerry," returned the general, bending a solemn look upon the porter, "you have been playing with edged tools, and your days are numbered. You have been reading the Afro-American Banner."

He shook open the paper, which he had retained in his hand, and read from one of the advertisements:—

"'Kinky, curly hair made straight in two applications. Dark skins lightened two shades; mulattoes turned perfectly white.'

"This stuff is rank poison, Jerry," continued the general with a mock solemnity which did not impose upon Jerry, who nevertheless listened with an air of great alarm. He suspected that the general was making fun of him; but he also knew that the general would like to think that Jerry believed him in earnest; and to please the white folks was Jerry's consistent aim in life. "I can see the signs of decay in your face, and your hair will all fall out in a week or two at the latest,—mark my words!"

230

McBane had listened to this pleasantry with a sardonic sneer. It was a waste of valuable time. To Carteret it seemed in doubtful taste. These grotesque advertisements had their tragic side. They were proof that the negroes had read the handwriting on the wall. These pitiful attempts to change their physical characteristics were an acknowledgment, on their own part, that the negro was doomed, and that the white man was to inherit the earth and hold all other races under his heel. For, as the months had passed, Carteret's thoughts, centring more and more upon the negro, had led him farther and farther, until now he was firmly convinced that there was no permanent place for the negro in the United States, if indeed anywhere in the world, except under the ground. More pathetic even than Jerry's efforts to escape from the universal doom of his race was his ignorance that even if he could, by some strange alchemy, bleach his skin and straighten his hair, there would still remain, underneath it all, only the unbleached darky,—the ass in the lion's skin.

When the general had finished his facetious lecture, Jerry backed out of the room shamefacedly, though affecting a greater confusion than he really felt. Jerry had not reasoned so closely as Carteret, but he had realized that it was a distinct advantage to be white,—an advantage which white people had utilized to secure all the best things in the world; and he had entertained the vague hope that by changing his complexion he might share this prerogative. While he suspected the general's sincerity, he nevertheless felt a little apprehensive lest the general's prediction about the effects of the face-bleach and other preparations might prove true,—the general was a white gentleman and ought to know,—and decided to abandon their use.

This purpose was strengthened by his next interview with the major. When Carteret summoned him, an hour later, after the other gentlemen had taken their leave, Jerry had washed his head thoroughly and there remained no trace of the pomade. An attempt to darken the lighter spots in his cuticle by the application of printer's ink had not proved equally successful,—the retouching left the spots as much too dark as they had formerly been too light.

"Jerry," said Carteret sternly, "when I hired you to work for the Chronicle, you were black. The word 'negro' means 'black.' The best negro is a black negro, of the pure type, as it came from the hand of God. If you wish to get along well with the white people, the blacker you are the better,—white people do not like negroes who want to be white. A man should be content to remain as God made him and where God placed him. So no more of this nonsense. Are you going to vote at the next election?"

"What would you 'vise me ter do, suh?" asked Jerry cautiously.

"I do not advise you. You ought to have sense enough to see where your own interests lie. I put it to you whether you cannot trust yourself more safely in the hands of white gentlemen, who are your true friends, than in the hands of ignorant and purchasable negroes and unscrupulous white scoundrels?"

"Dere's no doubt about it, suh," assented Jerry, with a vehemence proportioned to his desire to get back into favor. "I ain' gwine ter have nothin' ter do wid de 'lection, suh! Ef I don' vote, I kin keep my job, can't I, suh?"

The major eyed Jerry with an air of supreme disgust. What could be expected of a race so utterly devoid of tact? It seemed as though this negro thought a white gentleman might want to bribe him to remain away from the polls; and the negro's willingness to accept the imaginary bribe demonstrated the venal nature of the colored race,—its entire lack of moral principle!

"You will retain your place, Jerry," he said severely, "so long as you perform your duties to my satisfaction and behave yourself properly."

With this grandiloquent subterfuge Carteret turned to his next article on white supremacy. Jerry did not delude himself with any fine-spun sophistry. He knew perfectly well that he held his job upon the condition that he stayed away from the polls at the approaching election. Jerry was a fool—

> "The world of fools hath such a store,
> That he who would not see an ass,
> Must stay at home and shut his door
> And break his looking-glass."

But while no one may be entirely wise, there are degrees of folly, and Jerry was not all kinds of a fool.

XXIX
MUTTERINGS OF THE STORM

EVENTS moved rapidly during the next few days. The reproduction, in the Chronicle, of the article from the Afro-

American Banner, with Carteret's inflammatory comment, took immediate effect. It touched the Southern white man in his most sensitive spot. To him such an article was an insult to white womanhood, and must be resented by some active steps,—mere words would be no answer at all. To meet words with words upon such a subject would be to acknowledge the equality of the negro and his right to discuss or criticise the conduct of the white people.

The colored people became alarmed at the murmurings of the whites, which seemed to presage a coming storm. A number of them sought to arm themselves, but ascertained, upon inquiring at the stores, that no white merchant would sell a negro firearms. Since all the dealers in this sort of merchandise were white men, the negroes had to be satisfied with oiling up the old army muskets which some of them possessed, and the few revolvers with which a small rowdy element generally managed to keep themselves supplied. Upon an effort being made to purchase firearms from a Northern city, the express company, controlled by local men, refused to accept the consignment. The white people, on the other hand, procured both arms and ammunition in large quantities, and the Wellington Grays drilled with great assiduity at their armory.

All this went on without any public disturbance of the town's tranquillity. A stranger would have seen nothing to excite his curiosity. The white people did their talking among themselves, and merely grew more distant in their manner toward the colored folks, who instinctively closed their ranks as the whites drew away. With each day that passed the feeling grew more tense. The editor of the Afro-American Banner, whose office had been quietly garrisoned for several nights by armed negroes, became frightened, and disappeared from the town between two suns.

The conspirators were jubilant at the complete success of their plans. It only remained for them to so direct this aroused public feeling that it might completely accomplish the desired end,—to change the political complexion of the city government and assure the ascendancy of the whites until the amendment should go into effect. A revolution, and not a riot, was contemplated.

With this end in view, another meeting was called at Carteret's office.

"We are now ready," announced General Belmont, "for the final act of this drama. We must decide promptly, or events may run away from us."

"What do you suggest?" asked Carteret.

"Down in the American tropics," continued the general, "they have a way of doing things. I was in Nicaragua, ten years ago, when Paterno's revolution drove out Igorroto's government. It was as easy as falling off a log. Paterno had the arms and the best men. Igorroto was not looking for trouble, and the guns were at his breast before he knew it. We have the guns. The negroes are not expecting trouble, and are easy to manage compared with the fiery mixture that flourishes in the tropics."

"I should not advocate murder," returned Carteret. "We are animated by high and holy principles. We wish to right a wrong, to remedy an abuse, to save our state from anarchy and our race from humiliation. I don't object to frightening the negroes, but I am opposed to unnecessary bloodshed."

"I'm not quite so particular," struck in McBane. "They need to be taught a lesson, and a nigger more or less would n't be missed. There's too many of 'em now."

"Of course," continued Carteret, "if we should decide upon a certain mode of procedure, and the negroes should resist, a different reasoning might apply; but I will have no premeditated murder."

"In Central and South America," observed the general reflectively, "none are hurt except those who get in the way."

"There'll be no niggers hurt," said McBane contemptuously, "unless they strain themselves running. One white man can chase a hundred of 'em. I've managed five hundred at a time. I'll pay for burying all the niggers that are killed."

The conference resulted in a well-defined plan, to be put into operation the following day, by which the city government was to be wrested from the Republicans and their negro allies.

"And now," said General Belmont, "while we are cleansing the Augean stables, we may as well remove the cause as the effect. There are several negroes too many in this town, which will be much the better without them. There's that yellow lawyer, Watson. He's altogether too mouthy, and has too much business. Every nigger that gets into trouble sends for Watson, and white lawyers, with families to support and social positions to keep up, are deprived of their legitimate source of income."

"There's that damn nigger real estate agent," blurted out McBane. "Billy Kitchen used to get most of the nigger business, but this darky has almost driven him to the poorhouse. A white business man is entitled to a living in his own profession and his own home. That nigger don't belong, here nohow. He came from the North a year or two ago, and is hand in glove with Barber, the nigger editor, which is enough of itself to damn him. *He'll* have to go!"

"How about the collector of the port?"

"We'd better not touch him. It would bring the government down upon us, which we want to avoid. We don't need to worry about the nigger preachers either. They want to stay here, where the loaves and the fishes are. We can make 'em write letters to the newspapers justifying our course, as a condition of their remaining."

"What about Billings?" asked McBane. Billings was the white Republican mayor. "Is that skunk to be allowed to stay in town?"

"No," returned the general, "every white Republican office-holder ought to be made to go. This town is only big enough for Democrats, and negroes who can be taught to keep their place."

"What about the colored doctor," queried McBane, "with the hospital, and the diamond ring, and the carriage, and the other fallals?"

"I shouldn't interfere with Miller," replied the general decisively. "He's a very good sort of a negro, does n't meddle with politics, nor tread on any one else's toes. His father was a good citizen, which counts in his favor. He's spending money in the community too, and contributes to its prosperity."

"That sort of nigger, though, sets a bad example," retorted McBane. "They make it all the harder to keep the rest of 'em down."

"'One swallow does not make a summer,'" quoted the general. "When we get things arranged, there'll be no trouble. A stream cannot rise higher than its fountain, and a smart nigger without a constituency will no longer be an object of fear. I say, let the doctor alone."

"He'll have to keep mighty quiet, though," muttered McBane discontentedly. "I don't like smart niggers. I've had to shoot several of them, in the course of my life."

"Personally, I dislike the man," interposed Carteret, "and if I consulted my own inclinations, would say expel him with the rest; but my grievance is a personal one, and to gratify it in that way would be a loss to the community. I wish to be strictly impartial in this matter, and to take no step which cannot be entirely justified by a wise regard for the public welfare."

"What's the use of all this hypocrisy, gentlemen?" sneered McBane. "Every last one of us has an axe to grind! The major may as well put an edge on his. We'll never get a better chance to have things our way. If this nigger doctor annoys the major, we'll run him out with the rest. This is a white man's country, and a white man's city, and no nigger has any business here when a white man wants him gone!"

Carteret frowned darkly at this brutal characterization of their motives. It robbed the enterprise of all its poetry, and put a solemn act of revolution upon the plane of a mere vulgar theft of power. Even the general winced.

"I would not consent," he said irritably, "to Miller's being disturbed."

McBane made no further objection.

There was a discreet knock at the door.

"Come in," said Carteret.

Jerry entered. "Mistuh Ellis wants ter speak ter you a minute, suh," he said.

Carteret excused himself and left the room.

238

"Jerry," said the general, "you lump of ebony, the sight of you reminds me! If your master does n't want you for a minute, step across to Mr. Brown's and tell him to send me three cocktails."

"Yas, suh," responded Jerry, hesitating. The general had said nothing about paying.

"And tell him, Jerry, to charge them. I 'm short of change to-day."

" Yas, suh; yas, suh," replied Jerry, as he backed out of the presence, adding, when he had reached the hall: "Dere ain' no change fer Jerry dis time, sho': I'll jes' make dat *fo'* cocktails, an' de gin'l won't never know de diffe'nce. I ain' gwine 'cross de road fer nothin', not ef I knows it."

Half an hour later, the conspirators dispersed. They had fixed the hour of the proposed revolution, the course to be pursued, the results to be obtained; but in stating their equation they had overlooked one factor,—God, or Fate, or whatever one may choose to call the Power that holds the destinies of man in the hollow of his hand.

XXX
THE MISSING PAPERS

MRS. CARTERET was very much disturbed. It was supposed that the shock of her aunt's death had affected her health, for since that event she had fallen into a nervous condition which gave the major grave concern. Much to the general surprise, Mrs. Ochiltree had left no will, and no property of any considerable value except her homestead, which descended to Mrs. Carteret as the natural heir. Whatever she may have had on hand in the way of ready money had undoubtedly been abstracted from the cedar chest by the midnight marauder, to whose visit her death was immediately due. Her niece's grief was held to mark a deep-seated affection for the grim old woman who had reared her.

Mrs. Carteret's present state of mind, of which her nervousness was a sufficiently accurate reflection, did in truth date from her aunt's death, and also in part from the time of the conversation with Mrs. Ochiltree, one afternoon, during and after the drive past Miller's new hospital. Mrs. Ochiltree had grown steadily more and more childish after that time, and her niece had never succeeded in making her pick up the thread of thought where it had been dropped. At any rate, Mrs. Ochiltree had made no further disclosure upon the subject.

An examination, not long after her aunt's death, of the papers found near the cedar chest on the morning after the murder had contributed to Mrs. Carteret's enlightenment, but had not promoted her peace of mind.

When Mrs. Carteret reached home, after her hurried exploration of the cedar chest, she thrust into a bureau drawer the envelope she had found. So fully was her mind occupied, for several days, with the funeral, and with the excitement attending the arrest of Sandy Campbell, that she deferred the examination of the contents of the envelope until near the end of the week.

One morning, while alone in her chamber, she drew the envelope from the drawer, and was holding it in her hand, hesitating as to whether or not she should open it, when the baby in the next room began to cry.

The child's cry seemed like a warning, and yielding to a vague uneasiness, she put the paper back.

"Phil," she said to her husband at luncheon, "Aunt Polly said some strange things to me one day before she died,—I don't know whether she was quite in her right mind or not; but suppose that my father had left a will by which it was provided that half his property should go to that woman and her child?"

"It would never have gone by such a will," replied the major easily. "Your Aunt Polly was in her dotage, and merely dreaming. Your father would never have been such a fool; but even if he had, no such will could have stood the test of the courts. It would clearly have been due to the improper influence of a designing woman."

"So that legally, as well as morally," said Mrs. Carteret, "the will would have been of no effect?"

"Not the slightest. A jury would soon have broken down the legal claim. As for any moral obligation, there would have been nothing moral about the affair. The only possible consideration for such a gift was an immoral one. I don't wish to speak harshly of your father, my dear, but his conduct was gravely reprehensible. The woman herself had no right or claim whatever; she would have been whipped and expelled from the town, if justice—blind, bleeding justice, then prostrate at the feet of slaves and aliens—could have had her way!"

"But the child"—

"The child was in the same category. Who was she, to have inherited the estate of your ancestors, of which, a few years before, she would herself have formed a part?

The child of shame, it was hers to pay the penalty. But the discussion is all in the air, Olivia. Your father never did and never would have left such a will."

This conversation relieved Mrs. Carteret's uneasiness. Going to her room shortly afterwards, she took the envelope from her bureau drawer and drew out a bulky paper. The haunting fear that it might be such a will as her aunt had suggested was now removed; for such an instrument, in the light of what her husband had said confirming her own intuitions, would be of no valid effect. It might be just as well, she thought, to throw the paper in the fire without looking at it. She wished to think as well as might be of her father, and she felt that her respect for his memory would not be strengthened by the knowledge that he had meant to leave his estate away from her; for her aunt's words had been open to the construction that she was to have been left destitute. Curiosity strongly prompted her to read the paper. Perhaps the will contained no such provision as she had feared, and it might convey some request or direction which ought properly to be complied with.

She had been standing in front of the bureau while these thoughts passed through her mind, and now, dropping the envelope back into the drawer mechanically, she unfolded the document. It was written on legal paper, in her father's own hand.

Mrs. Carteret was not familiar with legal verbiage, and there were several expressions of which she did not perhaps appreciate the full effect; but a very hasty glance enabled her to ascertain the purport of the paper. It was a will, by which, in one item, her father devised to his daughter Janet, the child of the woman known as Julia

Brown, the sum of ten thousand dollars, and a certain plantation or tract of land a short distance from the town of Wellington. The rest and residue of his estate, after deducting all legal charges and expenses, was bequeathed to his beloved daughter, Olivia Merkell.

Mrs. Carteret breathed a sigh of relief. Her father had not preferred another to her, but had left to his lawful daughter the bulk of his estate. She felt at the same time a growing indignation at the thought that that woman should so have wrought upon her father's weakness as to induce him to think of leaving so much valuable property to her bastard,—property which by right should go, and now would go, to her own son, to whom by every rule of law and decency it ought to descend.

A fire was burning in the next room, on account of the baby,—there had been a light frost the night before, and the air was somewhat chilly. For the moment the room was empty. Mrs. Carteret came out from her chamber and threw the offending paper into the fire, and watched it slowly burn. When it had been consumed, the carbon residue of one sheet still retained its form, and she could read the words on the charred portion. A sentence, which had escaped her eye in her rapid reading, stood out in ghostly black upon the gray background:—

"All the rest and residue of my estate I devise and bequeath to my daughter Olivia Merkell, the child of my beloved first wife."

Mrs. Carteret had not before observed the word "first." Instinctively she stretched toward the fire the poker which she held in her hand, and at its touch the shadowy remnant fell to pieces, and nothing but ashes remained upon the hearth.

Not until the next morning did she think again of the envelope which had contained the paper she had burned. Opening the drawer where it lay, the oblong blue envelope confronted her. The sight of it was distasteful. The indorsed side lay uppermost, and the words seemed like a mute reproach:—

"The Last Will and Testament of Samuel Merkell."

Snatching up the envelope, she glanced into it mechanically as she moved toward the next room, and perceived a thin folded paper which had heretofore escaped her notice. When opened, it proved to be a certificate of marriage, in due form, between Samuel Merkell and Julia Brown. It was dated from a county in South Carolina, about two years before her father's death.

For a moment Mrs. Carteret stood gazing blankly at this faded slip of paper. Her father *had* married this woman!—at least he had gone through the form of marriage with her, for to him it had surely been no more than an empty formality. The marriage of white and colored persons was forbidden by law. Only recently she had read of a case where both the parties to such a crime, a colored man and a white woman, had been sentenced to long terms in the penitentiary. She even recalled the circumstances. The couple had been living together unlawfully,—they were very low people, whose private lives were beneath the public notice,—but influenced by a religious movement pervading the community, had sought, they said at the trial, to secure the blessing of God upon their union. The higher law, which imperiously demanded that the purity and prestige of the white race be preserved at any cost, had intervened at this point.

Mechanically she moved toward the fireplace, so

dazed by this discovery as to be scarcely conscious of her own actions. She surely had not formed any definite intention of destroying this piece of paper when her fingers relaxed unconsciously and let go their hold upon it. The draught swept it toward the fireplace. Ere scarcely touching the flames it caught, blazed fiercely, and shot upward with the current of air. A moment later the record of poor Julia's marriage was scattered to the four winds of heaven, as her poor body had long since mingled with the dust of earth.

The letter remained unread. In her agitation at the discovery of the marriage certificate, Olivia had almost forgotten the existence of the letter. It was addressed to "John Delamere, Esq., as Executor of my Last Will and Testament," while the lower left-hand corner bore the direction: "To be delivered only after my death, with seal unbroken."

The seal was broken already; Mr. Delamere was dead; the letter could never be delivered. Mrs. Carteret unfolded it and read:—

My Dear Delamere,—I have taken the liberty of naming you as executor of my last will, because you are my friend, and the only man of my acquaintance whom I feel that I can trust to carry out my wishes, appreciate my motives, and preserve the silence I desire.

I have, first, a confession to make. Inclosed in this letter you will find a certificate of marriage between my child Janet's mother and myself. While I have never exactly repented of this marriage, I have never had the courage to acknowledge it openly. If I had not married Julia, I fear Polly Ochiltree would have married me by main force,—as she would marry you or any other gentleman unfortunate enough to fall in the way of this twice-widowed man-hunter. When my wife died, three years ago, her sister Polly offered to keep house for me and the child. I would sooner have had the devil in the house, and yet I trembled with alarm,—there seemed no way of escape,—it was so clearly and obviously the proper thing.

But she herself gave me my opportunity. I was on the point of consenting, when she demanded, as a condition of her coming, that I discharge Julia, my late wife's maid. She was laboring under a misapprehension in regard to the girl, but I grasped at the straw, and did everything to foster her delusion. I declared solemnly that nothing under heaven would induce me to part with Julia. The controversy resulted in my permitting Polly to take the child, while I retained the maid.

Before Polly put this idea into my head, I had scarcely looked at Julia, but this outbreak turned my attention toward her. She was a handsome girl, and, as I soon found out, a good girl. My wife, who raised her, was a Christian woman, and had taught her modesty and virtue. She was free. The air was full of liberty, and equal rights, and all the abolition clap-trap, and she made marriage a condition of her remaining longer in the house. In a moment of weakness I took her away to a place where we were not known, and married her. If she had left me, I should have fallen a victim to Polly Ochiltree,—to which any fate was preferable.

And then, old friend, my weakness kept to the fore. I was ashamed of this marriage, and my new wife saw it. Moreover, she loved me,—too well, indeed, to wish to make me unhappy. The ceremony had satisfied her conscience, had set her right, she said, with God; for the opinions of men she did not care, since I loved her,—she only wanted to compensate me, as best she could, for the great honor I had done my handmaiden,—for she had read her Bible, and I was the Abraham to her Hagar, compared with whom she considered herself at a great advantage. It was her own proposition that nothing be said of this marriage. If any shame should fall on her, it would fall lightly, for it would be undeserved. When the child came, she still kept silence. No one, she argued, could blame an innocent child for the accident of birth, and in the sight of God this child had every right to exist; while among her own people illegitimacy would involve but little stigma.

I need not say that I was easily persuaded to accept this sacrifice; but touched by her fidelity, I swore to provide handsomely for them both. This I have tried to do by the will of which I ask you to act as executor. Had I left the child more, it might serve as a ground for attacking the will; my acknowledgment of the tie of blood is sufficient to justify a reasonable bequest.

I have taken this course for the sake of my daughter Olivia, who is dear to me, and whom I would not wish to make ashamed; and in deference to public opinion, which it is not easy to defy. If, after my death, Julia should choose to make our secret known, I shall of course be beyond the reach of hard words; but loyalty to my memory will probably keep her silent. A strong man would long since have acknowledged her before the world and taken the consequences; but, alas! I am only myself, and the atmosphere I live in does not encourage moral heroism. I should like to be different, but it is God who hath made us, and not we ourselves!

Nevertheless, old friend, I will ask of you one favor. If in the future this child of Julia's and of mine should grow to womanhood; if she should prove to have her mother's gentleness and love of virtue; if, in the new era which is opening up for her mother's race, to which, unfortunately, she must belong, she should become, in time, an educated woman; and if the time should ever come when, by virtue of her education or the development of her people, it would be to her a source of shame or unhappiness that she was an illegitimate child,—if you are still alive, old friend, and have the means of knowing or divining this thing, go to her and tell her, for me, that she is my lawful child, and ask her to forgive her father's weakness.

When this letter comes to you, I shall have passed to— the Beyond; but I am confident that you will accept this trust, for which I thank you now, in advance, most heartily.

The letter was signed with her father's name, the same signature which had been attached to the will.

Having firmly convinced herself of the illegality of the papers, and of her own right to destroy them, Mrs. Carteret ought to have felt relieved that she had thus removed all traces of her dead father's folly. True, the other daughter remained,—she had seen her on the street only the day before. The sight of this person she had always found offensive, and now, she felt, in view of what she had just learned, it must be even more so. Never, while this woman lived in the town, would she be able to throw the veil of forgetfulness over this blot upon her father's memory.

As the day wore on, Mrs. Carteret grew still less at ease. To herself, marriage was a serious thing,—to a right-thinking woman the most serious concern of life. A marriage certificate, rightfully procured, was scarcely less solemn, so far as it went, than the Bible itself. Her own she cherished as the apple of her eye. It was the evidence of her wifehood, the seal of her child's legitimacy, her patent of nobility,—the token of her own and her child's claim to social place and consideration. She had burned this pretended marriage certificate because it meant nothing. Nevertheless, she could not ignore the knowledge of another such marriage, of which every one in the town knew,—a celebrated case, indeed, where a white man, of a family quite as prominent as her father's, had married a colored woman during the military occupation of the state just after the civil war. The legality of the marriage had never been questioned. It had been fully consummated by twenty years of subsequent cohabitation. No amount of social persecution had ever shaken the position of the husband. With an iron will he had stayed on in the town, a living protest against the established customs of the South, so rudely interrupted for a few short years; and, though his children were negroes, though he had never appeared in public with his wife, no one had ever questioned the validity of his marriage or the legitimacy of his offspring.

The marriage certificate which Mrs. Carteret had burned dated from the period of the military occupation. Hence Mrs. Carteret, who was a good woman, and would not have done a dishonest thing, felt decidedly uncomfortable. She had destroyed the marriage certificate, but its ghost still haunted her.

Major Carteret, having just eaten a good dinner, was in a very agreeable humor when, that same evening, his wife brought up again the subject of their previous discussion.

"Phil," she asked, "Aunt Polly told me that once, long before my father died, when she went to remonstrate with him for keeping that woman in the house, he threatened to marry Julia if Aunt Polly ever said another word to him about the matter. Suppose he *had* married her, and had *then* left a will,—would the marriage have made any difference, so far as the will was concerned?"

Major Carteret laughed. "Your Aunt Polly," he said, "was a remarkable woman, with a wonderful imagination, which seems to have grown more vivid as her memory and judgment weakened. Why should your father marry his negro housemaid? Mr. Merkell was never rated as a fool,—he had one of the clearest heads in Wellington. I saw him only a day or two before he died, and I could swear before any court in Christendom that he was of sound mind and memory to the last. These notions of your aunt were mere delusions. Your father was never capable of such a folly."

"Of course I am only supposing a case," returned Olivia. "Imagining such a case, just for the argument, would the marriage have been legal?"

"That would depend. If he had married her during the military occupation, or over in South Carolina, the marriage would have been legally valid, though morally and socially outrageous."

"And if he had died afterwards, leaving a will?"

"The will would have controlled the disposition of his estate, in all probability."

"Suppose he had left no will?"

"You are getting the matter down pretty fine, my dear! The woman would have taken one third of the real estate for life, and could have lived in the homestead until she died. She would also have had half the other property,—the money and goods and furniture, everything except the land,—and the negro child would have shared with you the balance of the estate. That, I believe, is according to the law of descent and distribution."

Mrs. Carteret lapsed into a troubled silence. Her father *had* married the woman. In her heart she had no doubt of the validity of the marriage, so far as the law was concerned; if one marriage of such a kind would stand, another contracted under similar conditions was equally as good. If the marriage had been valid, Julia's child had been legitimate. The will she had burned gave this sister of hers—she shuddered at the word—but a small part of the estate. Under the law, which intervened now that there was no will, the property should have been equally divided. If the woman had been white,— but the woman had *not* been white, and the same rule of moral conduct did not, *could* not, in the very nature of things, apply, as between white people! For, if this were not so, slavery had been, not merely an economic mistake, but a great crime against humanity. If it had been such a crime, as for a moment she dimly perceived it might have been, then through the long centuries there had been piled up a catalogue of wrong and outrage which, if the law of compensation be a law of nature, must some time, somewhere, in some way, be atoned for. She herself had not escaped the penalty, of which, she realized, this burden placed upon her conscience was but another installment.

If she should make known the facts she had learned, it would mean what?—a division of her father's estate, a recognition of the legality of her father's relations with Julia. Such a stain upon her father's memory would be infinitely worse than if he had not married her. To have lived with her without marriage was a social misdemeanor, at which society in the old days had winked, or at most had frowned. To have married her was to have committed the unpardonable social sin. Such a scandal Mrs. Carteret could not have endured. Should she seek to make restitution, it would necessarily involve the disclosure of at least some of the facts. Had she not destroyed the will, she might have compromised with her conscience by producing it and acting upon its terms, which had been so stated as not to disclose the marriage. This was now rendered impossible by her own impulsive act; she could not mention the will at all, without admitting that she had destroyed it.

Mrs. Carteret found herself in what might be called, vulgarly, a moral "pocket." She could, of course, remain silent. Mrs. Carteret was a good woman, according to her lights, with a cultivated conscience, to which she had always looked as her mentor and infallible guide.

Hence Mrs. Carteret, after this painful discovery, remained for a long time ill at ease,—so disturbed, indeed, that her mind reacted upon her nerves, which had never been strong; and her nervousness affected her strength, which had never been great, until Carteret, whose love for her had been deepened and strengthened by the advent of his son, became alarmed for her health, and spoke very seriously to Dr. Price concerning it.

XXXI
THE SHADOW OF A DREAM

MRS. CARTERET awoke, with a start, from a troubled dream. She had been sailing across a sunlit sea, in a beautiful boat, her child lying on a bright-colored cushion at her feet. Overhead the swelling sail served as an awning to keep off the sun's rays, which far ahead were reflected with dazzling brilliancy from the shores of a golden island. Her son, she dreamed, was a fairy prince, and yonder lay his kingdom, to which he was being borne, lying there at her feet, in this beautiful boat, across the sunlit sea.

Suddenly and without warning the sky was over-cast. A squall struck the boat and tore away the sail. In the distance a huge billow—a great white wall of water— came sweeping toward their frail craft, threatening it with instant destruction. She clasped her child to her bosom, and a moment later found herself struggling in the sea, holding the child's head above the water. As she floated there, as though sustained by some unseen force, she saw in the distance a small boat approaching over the storm-tossed waves. Straight toward her it came, and she had reached out her hand to grasp its side, when the rower looked back, and she saw that it was her sister. The recognition had been mutual. With a sharp movement of one oar the boat glided by, leaving her clutching at the empty air.

She felt her strength begin to fail. Despairingly she signaled with her disengaged hand; but the rower, after one mute, reproachful glance, rowed on. Mrs. Carteret's strength grew less and less. The child became heavy as lead. Herself floating in the water, as though it were her native element, she could no longer support the child. Lower and lower it sank,—she was powerless to save it or to accompany it,—until, gasping wildly for breath, it threw up its little hands and sank, the cruel water gurgling over its head,—when she awoke with a start and a chill, and lay there trembling for several minutes before she heard little Dodie in his crib, breathing heavily.

She rose softly, went to the crib, and changed the child's position to an easier one. He breathed more freely, and she went back to bed, but not to sleep.

She had tried to put aside the distressing questions raised by the discovery of her father's will and the papers accompanying it. Why should she be burdened with such a responsibility, at this late day, when the touch of time had well-nigh healed these old sores? Surely, God had put his curse not alone upon the slave, but upon the stealer of men! With other good people she had thanked Him that slavery was no more, and that those who once had borne its burden upon their consciences could stand erect and feel that they themselves were free. The weed had been cut down, but its roots remained, deeply imbedded in the soil, to spring up and trouble a new generation. Upon her weak shoulders was placed the burden of her father's weakness, her father's folly. It was left to her to acknowledge or not this shameful marriage and her sister's rights in their father's estate.

Balancing one consideration against another she had almost decided that she might ignore this tie. To herself, Olivia Merkell,—Olivia Carteret,—the stigma of base birth would have meant social ostracism, social ruin, the averted face, the finger of pity or of scorn. All the tradi-

254

tional weight of public disapproval would have fallen upon her as the unhappy fruit of an unblessed union. To this other woman it could have had no such significance,—it had been the lot of her race. To them, twenty-five years before, sexual sin had never been imputed as more than a fault. She had lost nothing by her supposed illegitimacy; she would gain nothing by the acknowledgment of her mother's marriage.

On the other hand, what would be the effect of this revelation upon Mrs. Carteret herself? To have it known that her father had married a negress would only be less dreadful than to have it appear that he had committed some terrible crime. It was a crime now, by the laws of every Southern State, for white and colored persons to intermarry. She shuddered before the possibility that at some time in the future some person, none too well informed, might learn that her father had married a colored woman, and might assume that she, Olivia Carteret, or her child, had sprung from this shocking *mésalliance*,—a fate to which she would willingly have preferred death. No, this marriage must never be made known; the secret should remain buried forever in her own heart!

But there still remained the question of her father's property and her father's will. This woman was her father's child,—of that there could be no doubt, it was written in her features no less than in her father's will. As his lawful child,—of which, alas! there could also be no question,—she was entitled by law to half his estate. Mrs. Carteret's problem had sunk from the realm of sentiment to that of material things, which, curiously enough, she found much more difficult. For, while the negro, by the traditions of her people, was barred from the world of sentiment, his rights of property were recognized. The question had become, with Mrs. Carteret, a question of *meum* and *tuum*. Had the girl Janet been poor, ignorant, or degraded, as might well have been her fate, Mrs. Carteret might have felt a vicarious remorse for her aunt's suppression of the papers; but fate had compensated Janet for the loss; she had been educated, she had married well; she had not suffered for lack of the money of which she had been defrauded, and did not need it now. She had a child, it is true, but this child's career would be so circumscribed by the accident of color that too much wealth would only be a source of unhappiness; to her own child, on the contrary, it would open every door of life.

It would be too lengthy a task to follow the mind and conscience of this much-tried lady in their intricate workings upon this difficult problem; for she had a mind as logical as any woman's, and a conscience which she wished to keep void of offense. She had to confront a situation involving the element of race, upon which the moral standards of her people were hopelessly confused. Mrs. Carteret reached the conclusion, ere daylight dawned, that she would be silent upon the subject of her father's second marriage. Neither party had wished it known,—neither Julia nor her father,—and she would respect her father's wishes. To act otherwise would be to defeat his will, to make known what he had carefully concealed, and to give Janet a claim of title to one half her father's estate, while he had only meant her to have the ten thousand dollars named in the will.

By the same reasoning, she must carry out her father's

will in respect to this bequest. Here there was another difficulty. The mining investment into which they had entered shortly after the birth of little Dodie had tied up so much of her property that it would have been difficult to procure ten thousand dollars immediately; while a demand for half the property at once would mean bankruptcy and ruin. Moreover, upon what ground could she offer her sister any sum of money whatever? So sudden a change of heart, after so many years of silence, would raise the presumption of some right on the part of Janet in her father's estate. Suspicion once aroused, it might be possible to trace this hidden marriage, and establish it by legal proof. The marriage once verified, the claim for half the estate could not be denied. She could not plead her father's will to the contrary, for this would be to acknowledge the suppression of the will, in itself a criminal act.

There was, however, a way of escape. This hospital which had recently been opened was the personal property of her sister's husband. Some time in the future, when their investments matured, she would present to the hospital a sum of money equal to the amount her father had meant his colored daughter to have. Thus indirectly both her father's will and her own conscience would be satisfied.

Mrs. Carteret had reached this comfortable conclusion, and was falling asleep, when her attention was again drawn by her child's breathing. She took it in her own arms and soon fell asleep.

"By the way, Olivia," said the major, when leaving the house next morning for the office, "if you have any business down town to-day, transact it this forenoon. Under no circumstances must you or Clara or the baby leave the house after midday."

"Why, what's the matter, Phil?"

"Nothing to alarm you, except that there may be a little political demonstration which may render the streets unsafe. You are not to say anything about it where the servants might hear."

"Will there be any danger for you, Phil?" she demanded with alarm.

"Not the slightest, Olivia dear. No one will be harmed; but it is best for ladies and children to stay indoors."

Mrs. Carteret's nerves were still more or less unstrung from her mental struggles of the night, and the memory of her dream came to her like a dim foreboding of misfortune. As though in sympathy with its mother's feelings, the baby did not seem as well as usual. The new nurse was by no means an ideal nurse,—Mammy Jane understood the child much better. If there should be any trouble with the negroes, toward which her husband's remark seemed to point,—she knew the general political situation, though not informed in regard to her husband's plans,—she would like to have Mammy Jane near her, where the old nurse might be protected from danger or alarm.

With this end in view she dispatched the nurse, shortly after breakfast, to Mammy Jane's house in the negro settlement on the other side of the town, with a message asking the old woman to come immediately to Mrs. Carteret's. Unfortunately, Mammy Jane had gone to visit a sick woman in the country, and was not expected to return for several hours.

XXXII
THE STORM BREAKS

THE Wellington riot began at three o'clock in the afternoon of a day as fair as was ever selected for a deed of darkness. The sky was clear, except for a few light clouds that floated, white and feathery, high in air, like distant islands in a sapphire sea. A salt-laden breeze from the ocean a few miles away lent a crisp sparkle to the air.

At three o'clock sharp the streets were filled, as if by magic, with armed white men. The negroes, going about, had noted, with uneasy curiosity, that the stores and places of business, many of which closed at noon, were unduly late in opening for the afternoon, though no one suspected the reason for the delay; but at three o'clock every passing colored man was ordered, by the first white man be met, to throw up his hands. If he complied, he was searched, more or less roughly, for firearms, and then warned to get off the street. When he met another group of white men the scene was repeated. The man thus summarily held up seldom encountered more than two groups before disappearing across lots to his own home or some convenient hiding-place. If he resisted any demand of those who halted him—But the records of the day are historical; they may be found in the newspapers of the following date, but they are more firmly engraved upon the hearts and memories of the people of Wellington. For Many months there were negro families in the town whose children screamed with fear and ran to their mothers for protection at the mere sight of a white man.

Dr. Miller had received a call, about one o'clock, to attend a case at the house of a well-to-do colored farmer, who lived some three or four miles from the town, upon the very road, by the way, along which Miller had driven so furiously a few weeks before, in the few hours that intervened before Sandy Campbell would probably have been burned at the stake. The drive to his patient's home, the necessary inquiries, the filling of the prescription from his own medicine-case, which he carried along with him, the little friendly conversation about the weather and the crops, and, the farmer being an intelligent and thinking man, the inevitable subject of the future of their race,—these, added to the return journey, occupied at least two hours of Miller's time.

As he neared the town on his way back, he saw ahead of him half a dozen men and women approaching, with fear written in their faces, in every degree from apprehension to terror. Women were weeping and children crying, and all were going as fast as seemingly lay in their power, looking behind now and then as if pursued by some deadly enemy. At sight of Miller's buggy they made a dash for cover, disappearing, like a covey of frightened partridges, in the underbrush along the road.

Miller pulled up his horse and looked after them in startled wonder.

"What on earth can be the matter?" he muttered, struck with a vague feeling of alarm. A psychologist, seeking to trace the effects of slavery upon the human mind, might find in the South many a curious illustration of this curse, abiding long after the actual physical bondage had terminated. In the olden time the white South labored under the constant fear of negro insurrections. Knowing that they themselves, if in the negroes' place, would have risen in the effort to throw off the yoke, all their reiterated theories of negro subordination and inferiority could not remove that lurking fear, founded upon the obscure consciousness that the slaves ought to have risen. Conscience, it has been said, makes cowards of us all. There was never, on the continent of America, a successful slave revolt, nor one which lasted more than a few hours, or resulted in the loss of more than a few white lives; yet never was the planter quite free from the fear that there might be one.

On the other hand, the slave had before his eyes always the fear of the master. There were good men, according to their lights,—according to their training and environment,—among the Southern slave-holders, who treated their slaves kindly, as slaves, from principle, because they recognized the claims of humanity, even under the dark skin of a human chattel. There was many a one who protected or pampered his negroes, as the case might be, just as a man fondles his dog,—because they were his; they were a part of his estate, an integral part of the entity of property and person which made up the aristocrat; but with all this kindness, there was always present, in the consciousness of the lowest slave, the knowledge that he was in his master's power, and that he could make no effectual protest against the abuse of that authority. There was also the knowledge, among those who could think at all, that the best of masters was himself a slave to a system, which hampered his movements but scarcely less than those of his bondmen.

When, therefore, Miller saw these men and women scampering into the bushes, he divined, with this slumbering race consciousness which years of culture had not obliterated, that there was some race trouble on foot. His intuition did not long remain unsupported. A black head was cautiously protruded from the shrubbery, and a black voice—if such a description be allowable—addressed him:—

"Is dat you, Doctuh Miller?"

"Yes. Who are you, and what's the trouble?"

"What 's de trouble, suh? Why, all hell's broke loose in town yonduh. De w'ite folks is riz 'gins' de niggers, an' say dey 're gwine ter kill eve'y nigger dey kin lay han's on."

Miller's heart leaped to his throat, as he thought of his wife and child. This story was preposterous; it could not be true, and yet there must be something in it. He tried to question his informant, but the man was so overcome with excitement and fear that Miller saw clearly that he must go farther for information. He had read in the Morning Chronicle, a few days before, the obnoxious editorial quoted from the Afro-American Banner, and had noted the comment upon it by the white editor. He had felt, as at the time of its first publication, that the editorial was ill-advised. It could do no good, and was calculated to arouse the animosity of those whose friendship, whose tolerance, at least, was necessary and almost indispensable to the colored people. They were living, at the best, in a sort of armed neutrality with the whites; such a publication, however serviceable elsewhere, could have no other effect in Wellington than to endanger this truce and defeat the hope of a possible future friendship. The right of free speech entitled Barber to publish it; a larger measure of common-sense would have made him withhold it. Whether it was the republication of this article that had stirred up anew the sleeping dogs of race prejudice and whetted their thirst for blood, he could not yet tell; but at any rate, there was mischief on foot.

"Fer God's sake, doctuh, don' go no closeter ter dat town," pleaded his informant, "er you 'll be killt sho'. Come on wid us, suh, an' tek keer er yo'se'f. We're gwine ter hide in de swamps till dis thing is over!"

"God, man!" exclaimed Miller, urging his horse forward, "my wife and child are in the town!"

Fortunately, he reflected, there were no patients confined in the hospital,—if there should be anything in this preposterous story. To one unfamiliar with Southern life, it might have seemed impossible that these good Christian people, who thronged the churches on Sunday, and wept over the sufferings of the lowly Nazarene, and sent missionaries to the heathen, could be hungering and thirsting for the blood of their fellow men; but Miller cherished no such delusion. He knew the history of his country; he had the threatened lynching of Sandy Campbell vividly in mind; and he was fully persuaded that to race prejudice, once roused, any horror was possible. That women or children would be molested of set purpose he did not believe, but that they might suffer by accident was more than likely.

As he neared the town, dashing forward at the top of his horse's speed, he heard his voice called in a loud and agitated tone, and, glancing around him, saw a familiar form standing by the roadside, gesticulating vehemently.

He drew up the horse with a suddenness that threw the faithful and obedient animal back upon its haunches. The colored lawyer, Watson, came up to the buggy. That he was laboring under great and unusual excitement was quite apparent from his pale face and frightened air.

"What's the matter, Watson?" demanded Miller, hoping now to obtain some reliable information.

"Matter!" exclaimed the other. "Everything's the matter! The white people are up in arms. They have disarmed the colored people, killing half a dozen in the process, and wounding as many more. They have forced the mayor and aldermen to resign, have formed a provisional city government *à la française*, and have ordered me and half a dozen other fellows to leave town in forty-eight hours, under pain of sudden death. As they seem to mean it, I shall not stay so long. Fortunately, my wife and children are away. I knew you were out here, however, and I thought I'd come out and wait for you, so that we might talk the matter over. I don't imagine they mean you any harm, personally, because you tread on nobody's toes; but you 're too valuable a man for the race to lose, so I thought I 'd give you warning. I shall want to sell you my property, too, at a bargain. For I'm worth too much to my family to dream of ever attempting to live here again."

"Have you seen anything of my wife and child?" asked Miller, intent upon the danger to which they might be exposed.

"No; I did n't go to the house. I inquired at the drugstore and found out where you had gone. You need n't fear for them,—it is not a war on women and children."

"War of any kind is always hardest on the women and children," returned Miller; "I must hurry on and see that mine are safe."

"They'll not carry the war so far into Africa as that," returned Watson; "but I never saw anything like it. Yesterday I had a hundred white friends in the town, or thought I had,—men who spoke pleasantly to me on the street, and sometimes gave me their hands to shake. Not one of them said to me today: 'Watson, stay at home this afternoon.' I might have been killed, like any one of half a dozen others who have bit the dust, for any word that one of my 'friends' had said to warn me. When the race cry is started in this neck of the woods, friendship, religion, humanity, reason, all shrivel up like dry leaves in a raging furnace."

The buggy, into which Watson had climbed, was meanwhile rapidly nearing the town.

"I think I'll leave you here, Miller," said Watson, as they approached the outskirts, "and make my way home by a roundabout path, as I should like to get there unmolested. Home!—a beautiful word that, isn't it, for an exiled wanderer? It might not be well, either, for us to be seen together. If you put the hood of your buggy down, and sit well back in the shadow, you may be able to reach home without interruption; but avoid the main streets. I'll see you again this evening, if we're both alive, and I can reach you; for my time is short. A committee are to call in the morning to escort me to the train. I am to be dismissed from the community with public honors."

Watson was climbing down from the buggy, when a small party of men were seen approaching and big Josh Green, followed by several other resolute-looking colored men, came up and addressed them.

"Dr. Miller," cried Green, "Mr. Watson,—we're lookin' fer a leader. De w'ite folks are killin' de niggers, an' we ain' gwine ter stan' up an' be shot down like dogs. We're gwine ter defen' ou' lives, an' we ain' gwine ter run away f'm no place where we've got a right ter be; an' woe be ter de w'ite man w'at lays han's on us! Dere's two niggers in dis town ter eve'y w'ite man, an' ef we've got ter be killt, we'll take some w'ite folks 'long wid us, ez sho' ez dere 's a God in heaven,—ez I s'pose dere is, dough He mus' be 'sleep, er busy somewhar e'se ter-day. Will you-all come an' lead us?"

"Gentlemen," said Watson, "what is the use? The negroes will not back you up. They have n't the arms, nor the moral courage, nor the leadership."

"We'll git de arms, an' we'll git de courage, ef you'll come an' lead us! We wants leaders,—dat's w'y we come ter you!"

"What's the use?" returned Watson despairingly. "The odds are too heavy. I've been ordered out of town; if I stayed, I'd be shot on sight, unless I had a body-guard around me."

"We'll be yo' body-guard!" shouted half a dozen voices.

"And when my body-guard was shot, what then? I have a wife and children. It is my duty to live for them. If I died, I should get no glory and no reward, and my family would be reduced to beggary,—to which they'll soon be near enough as it is. This affair will blow over in a day or two. The white people will be ashamed of themselves to-morrow, and apprehensive of the consequences for some time to come. Keep quiet, boys, and trust in God. You won't gain anything by resistance."

"'God he'ps dem dat he'ps demselves,'" returned Josh stoutly. "Ef Mr. Watson won't lead us, will you, Dr. Miller?" said the spokesman, turning to the doctor.

For Miller it was an agonizing moment. He was no coward, morally or physically. Every manly instinct urged him to go forward and take up the cause of these leaderless people, and, if need be, to defend their lives and their rights with his own,—but to what end?

"Listen, men," he said. "We would only be throwing our lives away. Suppose we made a determined stand and won a temporary victory. By morning every train, every boat, every road leading into Wellington, would be crowded with white men,—as they probably will be any way,—with arms in their hands, curses on their lips, and vengeance in their hearts. In the minds of those who make and administer the laws, we have no standing in the court of conscience. They would kill us in the fight, or they would hang us afterwards,—one way or another, we should be doomed. I should like to lead you; I should like to arm every colored man in this town, and have them stand firmly in line, not for attack, but for defense; but if I attempted it, and they should stand by me, which is questionable,—for I have met them fleeing from the town,—my life would pay the forfeit. Alive, I may be of some use to you, and you are welcome to my life in that way,—I am giving it freely. Dead, I should be a mere lump of carrion. Who remembers even the names of those who have been done to death in the Southern States for the past twenty years?"

"I 'members de name er one of 'em," said Josh, "an' I 'members de name er de man dat killt 'im, an' I s'pec' his time is mighty nigh come."

"My advice is not heroic, but I think it is wise. In this riot we are placed as we should be in a war: we have no territory, no base of supplies, no organization, no outside sympathy,—we stand in the position of a race, in a case like this, without money and without friends. Our time will come,—the time when we can command respect for our rights; but it is not yet in sight. Give it up, boys, and wait. Good may come of this, after all."

Several of the men wavered, and looked irresolute.

"I reckon that's all so, doctuh," returned Josh, "an', de way you put it, I don' blame you ner Mr. Watson; but all dem reasons ain' got no weight wid me. I'm gwine in dat town, an' ef any w'ite man 'sturbs me, dere'll be trouble,—dere'll be double trouble,—I feels it in my bones!"

"Remember your old mother, Josh," said Miller.

"Yas, suh, I'll 'member her; dat 's all I kin do now. I don' need ter wait fer her no mo', fer she died dis mo'nin'. I'd lack ter see her buried, suh, but I may not have de chance. Ef I gits killt, will you do me a favor?"

"Yes, Josh; what is it?"

"Ef I should git laid out in dis commotion dat's gwine on, will you collec' my wages f'm yo' brother, and see dat de ole 'oman is put away right?"

"Yes, of course."

"Wid a nice coffin, an' a nice fune'al, an' a head-bo'd an' a foot-bo'd?"

"Yes."

"All right, suh! Ef I don' live ter do it, I'll know it'll be 'tended ter right. Now we're gwine out ter de cotton compress, an' git a lot er colored men tergether, an' ef de w'ite folks 'sturbs me, I should n't be s'prise' ef dere 'd be a mix-up;—an' ef dere is, me an *one* w'ite man'll stan' befo' de jedgment th'one er God dis day; an' it won't be me w'at'll be 'feared er de jedgment. Come along, boys! Dese gentlemen may have somethin' ter live fer; but ez fer my pa't, I'd ruther be a dead nigger any day dan a live dog!"

XXXIII
INTO THE LION'S JAWS

THE party under Josh's leadership moved off down the road. Miller, while entirely convinced that he had acted wisely in declining to accompany them, was yet conscious of a distinct feeling of shame and envy that he, too, did not feel impelled to throw away his life in a hopeless struggle.

Watson left the buggy and disappeared by a path at the roadside. Miller drove rapidly forward. After entering the town, he passed several small parties of white men, but escaped scrutiny by sitting well back in his buggy, the presumption being that a well-dressed man with a good horse and buggy was white. Torn with anxiety, he reached home at about four o'clock. Driving the horse into the yard, he sprang down from the buggy and hastened to the house, which he found locked, front and rear.

A repeated rapping brought no response. At length he broke a window, and entered the house like a thief.

"Janet, Janet!" he called in alarm, "where are you? It is only I,—Will!"

There was no reply. He ran from room to room, only to find them all empty. Again he called his wife's name, and was about rushing from the house, when a muffled voice came faintly to his ear,

"Is dat you, Doctuh Miller?"

"Yes. Who are you, and where are my wife and child?"

He was looking around in perplexity, when the door of a low closet under the kitchen sink was opened from within, and a woolly head was cautiously protruded.

"Are you *sho'* dat 's you, doctuh?"

"Yes, Sally; where are"—

"An' not some w'ite man come ter bu'n down de house an' kill all de niggers?"

"No, Sally, it's me all right. Where is my wife? Where is my child?"

"Dey went over ter see Mis' Butler 'long 'bout two o'clock, befo' dis fuss broke out, suh. Oh, Lawdy, Lawdy, suh! Is all de cullud folks be'n killt 'cep'n' me an' you, suh? Fer de Lawd's sake, suh, you won' let 'em kill me, will you, suh? I'll wuk fer you fer nuthin' suh, all my bawn days, ef you'll save my life, suh!"

"Calm yourself, Sally. You'll be safe enough if you stay right here, I've no doubt. They'll not harm women,—of that I'm sure enough, although I have n't yet got the bearings of this deplorable affair. Stay here and look after the house. I must find my wife and child!"

The distance across the city to the home of the Mrs. Butler whom his wife had gone to visit was exactly one mile. Though Miller had a good horse in front of him, he was two hours in reaching his destination. Never will the picture of that ride fade from his memory. In his dreams he repeats it night after night, and sees the sights that wounded his eyes, and feels the thoughts—the haunting spirits of the thoughts—that tore his heart as he rode through hell to find those whom he was seeking.

For a short distance he saw nothing, and made rapid progress. As he turned the first corner, his horse shied at the dead body of a negro, lying huddled up in the collapse which marks sudden death. What Miller shuddered at was not so much the thought of death, to the sight of which his profession had accustomed him, as the suggestion of what it signified. He had taken with allowance the wild statement of the fleeing fugitives. Watson, too, had been greatly excited, and Josh Green's group were desperate men, as much liable to be misled by their courage as the others by their fears; but here was proof that murder had been done,—and his wife and children were in the town. Distant shouts, and the sound of firearms, increased his alarm. He struck his horse with the whip, and dashed on toward the heart of the city, which he must traverse in order to reach Janet and the child.

At the next corner lay the body of another man, with the red blood oozing from a ghastly wound in the forehead. The negroes seemed to have been killed, as the band plays in circus parades, at the street intersections, where the example would be most effective. Miller, with a wild leap of the heart, had barely passed this gruesome spectacle, when a sharp voice commanded him to halt, and emphasized the order by covering him with a revolver. Forgetting the prudence he had preached to others, he had raised his whip to strike the horse, when several hands seized the bridle.

"Come down, you damn fool," growled an authoritative voice. "Don't you see we're in earnest? Do you want to get killed?"

"Why should I come down?" asked Miller.

"Because we've ordered you to come down! This is the white people's day, and when they order, a nigger must obey. We're going to search you for weapons."

"Search away. You'll find nothing but a case of surgeon's tools, which I 'm more than likely to need before this day is over, from all indications."

"No matter; we'll make sure of it! That's what we're here for. Come down, if you don't want to be pulled down!"

Miller stepped down from his buggy. His interlocutor, who made no effort at disguise, was a clerk in a dry-goods store where Miller bought most of his family and hospital supplies. He made no sign of recognition, however, and Miller claimed no acquaintance. This man, who had for several years emptied Miller's pockets in the course of more or less legitimate trade, now went through them, aided by another man, more rapidly than ever before, the searchers convincing themselves that Miller carried no deadly weapon upon his person. Meanwhile, a third ransacked the buggy with like result. Miller recognized several others of the party, who made not the slightest attempt at disguise, though no names were called by any one.

"Where are you going?" demanded the leader.

"I am looking for my wife and child," replied Miller.

"Well, run along, and keep them out of the streets when you find them; and keep your hands out of this affair, if you wish to live in this town, which from now on will be a white man's town, as you niggers will be pretty firmly convinced before night."

Miller drove on as swiftly as might be.

At the next corner he was stopped again. In the white man who held him up, Miller recognized a neighbor of his own. After a short detention and a perfunctory search, the white man remarked apologetically:—

"Sorry to have had to trouble you, doctuh, but them's the o'ders. It ain't men like you that we're after, but the vicious and criminal class of niggers."

Miller smiled bitterly as he urged his horse forward.

He was quite well aware that the virtuous citizen who had stopped him had only a few weeks before finished a term in the penitentiary, to which he had been sentenced for stealing. Miller knew that he could have bought all the man owned for fifty dollars, and his soul for as much more.

A few rods farther on, he came near running over the body of a wounded man who lay groaning by the wayside. Every professional instinct urged him to stop and offer aid to the sufferer; but the uncertainty concerning his wife and child proved a stronger motive and urged him resistlessly forward. Here and there the ominous sound of firearms was audible. He might have thought this merely a part of the show, like the "powder play" of the Arabs, but for the bloody confirmation of its earnestness which had already assailed his vision. Somewhere in this seething caldron of unrestrained passions were his wife and child, and he must hurry on.

His progress was painfully slow. Three times he was stopped and searched. More than once his way was barred, and he was ordered to turn back, each such occasion requiring a detour which consumed many minutes. The man who last stopped him was a well-known Jewish merchant. A Jew—God of Moses!—had so far forgotten twenty centuries of history as to join in the persecution of another oppressed race! When almost reduced to despair by these innumerable delays, he perceived, coming toward him, Mr. Ellis, the sub-editor of the Morning Chronicle. Miller had just been stopped and questioned again, and Ellis came up as he was starting once more upon his endless ride.

"Dr. Miller," said Ellis kindly, "it is dangerous for you on the streets. Why tempt the danger?"

"I am looking for my wife and child," returned Miller in desperation. "They are somewhere in this town,—I don't know where,—and I must find them."

Ellis had been horror-stricken by the tragedy of the afternoon, the wholly superfluous slaughter of a harmless people, whom a show of force would have been quite sufficient to overawe. Elaborate explanations were afterwards given for these murders, which were said, perhaps truthfully, not to have been premeditated, and many regrets were expressed. The young man had been surprised, quite as much as the negroes themselves, at the ferocity displayed. His own thoughts and feelings were attuned to anything but slaughter. Only that morning he had received a perfumed note, calling his attention to what the writer described as a very noble deed of his, and requesting him to call that evening and receive the writer's thanks. Had he known that Miss Pemberton, several weeks after their visit to the Sound, had driven out again to the hotel and made some inquiries among the servants, he might have understood better the meaning of this missive. When Miller spoke of his wife and child, some subtle thread of suggestion coupled the note with Miller's plight.

"I'll go with you, Dr. Miller," he said, "if you'll permit me. In my company you will not be disturbed."

He took a seat in Miller's buggy after which it was not molested.

Neither of them spoke. Miller was sick at heart; he could have wept with grief, even had the welfare of his own dear ones not been involved in this regrettable affair. With prophetic instinct he foresaw the hatreds to which this day would give birth; the long years of constraint and distrust which would still further widen the breach between two peoples whom fate had thrown together in one community.

There was nothing for Ellis to say. In his heart he could not defend the deeds of this day. The petty annoyances which the whites had felt at the spectacle of a few negroes in office; the not unnatural resentment of a proud people at what had seemed to them a presumptuous freedom of speech and lack of deference on the part of their inferiors,—these things, which he knew were to be made the excuse for overturning the city government, he realized full well were no sort of justification for the wholesale murder or other horrors which might well ensue before the day was done. He could not approve the acts of his own people; neither could he, to a negro, condemn them. Hence he was silent.

"Thank you, Mr. Ellis," exclaimed Miller, when they had reached the house where he expected to find his wife. "This is the place where I was going. I am—under a great obligation to you."

"Not at all, Dr. Miller. I need not tell you how much I regret this deplorable affair."

Ellis went back down the street. Fastening his horse to the fence, Miller sprang forward to find his wife and child. They would certainly be there, for no colored woman would be foolhardy enough to venture on the streets after the riot had broken out.

As he drew nearer, he felt a sudden apprehension. The house seemed strangely silent and deserted. The doors were closed, and the venetian blinds shut tightly. Even a dog which had appeared slunk timidly back under the house, instead of barking vociferously according to the usual habit of his kind.

XXXIV
THE VALLEY OF THE SHADOW

MILLER knocked at the door. There was no response. He went round to the rear of the house. The dog had slunk behind the woodpile. Miller knocked again, at the back door, and, receiving no reply, called aloud.

"Mrs. Butler! It is I, Dr. Miller. Is my wife here?"

The slats of a near-by blind opened cautiously.

"Is it really you, Dr. Miller?"

"Yes, Mrs. Butler. I am looking for my wife and child,—are they here?"

"No, sir; she became alarmed about you, soon after the shooting commenced, and I could not keep her. She left for home half an hour ago. It is coming on dusk, and she and the child are so near white that she did not expect to be molested."

"Which way did she go?"

"She meant to go by the main street. She thought it would be less dangerous than the back streets. I tried to get her to stay here, but she was frantic about you, and nothing I could say would keep her. Is the riot almost over, Dr. Miller? Do you think they will murder us all, and burn down our houses?"

"God knows," replied Miller, with a groan. "But I must find her, if I lose my own life in the attempt."

Surely, he thought, Janet would be safe. The white people of Wellington were not savages; or at least their temporary reversion to savagery would not go as far as to include violence to delicate women and children. Then there flashed into his mind Josh Green's story of his "silly" mother, who for twenty years had walked the earth as a child, as the result of one night's terror, and his heart sank within him.

Miller realized that his buggy, by attracting attention, had been a hindrance rather than a help in his progress across the city. In order to follow his wife, he must practically retrace his steps over the very route he had come. Night was falling. It would be easier to cross the town on foot. In the dusk his own color, slight in the daytime, would not attract attention, and by dodging in the shadows he might avoid those who might wish to intercept him. But he must reach Janet and the boy at any risk. He had not been willing to throw his life away hopelessly, but he would cheerfully have sacrificed it for those whom he loved.

He had gone but a short distance, and had not yet reached the centre of mob activity, when he intercepted a band of negro laborers from the cotton compress, with big Josh Green at their head.

"Hello, doctuh!" cried Josh, "does you wan' ter jine us?"

"I'm looking for my wife and child, Josh. They're somewhere in this den of murderers. Have any of you seen them?"

No one had seen them.

"You men are running a great risk," said Miller. "You are rushing on to certain death."

"Well, suh, maybe we is; but we're gwine ter die fightin'. Dey say de w'ite folks is gwine ter bu'n all de cullud schools an' chu'ches, an' kill all de niggers dey kin ketch. Dey're gwine ter bu'n yo' new hospittle, ef somebody don' stop 'em."

"Josh—men—you are throwing your lives away. It is

a fever; it will wear off to-morrow, or to-night. They'll not burn the schoolhouses, nor the hospital—they are not such fools, for they benefit the community; and they'll only kill the colored people who resist them. Every one of you with a gun or a pistol carries his death warrant in his own hand. I'd rather see the hospital burn than have one of you lose his life. Resistance only makes the matter worse,—the odds against you are too long."

"Things can't be any wuss, doctuh," replied one of the crowd sturdily. "A gun is mo' dange'ous ter de man in front of it dan ter de man behin' it. Dey're gwine ter kill us anyhow; an' we're tired,—we read de newspapers,—an' we 're tired er bein' shot down like dogs, widout jedge er jury. We'd ruther die fightin' dan be stuck like pigs in a pen!"

"God help you!" said Miller. "As for me, I must find my wife and child."

"Good-by, doctuh," cried Josh, brandishing a huge knife. "'Member 'bout de ole 'oman, ef you lives thoo dis. Don' fergit de headbo'd an' de footbo'd, an' a silver plate on de coffin, ef dere's money ernuff."

They went their way, and Miller hurried on. They might resist attack; he thought it extremely unlikely that they would begin it; but he knew perfectly well that the mere knowledge that some of the negroes contemplated resistance would only further inflame the infuriated whites. The colored men might win a momentary victory, though it was extremely doubtful; and they would as surely reap the harvest later on. The qualities which in a white man would win the applause of the world would in a negro be taken as the marks of savagery. So thoroughly diseased was public opinion in matters of race that the negro who

278

died for the common rights of humanity might look for no meed of admiration or glory. At such a time, in the white man's eyes, a negro's courage would be mere desperation; his love of liberty, a mere animal dislike of restraint. Every finer human instinct would be interpreted in terms of savagery. Or, if forced to admire, they would none the less repress. They would applaud his courage while they stretched his neck, or carried off the fragments of his mangled body as souvenirs, in much the same way that savages preserve the scalps or eat the hearts of their enemies.

But concern for the fate of Josh and his friends occupied only a secondary place in Miller's mind for the moment. His wife and child were somewhere ahead of him. He pushed on. He had covered about a quarter of a mile more, and far down the street could see the signs of greater animation, when he came upon the body of a woman lying upon the sidewalk. In the dusk he had almost stumbled over it, and his heart came up in his mouth. A second glance revealed that it could not be his wife. It was a fearful portent, however, of what her fate might be. The "war" had reached the women and children. Yielding to a professional instinct, he stooped, and saw that the prostrate form was that of old Aunt Jane Letlow. She was not yet quite dead, and as Miller, with a tender touch, placed her head in a more comfortable position, her lips moved with a last lingering flicker of consciousness:—

"Comin', missis, comin'!"

Mammy Jane had gone to join the old mistress upon whose memory her heart was fixed; and yet not all her reverence for her old mistress, nor all her deference to the whites, nor all their friendship for her, had been able to save her from this raging devil of race hatred which momentarily possessed the town.

Perceiving that he could do no good, Miller hastened onward, sick at heart. Whenever he saw a party of white men approaching,—these brave reformers never went singly,—he sought concealment in the shadow of a tree or the shrubbery in some yard until they had passed. He had covered about two thirds of the distance homeward, when his eyes fell upon a group beneath a lamp-post, at sight of which he turned pale with horror, and rushed forward with a terrible cry.

XXXV
"MINE ENEMY, O MINE ENEMY!"

THE proceedings of the day—planned originally as a "demonstration," dignified subsequently as a "revolution," under any name the culmination of the conspiracy formed by Carteret and his colleagues—had by seven o'clock in the afternoon developed into a murderous riot. Crowds of white men and half-grown boys, drunk with whiskey or with license, raged through the streets, beating, chasing, or killing any negro so unfortunate as to fall into their hands. Why any particular negro was assailed, no one stopped to inquire; it was merely a white mob thirsting for black blood, with no more conscience or discrimination than would be exercised by a wolf in a sheepfold. It was race against race, the whites against the negroes; and it was a one-sided affair, for until Josh Green got together his body of armed men, no effective resistance had been made by any colored person, and the individuals who had been killed had so far left no marks upon the enemy by which they might be remembered.

"Kill the niggers!" rang out now and then through the dusk, and far down the street and along the intersecting thoroughfares distant voices took up the ominous refrain,—"Kill the niggers! Kill the damned niggers!"

Now, not a dark face had been seen on the street for half an hour, until the group of men headed by Josh made their appearance in the negro quarter. Armed with guns and axes, they presented quite a formidable appearance as they made their way toward the new hospital, near which stood a schoolhouse and a large church, both used by the colored people. They did not reach their destination without having met a number of white men, singly or in twos or threes; and the rumor spread with incredible swiftness that the negroes in turn were up in arms, determined to massacre all the whites and burn the town. Some of the whites became alarmed, and recognizing the power of the negroes, if armed and conscious of their strength, were impressed by the immediate necessity of overpowering and overawing them. Others, with appetites already whetted by slaughter, saw a chance, welcome rather than not, of shedding more black blood. Spontaneously the white mob flocked toward the hospital, where rumor had it that a large body of desperate negroes, breathing threats of blood and fire, had taken a determined stand.

It had been Josh's plan merely to remain quietly and peaceably in the neighborhood of the little group of public institutions, molesting no one, unless first attacked, and merely letting the white people see that they meant to protect their own; but so rapidly did the rumor spread, and so promptly did the white people act, that by the time Josh and his supporters had reached the top of the rising ground where the hospital stood, a crowd of white men much more numerous than their own party were following them at a short distance.

Josh, with the eye of a general, perceived that some of his party were becoming a little nervous, and decided that they would feel safer behind shelter.

"I reckon we better go inside de hospittle, boys," he exclaimed. "Den we'll be behind brick walls, an' dem, other fellows 'll be outside, an' ef dere's any fightin', we'll have de best show. We ain' gwine ter do no shootin' till we're pestered, an' dey'll be less likely ter pester us ef dey can't git at us widout runnin' some resk. Come along in! Be men! De gov'ner er de President is gwine ter sen' soldiers ter stop dese gwines-on, an' meantime we kin keep dem white devils f'm bu'nin' down our hospittles an' chu'ch-houses. W'en dey comes an' fin's out dat we jest means ter pertect out prope'ty, dey'll go 'long 'bout deir own business. Er, ef dey wants a scrap, dey kin have it! Come erlong, boys!"

Jerry Letlow, who had kept out of sight during the day, had started out, after night had set in, to find Major Carteret. Jerry was very much afraid. The events of the day had filled him with terror. Whatever the limitations of Jerry's mind or character may have been, Jerry had a keen appreciation of the danger to the negroes when they came in conflict with the whites, and he had no desire to imperil his own skin. He valued his life for his own sake, and not for any altruistic theory that it might be of service to others. In other words, Jerry was something of a coward. He had kept in hiding all day, but finding, toward evening, that the riot did not abate, and fearing, from the rumors which came to his ears, that all the negroes would be exterminated, he had set out, somewhat desperately, to try to find his white patron and protector. He had been cautious to avoid meeting any white men, and, anticipating no danger from those of his own race, went toward the party which he saw approaching, whose path would cross his own. When they were only a few yards apart, Josh took a step forward and caught Jerry by the arm.

"Come along, Jerry, we need you! Here's another man, boys. Come on now, and fight fer yo' race!"

In vain Jerry protested. "I don' want ter fight," he howled. "De w'ite folks ain' gwine ter pester me; dey 're my frien's. Tu'n me loose,—tu'n me loose, er we all gwine ter git killed!"

The party paid no attention to Jerry's protestations. Indeed, with the crowd of whites following behind, they were simply considering the question of a position from which they could most effectively defend themselves and the building which they imagined to be threatened. If Josh had released his grip of Jerry, that worthy could easily have escaped from the crowd; but Josh maintained his hold almost mechanically, and, in the confusion, Jerry found himself swept with the rest into the hospital, the doors of which were promptly barricaded with the heavier pieces of furniture, and the windows manned by several men each, Josh, with the instinct of a born commander, posting his forces so that they could cover with their guns all the approaches to the building. Jerry still continuing to make himself troublesome, Josh, in a moment of impatience, gave him a terrific box on the ear, which stretched him out upon the floor unconscious.

"Shet up," he said; "ef you can't stan' up like a man, keep still, and don't interfere wid men w'at will fight!"

The hospital, when Josh and his men took possession, had been found deserted. Fortunately there were no patients for that day, except one or two convalescents, and these, with the attendants, had joined the exodus of the colored people from the town.

A white man advanced from the crowd without toward the main entrance to the hospital. Big Josh, looking out from a window, grasped his gun more firmly, as his eyes fell upon the man who had murdered his father and darkened his mother's life. Mechanically he raised his rifle, but lowered it as the white man lifted up his hand as a sign that he wished to speak.

"You niggers," called Captain McBane loudly,—it was that worthy,—"you niggers are courtin' death, an' you won't have to court her but a minute er two mo' befo' she'll have you. If you surrender and give up your arms, you'll be dealt with leniently,—you may get off with the chain-gang or the penitentiary. If you resist, you'll be shot like dogs."

"Dat's no news, Mr. White Man," replied Josh, appearing boldly at the window. "We're use' ter bein' treated like dogs by men like you. If you w'ite people will go 'long an' ten' ter yo' own business an' let us alone, we'll ten' ter ou'n. You've got guns, an' we've got jest as much right ter carry 'em as you have. Lay down yo'n, an' we'll lay down on'n,—we did n' take 'em, up fust; but we ain' gwine ter let you bu'n down ou' chu'ches an' school' ouses, er dis hospittle, an' we ain' comin' out er dis house, where we ain' disturbin' nobody, fer you ter shoot us down er sen' us ter jail. You hear me!"

"All right," responded McBane. "You've had fair warning. Your blood be on your"—

His speech was interrupted by a shot from the crowd, which splintered the window-casing close to Josh's head. This was followed by half a dozen other shots, which were replied to, almost simultaneously, by a volley from within, by which one of the attacking party was killed and another wounded.

This roused the mob to frenzy.

"Vengeance! vengeance!" they yelled. "Kill the niggers!"

A negro had killed a white man,—the unpardonable sin, admitting neither excuse, justification, nor extenuation. From time immemorial it had been bred in the Southern white consciousness, and in the negro consciousness also, for that matter, that the person of a white man was sacred from the touch of a negro, no matter what the provocation. A dozen colored men lay dead in the streets of Wellington, inoffensive people, slain in cold blood because they had been bold enough to question the authority of those who had assailed them, or frightened enough to flee when they had been ordered to stand still; but their lives counted nothing against that of a riotous white man, who had courted death by attacking a body of armed men.

The crowd, too, surrounding the hospital, had changed somewhat in character. The men who had acted as leaders in the early afternoon, having accomplished their pur-

285

pose of overturning the local administration and establishing a provisional government of their own, had withdrawn from active participation in the rioting, deeming the negroes already sufficiently overawed to render unlikely any further trouble from that source. Several of the ringleaders had indeed begun to exert themselves to prevent further disorder, or any loss of property, the possibility of which had become apparent; but those who set in motion the forces of evil cannot always control them afterwards. The baser element of the white population, recruited from the wharves and the saloons, was now predominant.

Captain McBane was the only one of the revolutionary committee who had remained with the mob, not with any purpose to restore or preserve order, but because he found the company and the occasion entirely congenial. He had had no opportunity, at least no tenable excuse, to kill or maim a negro since the termination of his contract with the state for convicts, and this occasion had awakened a dormant appetite for these diversions. We are all puppets in the hands of Fate, and seldom see the strings that move us. McBane had lived a life of violence and cruelty. As a man sows, so shall he reap. In works of fiction, such men are sometimes converted. More often, in real life, they do not change their natures until they are converted into dust. One does well to distrust a tamed tiger.

On the outskirts of the crowd a few of the better class, or at least of the better clad, were looking on. The double volley described had already been fired, when the number of these was augmented by the arrival of Major Carteret and Mr. Ellis, who had just come from the Chronicle office, where the next day's paper had been in hasty preparation. They pushed their way towards the front of the crowd.

"This must be stopped, Ellis," said Carteret. "They are burning houses and killing women and children. Old Jane, good old Mammy Jane, who nursed my wife at her bosom, and has waited on her and my child within a few weeks, was killed only a few rods from my house, to which she was evidently fleeing for protection. It must have been by accident,—I cannot believe that any white man in town would be dastard enough to commit such a deed intentionally! I would have defended her with my own life! We must try to stop this thing!"

"Easier said than done," returned Ellis. "It is in the fever stage, and must burn itself out. We shall be lucky if it does not burn the town out. Suppose the negroes should also take a hand at the burning? We have advised the people to put the negroes down, and they are doing the job thoroughly."

"My God!" replied the other, with a gesture of impatience, as he continued to elbow his way through the crowd; "I meant to keep them in their places,—I did not intend wholesale murder and arson."

Carteret, having reached the front of the mob, made an effort to gain their attention.

"Gentlemen! " he cried in his loudest tones. His voice, unfortunately, was neither loud nor piercing.

"Kill the niggers!" clamored the mob.

"Gentlemen, I implore you"—

The crash of a dozen windows, broken by stones and pistol shots, drowned his voice.

"Gentlemen!" he shouted; "this is murder, it is madness; it is a disgrace to our city, to our state, to our civilization!"

"That's right!" replied several voices. The mob had recognized the speaker. "It *is* a disgrace, and we'll not put up with it a moment longer. Burn 'em out! Hurrah for Major Carteret, the champion of 'white supremacy'! Three cheers for the Morning Chronicle and 'no nigger domination'!"

"Hurrah, hurrah, hurrah!" yelled the crowd.

In vain the baffled orator gesticulated and shrieked in the effort to correct the misapprehension. Their oracle had spoken; not hearing what he said, they assumed it to mean encouragement and cooperation. Their present course was but the logical outcome of the crusade which the Morning Chronicle had preached, in season and out of season, for many months. When Carteret had spoken, and the crowd had cheered him, they felt that they had done all that courtesy required, and he was good-naturedly elbowed aside while they proceeded with the work in hand, which was now to drive out the negroes from the hospital and avenge the killing of their comrade.

Some brought hay, some kerosene, and others wood from a pile which had been thrown into a vacant lot near by. Several safe ways of approach to the building were discovered, and the combustibles placed and fired. The flames, soon gaining a foothold, leaped upward, catching here and there at the exposed woodwork, and licking the walls hungrily with long tongues of flame.

Meanwhile a desultory firing was kept up from the outside, which was replied to scatteringly from within the hospital. Those inside were either not good marksmen, or excitement had spoiled their aim. If a face appeared

288

at a window, a dozen pistol shots from the crowd sought the spot immediately.

Higher and higher leaped the flames. Suddenly from one of the windows sprang a black figure, waving a white handkerchief. It was Jerry Letlow. Regaining consciousness after the effect of Josh's blow had subsided, Jerry had kept quiet and watched his opportunity. From a safe vantage-ground he had scanned the crowd without, in search of some white friend. When he saw Major Carteret moving disconsolately away after his futile effort to stem the torrent, Jerry made a dash for the window. He sprang forth, and, waving his handkerchief as a flag of truce, ran toward Major Carteret, shouting frantically:—

"Majah Carteret—O majah! It's me, suh, Jerry, suh! I did n' go in dere myse'f, suh,—I wuz drag' in dere! I would n' do nothin' g'inst de w'ite folks, suh,—no, 'ndeed, I would n', suh!"

Jerry's cries were drowned in a roar of rage and a volley of shots from the mob. Carteret, who had turned away with Ellis, did not even hear his servant's voice. Jerry's poor flag of truce, his explanations, his reliance upon his white friends, all failed him in the moment of supreme need. In that hour, as in any hour when the depths of race hatred are stirred, a negro was no more than a brute beast, set upon by other brute beasts whose only instinct was to kill and destroy.

"Let us leave this inferno, Ellis," said Carteret, sick with anger and disgust. He had just become aware that a negro was being killed, though he did not know whom. "We can do nothing. The negroes have themselves to blame,—they tempted us beyond endurance. I counseled firmness, and firm measures were taken, and our purpose was accomplished. I am not responsible for these subsequent horrors,—I wash my hands of them. Let us go!"

The flames gained headway and gradually enveloped the burning building, until it became evident to those within as well as those without that the position of the defenders was no longer tenable. Would they die in the flames, or would they be driven out? The uncertainty soon came to an end.

The besieged had been willing to fight, so long as there seemed a hope of successfully defending themselves and their property; for their purpose was purely one of defense. When they saw the case was hopeless, inspired by Josh Green's reckless courage, they were still willing to sell their lives dearly. One or two of them had already been killed, and as many more disabled. The fate of Jerry Letlow had struck terror to the hearts of several others, who could scarcely hide their fear. After the building had been fired, Josh's exhortations were no longer able to keep them in the hospital. They preferred to fight and be killed in the open, rather than to be smothered like rats in a hole.

"Boys!" exclaimed Josh,—"men!—fer nobody but men would do w'at you have done,—the day has gone g'inst us. We kin see ou' finish; but fer my part, I ain' gwine ter leave dis worl' widout takin' a w'ite man 'long wid me, an' I sees my man right out yonder waitin',—I be'n waitin' fer him twenty years, but he won' have ter wait fer me mo' 'n 'bout twenty seconds. Eve'y one er you pick yo' man! We'll open de do', an, we'll give some w'ite men a chance ter be sorry dey ever started dis fuss!"

The door was thrown open suddenly, and through it rushed a dozen or more black figures, armed with knives, pistols, or clubbed muskets. Taken by sudden surprise, the white people stood motionless for a moment, but the approaching negroes had scarcely covered half the distance to which the heat of the flames had driven back the mob, before they were greeted with a volley that laid them all low but two. One of these, dazed by the fate of his companions, turned instinctively to flee, but had scarcely faced around before he fell, pierced in the back by a dozen bullets.

Josh Green, the tallest and biggest of them all, had not apparently been touched. Some of the crowd paused in involuntary admiration of this black giant, famed on the wharves for his strength, sweeping down upon them, a smile upon his face, his eyes lit up with a rapt expression which seemed to take him out of mortal ken. This impression was heightened by his apparent immunity from the shower of lead which less susceptible persons had continued to pour at him.

Armed with a huge bowie-knife, a relic of the civil war, which he had carried on his person for many years for a definite purpose, and which he had kept sharpened to a razor edge, he reached the line of the crowd. All but the bravest shrank back. Like a wedge he dashed through the mob, which parted instinctively before him, and all oblivious of the rain of lead which fell around him, reached the point where Captain McBane, the bravest man in the party, stood waiting to meet him. A pistol-flame flashed in his face, but he went on, and raising his powerful right arm, buried his knife to the hilt in the heart of his enemy. When the crowd dashed forward to wreak vengeance on his dead body, they found him with a smile still upon his face.

One of the two died as the fool dieth. Which was it, or was it both? "Vengeance is mine," saith the Lord, and it had not been left to Him. But they that do violence must expect to suffer violence. McBane's death was merciful, compared with the nameless horrors he had heaped upon the hundreds of helpless mortals who had fallen into his hands during his career as a contractor of convict labor.

Sobered by this culminating tragedy, the mob shortly afterwards dispersed. The flames soon completed their work, and this handsome structure, the fruit of old Adam Miller's industry, the monument of his son's philanthropy, a promise of good things for the future of the city, lay smouldering in ruins, a melancholy witness to the fact that our boasted civilization is but a thin veneer, which cracks and scales off at the first impact of primal passions.

XXXVI
FIAT JUSTITIA

By the light of the burning building, which illuminated the street for several blocks, Major Carteret and Ellis made their way rapidly until they turned into the street where the major lived. Reaching the house, Carteret tried the door and found it locked. A vigorous ring at the bell brought no immediate response. Carteret had begun to pound impatiently upon the door, when it was cautiously opened by Miss Pemberton, who was pale, and trembled with excitement.

"Where is Olivia?" asked the major.

"She is upstairs, with Dodie and Mrs. Albright's hospital nurse. Dodie has the croup. Virgie ran away after the riot broke out. Sister Olivia had sent for Mammy Jane, but she did not come. Mrs. Albright let her white nurse come over."

"I'll go up at once," said the major anxiously. "Wait for me, Ellis,—I'll be down in a few minutes."

"Oh, Mr. Ellis," exclaimed Clara, coming toward him with both hands extended, "can nothing be done to stop this terrible affair?"

"I wish I could do something," he murmured fervently, taking both her trembling hands in his own broad palms, where they rested with a surrendering trustfulness which he has never since had occasion to doubt. "It has gone too far, already, and the end, I fear, is not yet; but it cannot grow much worse."

The editor hurried upstairs. Mrs. Carteret, wearing a worried and haggard look, met him at the threshold of the nursery.

"Dodie is ill," she said. "At three o'clock, when the trouble began, I was over at Mrs. Albright's,—I had left Virgie with the baby. When I came back, she and all the other servants had gone. They had heard that the white people were going to kill all the negroes, and fled to seek safety. I found Dodie lying in a draught, before an open window, gasping for breath. I ran back to Mrs. Albright's, —I had found her much better to-day,—and she let her nurse come over. The nurse says that Dodie is threatened with membranous croup."

"Have you sent for Dr. Price?"

"There was no one to send,—the servants were gone,

and the nurse was afraid to venture out into the street. I telephoned for Dr. Price, and found that he was out of town; that he had gone up the river this morning to attend a patient, and would not be back until to-morrow. Mrs. Price thought that he had anticipated some kind of trouble in the town to-day, and had preferred to be where he could not be called upon to assume any responsibility."

"I suppose you tried Dr. Ashe?"

"I could not get him, nor any one else, after that first call. The telephone service is disorganized on account of the riot. We need medicine and ice. The drugstores are all closed on account of the riot, and for the same reason we couldn't get any ice."

Major Carteret stood beside the brass bedstead upon which his child was lying—his only child, around whose curly head clustered all his hopes; upon whom all his life for the past year had been centred. He stooped over the bed, beside which the nurse had stationed herself. She was wiping the child's face, which was red and swollen and covered with moisture, the nostrils working rapidly, and the little patient vainly endeavoring at intervals to cough up the obstruction to his breathing.

"Is it serious?" he inquired anxiously. He had always thought of the croup as a childish ailment, that yielded readily to proper treatment; but the child's evident distress impressed him with sudden fear.

"Dangerous," replied the young woman laconically. You came none too soon. If a doctor is n't got at once, the child will die,—and it must be a good doctor."

"Whom can I call?" he asked. "You know them all, I suppose. Dr. Price, our family physician, is out of town."

"Dr. Ashe has charge of his cases when he is away," replied the nurse. "If you can't find him, try Dr. Hooper. The child is growing worse every minute. On your way back you'd better get some ice, if possible."

The major hastened downstairs.

"Don't wait for me, Ellis," he said. "I shall be needed here for a while. I'll get to the office as soon as possible. Make up the paper, and leave another stick out for me to the last minute, but fill it up in case I'm not on hand by twelve. We must get the paper out early in the morning."

Nothing but a matter of the most vital importance would have kept Major Carteret away from his office this night. Upon the presentation to the outer world of the story of this riot would depend the attitude of the great civilized public toward the events of the last ten hours. The Chronicle was the source from which the first word would be expected; it would give the people of Wellington their cue as to the position which they must take in regard to this distressful affair, which had so far transcended in ferocity the most extreme measures which the conspirators had anticipated. The burden of his own responsibility weighed heavily upon him, and could not be shaken off; but he must do first the duty nearest to him,—he must first attend to his child.

Carteret hastened from the house, and traversed rapidly the short distance to Dr. Ashe's office. Far down the street he could see the glow of the burning hospital, and he had scarcely left his own house when the fusillade of shots, fired when the colored men emerged from the burning building, was audible. Carteret would have hastened back to the scene of the riot, to see what was now going on, and to make another effort to stem the tide of bloodshed; but before the dread of losing his child, all other interests fell into the background. Not all the negroes in Wellington could weigh in the balance for one instant against the life of the feeble child now gasping for breath in the house behind him.

Reaching the house, a vigorous ring brought the doctor's wife to the door.

"Good-evening, Mrs. Ashe. Is the doctor at home?"

"No, Major Carteret. He was called to attend Mrs. Wells, who was taken suddenly ill, as a result of the trouble this afternoon. He will be there all night, no doubt."

"My child is very ill, and I must find some one."

"Try Dr. Yates. His house is only four doors away."

A ring at Dr. Yates's door brought out a young man.

"Is Dr. Yates in?"

"Yes, sir."

"Can I see him?"

"You might see him, sir, but that would be all. His horse was frightened by the shooting on the streets, and ran away and threw the doctor, and broke his right arm. I have just set it; he will not be able to attend any patients for several weeks. He is old and nervous, and the shock was great."

"Are you not a physician? " asked Carteret, looking at the young man keenly. He was a serious, gentlemanly looking young fellow, whose word might probably be trusted.

"Yes, I am Dr. Evans, Dr. Yates's assistant. I'm really little more than a student, but I'll do what I can."

"My only child is sick with the croup, and requires immediate attention."

296

"I ought to be able to handle a case of the croup," answered Dr. Evans, "at least in the first stages. I'll go with you, and stay by the child, and if the case is beyond me, I may keep it in check until another physician comes."

He stepped back into another room, and returning immediately with his hat, accompanied Carteret homeward. The riot had subsided; even the glow from the smouldering hospital was no longer visible. It seemed that the city, appalled at the tragedy, had suddenly awakened to a sense of its own crime. Here and there a dark face, emerging cautiously from some hiding-place, peered from behind fence or tree, but shrank hastily away at the sight of a white face. The negroes of Wellington, with the exception of Josh Green and his party, had not behaved bravely on this critical day in their history; but those who had fought were dead, to the last man; those who had sought safety in flight or concealment were alive to tell the tale.

"We pass right by Dr. Thompson's," said Dr. Evans. "If you haven't spoken to him, it might be well to call him for consultation, in case the child should be very bad."

"Go on ahead," said Carteret, "and I'll get him."

Evans hastened on, while Carteret sounded the old-fashioned knocker upon the doctor's door. A gray-haired negro servant, clad in a dress suit and wearing a white tie, came to the door.

"De doctuh, suh," he replied politely to Carteret's question, "has gone ter ampitate de ahm er a gent'eman who got one er his bones smashed wid a pistol bullet in de—fightin' dis afternoon, suh. He's jes' gone, suh, an' lef' wo'd dat he'd be gone a' hour er mo', suh."

Carteret hastened homeward. He could think of no other available physician. Perhaps no other would be needed, but if so, he could find out from Evans whom it was best to call.

When he reached the child's room, the young doctor was bending anxiously over the little frame. The little lips had become livid, the little nails, lying against the white sheet, were blue. The child's efforts to breathe were most distressing, and each gasp cut the father like a knife. Mrs. Carteret was weeping hysterically.

"How is he, doctor?" asked the major.

"He is very low," replied the young man. "Nothing short of tracheotomy—an operation to open the windpipe—will relieve him. Without it, in half or three quarters of an hour he will be unable to breathe. It is a delicate operation, a mistake in which would be as fatal as the disease. I have neither the knowledge nor the experience to attempt it, and your child's life is too valuable for a student to practice upon. Neither have I the instruments here."

"What shall we do?" demanded Carteret. "We have called all the best doctors, and none are available."

The young doctor's brow was wrinkled with thought. He knew a doctor who could perform the operation. He had heard, also, of a certain event at Carteret's house some months before, when an unwelcome physician had been excluded from a consultation,—but it was the last chance.

"There is but one other doctor in town who has performed the operation, so far as I know," he declared, "and that is Dr. Miller. If you can get him, he can save your child's life."

Carteret hesitated involuntarily. All the incidents, all the arguments, of the occasion when he had refused to admit the colored doctor to his house, came up vividly before his memory. He had acted in accordance with his lifelong beliefs, and had carried his point; but the present situation was different,—this was a case of imperative necessity, and every other interest or consideration must give way before the imminence of his child's peril. That the doctor would refuse the call, he did not imagine: it would be too great an honor for a negro to decline,—unless some bitterness might have grown out of the proceedings of the afternoon. That this doctor was a man of some education he knew; and he had been told that he was a man of fine feeling,—for a negro,—and might easily have taken to heart the day's events. Nevertheless, he could hardly refuse a professional call,—professional ethics would require him to respond. Carteret had no reason to suppose that Miller had ever learned of what had occurred at the house during Dr. Burns's visit to Wellington. The major himself had never mentioned the controversy, and no doubt the other gentlemen had been equally silent.

"I'll go for him myself," said Dr. Evans, noting Carteret's hesitation and suspecting its cause. "I can do nothing here alone, for a little while, and I may be able to bring the doctor back with me. He likes a difficult operation."

It seemed an age ere the young doctor returned, though it was really only a few minutes. The nurse did what she could to relieve the child's sufferings, which grew visibly more and more acute. The mother, upon the other side of the bed, held one of the baby's hands in her own, and controlled her feelings as best she might. Carteret paced the floor anxiously, going every few seconds to the head of the stairs to listen for Evans's footsteps on the piazza without. At last the welcome sound was audible, and a few strides took him to the door.

"Dr. Miller is at home, sir," reported Evans, as he came in. "He says that he was called to your house once before, by a third person who claimed authority to act, and that he was refused admittance. He declares that he will not consider such a call unless it come from you personally."

"That is true, quite true," replied Carteret. "His position is a just one. I will go at once. Will—will—my child live until I can get Miller here?"

"He can live for half an hour without an operation. Beyond that I could give you little hope."

Seizing his hat, Carteret dashed out of the yard and ran rapidly to Miller's house; ordinarily a walk of six or seven minutes, Carteret covered it in three, and was almost out of breath when he rang the bell of Miller's front door.

The ring was answered by the doctor in person.

"Dr. Miller, I believe?" asked Carteret.

"Yes, sir."

"I am Major Carteret. My child is seriously ill, and you are the only available doctor who can perform the necessary operation."

"Ah! You have tried all the others,—and then you come to me!"

"Yes, I do not deny it," admitted the major, biting his lip. He had not counted on professional jealousy as an obstacle to be met. "But I *have* come to you, as a physician, to engage your professional services for my child,—

my only child. I have confidence in your skill, or I should not have come to you. I request—nay, I implore you to lose no more time, but come with me at once! My child's life is hanging by a thread, and you can save it!"

"Ah!" replied the other, "as a father whose only child's life is in danger, you implore *me*, of all men in the world, to come and save it!"

There was a strained intensity in the doctor's low voice that struck Carteret, in spite of his own pre-occupation. He thought he heard, too, from the adjoining room, the sound of some one sobbing softly. There was some mystery here which he could not fathom unaided.

Miller turned to the door behind him and threw it open. On the white cover of a low cot lay a childish form in the rigidity of death, and by it knelt, with her back to the door, a woman whose shoulders were shaken by the violence of her sobs. Absorbed in her grief, she did not turn, or give any sign that she had recognized the intrusion.

"There, Major Carteret!" exclaimed Miller, with the tragic eloquence of despair, "there lies a specimen of your handiwork! There lies *my* only child, laid low by a stray bullet in this riot which you and your paper have fomented; struck down as much by your hand as though you had held the weapon with which his life was taken!"

"My God!" exclaimed Carteret, struck with horror. "Is the child dead?"

"There he lies," continued the other, "an innocent child,—there he lies dead, his little life snuffed out like a candle, because you and a handful of your friends thought you must override the laws and run this town at any cost!—and there kneels his mother, overcome by grief. We are alone in the house. It is not safe to leave her unattended. My duty calls me here, by the side of my dead child and my suffering wife! I cannot go with you. There is a just God in heaven!—as you have sown, so may you reap!"

Carteret possessed a narrow, but a logical mind, and except when confused or blinded by his prejudices, had always tried to be a just man. In the agony of his own predicament,—in the horror of the situation at Miller's house,—for a moment the veil of race prejudice was rent in twain, and he saw things as they were, in their correct proportions and relations,—saw clearly and convincingly that he had no standing here, in the presence of death, in the home of this stricken family. Miller's refusal to go with him was pure, elemental justice; he could not blame the doctor for his stand. He was indeed conscious of a certain involuntary admiration for a man who held in his hands the power of life and death, and could use it, with strict justice, to avenge his own wrongs. In Dr. Miller's place he would have done the same thing. Miller had spoken the truth,—as he had sown, so must he reap! He could not expect, could not ask, this father to leave his own household at such a moment.

Pressing his lips together with grim courage, and bowing mechanically, as though to Fate rather than the physician, Carteret turned and left the house. At a rapid pace he soon reached home. There was yet a chance for his child: perhaps some one of the other doctors had come; perhaps, after all, the disease had taken a favorable turn,—Evans was but a young doctor, and might have been mistaken. Surely, with doctors all around him, his child would not be permitted to die for lack of medical attention! He found the mother, the doctor, and the nurse still grouped, as he had left them, around the suffering child.

"How is he now?" he asked, in a voice that sounded like a groan.

"No better," replied the doctor; "steadily growing worse. He can go on probably for twenty minutes longer without an operation."

"Where is the doctor?" demanded Mrs. Carteret, looking eagerly toward the door. "You should have brought him right upstairs. There's not a minute to spare! Phil, Phil, our child will die!"

Carteret's heart swelled almost to bursting with an intense pity. Even his own great sorrow became of secondary importance beside the grief which his wife must soon feel at the inevitable loss of her only child. And it was his fault! Would that he could risk his own life to spare her and to save the child!

Briefly, and as gently as might be, he stated the result of his errand. The doctor had refused to come, for a good reason. He could not ask him again.

Young Evans felt the logic of the situation, which Carteret had explained sufficiently. To the nurse it was even clearer. If she or any other woman had been in the doctor's place, she would have given the same answer.

Mrs. Carteret did not stop to reason. In such a crisis a mother's heart usurps the place of intellect. For her, at that moment, there were but two facts in all the world. Her child lay dying. There was within the town, and within reach, a man who could save him. With an agonized cry she rushed wildly from the room.

Carteret sought to follow her, but she flew down the long stairs like a wild thing. The least misstep might have precipitated her to the bottom; but ere Carteret, with a remonstrance on his lips, had scarcely reached the uppermost step, she had thrown open the front door and fled precipitately out into the night.

XXXVII
THE SISTERS

MILLER'S doorbell rang loudly, insistently, as though demanding a response. Absorbed in his own grief, into which he had relapsed upon Carteret's departure, the sound was an unwelcome intrusion. Surely the man could not be coming back! If it were some one else—What else might happen to the doomed town concerned him not. His child was dead,—his distracted wife could not be left alone.

The doorbell rang—clamorously—appealingly. Through the long hall and the closed door of the room where he sat, he could hear some one knocking, and a faint voice calling.

"Open, for God's sake, open!"

It was a woman's voice,—the voice of a woman in distress. Slowly Miller rose and went to the door, which he opened mechanically.

A lady stood there, so near the image of his own wife, whom he had just left, that for a moment he was well-nigh startled. A little older, perhaps, a little fairer of complexion, but with the same form, the same features, marked by the same wild grief. She wore a loose wrapper, which clothed her like the drapery of a statue. Her long dark hair, the counterpart of his wife's, had fallen down, and hung disheveled about her shoulders. There was blood upon her knuckles, where she had beaten with them upon the door.

"Dr. Miller," she panted, breathless from her flight and laying her hand upon his arm appealingly,—when he shrank from the contact she still held it there,—"Dr. Miller,—you will come and save my child? You know what it is to lose a child! I am so sorry about your little boy! You will come to mine!"

"Your sorrow comes too late, madam," he said harshly. "My child is dead. I charged your husband with his murder, and he could not deny it. Why should I save your husband's child?"

"Ah, Dr. Miller! " she cried, with his wife's voice,— she never knew how much, in that dark hour, she owed to that resemblance—"it is *my* child, and I have never injured you. It is my child, Dr. Miller, my only child. I brought it into the world at the risk of my own life! I have nursed it, I have watched over it, I have prayed for it,— and it now lies dying! Oh, Dr. Miller, dear Dr. Miller, if you have a heart, come and save my child!"

"Madam," he answered more gently, moved in spite of himself, "my heart is broken. My people lie dead upon the streets, at the hands of yours. The work of my life is in ashes,—and, yonder, stretched out in death, lies my own child! God! woman, you ask too much of human nature! Love, duty, sorrow, *justice*, call me here. I cannot go!"

She rose to her full height. "Then you are a murderer," she cried wildly. "His blood be on your head, and a mother's curse beside!"

The next moment, with a sudden revulsion of feeling, she had thrown herself at his feet,—at the feet of a negro, this proud white woman,—and was clasping his knees wildly.

"O God!" she prayed, in tones which quivered with anguish, "pardon my husband's sins, and my own, and move this man's hard heart, by the blood of thy Son, who died to save us all!"

It was the last appeal of poor humanity. When the pride of intellect and caste is broken; when we grovel in the dust of humiliation; when sickness and sorrow come, and the shadow of death falls upon us, and there is no hope elsewhere,—we turn to God, who sometimes swallows the insult, and answers the appeal.

Miller raised the lady to her feet. He had been deeply moved,—but he had been more deeply injured. This was his wife's sister,—ah, yes! but a sister who had scorned and slighted and ignored the existence of his wife for all her life. Only Miller, of all the world, could have guessed what this had meant to Janet, and he had merely divined it through the clairvoyant sympathy of love. This woman could have no claim upon him because of this unacknowledged relationship. Yet, after all, she *was* his wife's sister, his child's kinswoman. She was a fellow creature, too, and in distress.

"Rise, madam," he said, with a sudden inspiration, lifting her gently. "I will listen to you on one condition. My child lies dead in the adjoining room, his mother by his side. Go in there, and make your request of her. I will abide by her decision."

The two women stood confronting each other across the

body of the dead child, mute witness of this first meeting between two children of the same father. Standing thus face to face, each under the stress of the deepest emotions, the resemblance between them was even more striking than it had seemed to Miller when he had admitted Mrs. Carteret to the house. But Death, the great leveler, striking upon the one hand and threatening upon the other, had wrought a marvelous transformation in the bearing of the two women. The sad-eyed Janet towered erect, with menacing aspect, like an avenging goddess. The other, whose pride had been her life, stood in the attitude of a trembling suppliant.

"*You* have come here," cried Janet, pointing with a tragic gesture to the dead child,—"*you*, to gloat over your husband's work. All my life you have hated and scorned and despised me. Your presence here insults me and my dead. What are you doing here?"

"Mrs. Miller," returned Mrs. Carteret tremulously, dazed for a moment by this outburst, and clasping her hands with an imploring gesture, "my child, my only child, is dying, and your husband alone can save his life. Ah, let me have my child," she moaned, heartrendingly. "It is my only one—my sweet child—my ewe lamb!"

"This was *my* only child!" replied the other mother; "and yours is no better to die than mine!"

"You are young," said Mrs. Carteret, "and may yet have many children,—this is my only hope! If you have a human heart, tell your husband to come with me. He leaves it to you; he will do as you command."

"Ah," cried Janet, "I have a human heart, and therefore I will not let him go. *My* child is dead!—O God, my child, my child!"

She threw herself down by the bedside, sobbing hysterically. The other woman knelt beside her, and put her arm about her neck. For a moment Janet, absorbed in her grief, did not repulse her.

"Listen," pleaded Mrs. Carteret. "You will not let my baby die? You are my sister;—the child is your own near kin!"

My child was nearer," returned Janet, rising again to her feet and shaking off the other woman's arm. "He was my son, and I have seen him die. I have been your sister for twenty-five years, and you have only now, for the first time, called me so!"

"Listen—sister," returned Mrs. Carteret. Was there no way to move this woman? Her child lay dying if he were not dead already. She would tell everything, and leave the rest to God. If it would save her child, she would shrink at no sacrifice. Whether the truth would still further incense Janet, or move her to mercy, she could not tell; she would leave the issue to God.

"Listen, sister! " she said. "I have a confession to make. You *are* my lawful sister. My father was married to your mother. You are entitled to his name, and to half his estate."

Janet's eyes flashed with bitter scorn.

"And you have robbed me all these years, and now tell me that as a reason why I should forgive the murder of my child?"

"No, no!" cried the other wildly, fearing the worst. "I have known of it only a few weeks,—since my Aunt Polly's death. I had not meant to rob you,—I had meant to make restitution. Sister! for our father's sake, who did you no wrong, give me my child's life!"

Janet's eyes slowly filled with tears—bitter tears— burning tears. For a moment even her grief at her child's loss dropped to second place in her thoughts. This, then, was the recognition for which, all her life, she had longed in secret. It had come, after many days, and in larger measure than she had dreamed; but it had come, not with frank kindliness and sisterly love, but in a storm of blood and tears; not freely given, from an open heart, but extorted from a reluctant conscience by the agony of a mother's fears. Janet had obtained her heart's desire, and now that it was at her lips, found it but apples of Sodom, filled with dust and ashes!

"Listen!" she cried, dashing her tears aside. "I have but one word for you,—one last word,—and then I hope never to see your face again! My mother died of want, and I was brought up by the hand of charity. Now, when I have married a man who can supply my needs, you offer me back the money which you and your friends have robbed me of! You imagined that the shame of being a negro swallowed up every other ignominy,—and in your eyes I am a negro, though I am your sister, and you are white, and people have taken me for you on the streets,—and you, therefore, left me nameless all my life! Now, when an honest man has given me a name of which I can be proud, you offer me the one of which you robbed me, and of which I can make no use. For twenty-five years I, poor, despicable fool, would have kissed your feet for a word, a nod, a smile. Now, when this tardy recognition comes, for which I have waited so long it is tainted, with fraud and crime and blood, and I must pay for it with my child's life!"

"And I must forfeit that of mine, it seems for withholding it so long," sobbed the other, as tottering, she turned to go. "It is but just."

"Stay—do not go yet!" commanded Janet imperiously, her pride still keeping back her tears. "I have not done. I throw you back your father's name, your father's wealth, your sisterly recognition. I want none of them,—they are bought too dear! ah, God, they are bought too dear! But that you may know that a woman may be foully wronged, and yet may have a heart to feel, even for one who has injured her, you may have your child's life, if my husband can save it! Will," she said, throwing open the door into the next room, "go with her!"

"God will bless you for a noble woman!" exclaimed Mrs. Carteret. "You do not mean all the cruel things you have said,—ah, no! I will see you again, and make you take them back; I cannot thank you now! Oh, doctor, let us go! I pray God we may not be too late!"

Together they went out into the night. Mrs. Carteret tottered under the stress of her emotions, and would have fallen, had not Miller caught and sustained her with his arm until they reached the house, where he turned over her fainting form to Carteret at the door.

"Is the child still alive?" asked Miller.

"Yes, thank God," answered the father, "but nearly gone."

"Come on up, Dr. Miller," called Evans from the head of the stairs. "There 's time enough, but none to spare."